Moral Philosophy

a guide to ethical theory

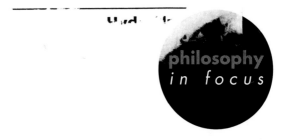

Moral Philosophy

a guide to ethical theory

philosophy
in focus

Gerald Jones
Daniel Cardinal
Jeremy Hayward

Academic consultant
Mary Warnock

HODDER
EDUCATION
AN HACHETTE UK COMPANY

Authors

Gerald Jones is Head of Humanities at the Mary Ward Centre, London; **Daniel Cardinal** is Head of Philosophy at Orpington College; **Jeremy Hayward** is a lecturer at the Institute of Education, London.

The academic consultant **Mary Warnock** is a philosopher who has written widely on many subjects. Her books include *An Intelligent Person's Guide to Ethics*, *Nature and Mortality* and *A Good Life: Thoughts on Life and Death* (forthcoming). Baroness Warnock has also been involved with several committees investigating applied ethics, including stem cell research and euthanasia and, most recently, the issue of the inclusion in mainstream education of pupils with special needs.

Acknowledgements

Cover artwork adapted from London Underground map, with permission; **p.92** *School of Athens*: akg-images/Erich Lessing; **p.219** Calvin & Hobbes: © Universal Press Syndicate 2006. Reprinted by permission; **p.229** *Point of View* Words & Music by Monica Bragato, Alfredo Comazzetto, Thomas Croquet, Christian Mazzalai, Laurent Mazzalai & Frederic Jean Moulin. © 2001 Suano Edizioni Musicali & Ghettoblaster SARL. Administered by Warner/Chappell Music Ltd, London W6 8BS. Reproduced by permission.

Every effort has been made to trace all copyright holders, but if any have been inadvertently overlooked the Publishers will be pleased to make the necessary arrangements at the first opportunity.

For Gill, Geoff and Jared

Although every effort has been made to ensure that website addresses are correct at time of going to press, Hodder Education cannot be held responsible for the content of any website mentioned in this book.

Hachette's policy is to use papers that are natural, renewable and recyclable products and made from wood grown in sustainable forests. The logging and manufacturing processes are expected to conform to the environmental regulations of the country of origin.

Orders: please contact Bookpoint Ltd, 130 Milton Park, Abingdon, Oxon OX14 4SB. Telephone: +44 (0)1235 827720. Fax: +44 (0)1235 400454. Lines are open from 9.00a.m. to 5.00p.m., Monday to Saturday, with a 24-hour message answering service. Visit our website at www.hoddereducation.co.uk

© Gerald Jones, Daniel Cardinal and Jeremy Hayward 2006
First published in 2006
Hodder Education,
an Hachette UK Company
338 Euston Road, London NW1 3BH

Impression number 10 9 8
Year 2013

Artwork by Richard Duszczak, Tony Jones/Art Construction, Tony Randell
Cover design and illustration by John Townson/Creation
Typeset in 11/13 Galliard by Dorchester Typesetting Group Ltd, Dorchester, Dorset
Printed and bound by CPI Group (UK) Ltd, Croydon CR0 4YY

A catalogue record for this title is available from the British Library

ISBN: 978 0 340 88805 6

Contents

Key to features

ACTIVITY
A practical task
to help you to
understand
the ideas.

experimenting with ideas
Plays around with
some of the concepts
discussed; looks at them
from different angles.

A direct quotation from
a key thinker.

•••••• ▶ criticism ◀ ••••••
Highlights and
evaluates some of
the difficulties
in various ideas.

**more
difficult**
A more in-depth
discussion of the ideas.

The series

This series is for students who are beginning to study philosophy. The books fill the middle ground between introductory texts, which do not always provide enough detail to help students with their essays and examinations, and more advanced academic texts which are often too complex for students new to philosophy to understand.

All of the study guides are written around the themes and texts for the AQA AS Level philosophy specification; this book is also suitable for students studying the ethics options within AS and A Level Religious Studies (see page 22). In addition to *Moral Philosophy: A Guide to Ethical Theory* there are five other guides available:

- Plato's *Republic*
- Descartes' *Meditations*
- Sartre's *Existentialism and Humanism*
- *Epistemology: the Theory of Knowledge*
- *Philosophy of Religion*.

The authors have substantial experience of teaching philosophy at A Level. They are also committed to making philosophy as accessible and engaging as possible. The study guides contain exercises to help students to grasp in a meaningful way the philosophical theories and ideas that they will face.

Some activities in this study guide are adopted from the resource book *Exploring Ethics*, also published by Hodder Murray. The resource book contains photocopiable games and exercises and is an ideal teacher accompaniment to this student guide. If you would like to order *Exploring Ethics*, please see contact details on p. iv.

Feedback and comments on these study guides would be welcome.

Words in SMALL CAPITALS are explained in the Glossary on page 235.

Philosophy and ethics

Three important questions

What should I do?

> *O'Brien moved the cage nearer. It was less than a metre
> from Winston's face. 'This mask will fit over your head
> leaving no exit. When I press this lever the door of the cage
> will slide up. Have you ever seen a rat leap through the
> air? They will leap on to your face and bore straight into it.
> Sometimes they attack the eyes first. Sometimes they burrow
> through the cheeks and devour the tongue.' The cage was
> nearer … Winston could see the whiskers and yellow teeth.
> Again the panic took hold of him. He was blind, helpless,
> mindless … The mask was closing over his face. The wire
> brushed his cheek. And then … a tiny fragment of hope …
> he had suddenly understood that in the whole world there
> was just one person to whom he could transfer his
> punishment – one body that he could thrust between himself
> and the rats. And he was shouting frantically, over and
> over. 'Do it to Julia! Do it to Julia! Not me! Julia! I don't
> care what you do to her. Tear her face off, strip her to the
> bones. Not me! Julia! Not me!'*
>
> *He was falling backwards … He was light years distant.
> But through the darkness that enveloped him he heard
> another metallic click, and knew that the cage door had
> clicked shut and not open.*[1]

George Orwell, *1984*

What would you do? In Orwell's novel Winston Smith is
tortured for many weeks by the State, but inside he stays true
to his lover, Julia. Finally, in Room 101, he encounters his
worst nightmare – a cage of starving rats ready to gnaw his
face off. This is Winston's breaking point and he betrays Julia,
by calling for her to take his place: let Julia be tortured, not
him. For his tormentors this betrayal is complete: they have
reached into the heart of Winston, found the person who is
most precious to him, and have destroyed this love. This
moment brings about Winston's release from torture, but

only because it is the end of his mental and moral resistance. He is no longer a threat to the State. He is set free, a pathetic figure, a man destroyed.

This sad everyman, Winston Smith, had a choice, a narrow one and a hideous one maybe, but still a choice: to be true to the only thing of value in his life – his love for Julia – or to betray it; to be courageous, or give in to this terrifying fear; to die without a face, or live without a soul. What would you choose?

What you choose to do, the way you choose to live, matters. The question 'what should I do?' is a question which may appear trivial in everyday circumstances ('what should I do with this tasteless chewing gum?'), but which, when asked more generally about life, is surely the most important a human being can ask. And what you decide to do says much about the principles you have, the values you hold and the things that are important to you. Most of the time you don't have to think too much about this: you live buried in a routine, following habits that suit you, treading well-worn paths to college or work – and the question 'what should I do?' remains a silent one, unanswered, or answered only subconsciously as you go about your daily life. But every now and then, usually at a moment of crisis, the question flares up at you in big capital letters. What on earth should I do? It becomes a terrifying question, a life-changing one. What should you do on learning that you or your partner is pregnant? What should you do if you find out your baby has Down's Syndrome? What should you do if you are tempted to be unfaithful to your partner? Or if a loved one is suffering a slow and painful death? And what should you do if you believe the government you live under is a tyrannical, murderous, oppressive regime (as in Winston Smith's case)?

The question 'what should I do?' is not a trivial one, as Socrates (469–399 BC) said, it is our whole way of life that is at issue.[2] Nor is it one that we can avoid or duck under. It's true that most of the time we don't really have to confront it, but nonetheless it is there, forming a backdrop to every day of our lives. What should you do? But moral philosophy is concerned with more than just this single question.

What should we do?

'We're on an island. We've been on the mountain-top and seen water all around. We saw no houses, no smoke, no footprints, no boats, no people … There aren't any grown-ups. We shall have to look after ourselves.' The meeting

*hummed and was silent. 'And another thing. We can't
have everybody talking at once. We'll have to have "Hands
up" like at school.' He held the conch before his face …
'That's what this shell's called. I'll give the conch to the next
person to speak. He can hold it when he's speaking.'
Jack was on his feet. 'We'll have rules!' he cried excitedly.
'Lots of rules! Then when anyone breaks 'em …'*[3]

William Golding, *Lord of the Flies*

Ralph, Jack and the other boys stranded on this desert island
face a different, but related, concern to the one we have
sketched above. These boys do not only have to decide what
each of them should do as individuals, such as become
hunters, keep the fire going, or avoid doing any work. They
also have to decide what they should do *as a group* – what
rules they should have and, as Jack says ominously, what to
do if anyone breaks these rules.

As with the first question (what should *I* do?) this issue, of
how we are going to live together, is fundamental to our
existence. We cannot, and do not, live in isolation from one
another – except in rare cases, most of us are born into, and
grow up within, a family or community. Humans are, as
Aristotle (384–322 BC) said, political animals.[4] The poet John
Donne put it even better: 'No man is an island entire of itself;
every man is a piece of the continent, a part of the main.'[5]
Whether we like it or not, we are connected to other people:
the choices we make affect them, and their choices affect us.
So morality is not just a private, personal, issue, but also a
public one that determines the way in which we live in
society.

Aristotle made it clear two and half thousand years ago that
ethics was not an isolated discipline relating only to each of us
as individuals. Ethics, in a personal sense, is also the
foundation for ethics in a public sense – determining how we
should all live together. Indeed Aristotle believed that in
order for us to flourish as individuals we must flourish
together in the right sort of society.

*For even if the good of the community coincides with that of
the individual, it is clearly a greater and more perfect
thing to achieve and preserve that of a community.*[6]

Aristotle

The public and policy dimension of ethics extends even
beyond human society, as humans share this planet with
other living things, and our survival seems interwoven with
theirs.

It is true that the question 'what should we do?' is less
confrontational, less immediate, than 'what should I do?' but

it is still a pressing question. Some of the biggest problems we face today are ethical ones that occur in the public arena, the resolution of which may determine our survival as a species. Should we continue to destroy the rainforests? Should we cut down on our consumption of fossil fuel, even if it results in a fall in our standard of living? Should rare species be protected, against the wishes of local farmers? Should certain types of euthanasia be made legal? Should embryonic stem cell research be permitted? Some of these questions touch on the morality of laws and policies, such as whether the laws that we have are GOOD or bad. Other questions go beyond the particular legal systems of a country, to ecological questions which affect all of us, and our descendants, as human beings.

You have survived a plane crash on a desert island, along with a group of other people the same age as you. There are no obvious authority figures in the group of survivors; no one knows when or if you'll be rescued; you may be on this small island for the rest of your life.

1 What would you do in this situation?
2 What do you think the priorities for the group should be? What things should be sorted out first?
3 What rules would you propose to enable you to do what *you* want to do?
4 What rules do you think are needed to enable the group to survive as a group?
5 Is there any conflict between the rules you've proposed for **3** and **4**?

What sort of person should I be?

'Just do your job, Nick. Do it well. Show people that you're honest and courageous and hard-working … '

I shook my head and said I couldn't.

'No?' He leaned back in his chair. 'And just why can't you?'

'For a couple of reasons,' I said. 'For one thing, I ain't real brave and hard-workin' and honest. For another, the voters don't want me to be.'

'And just how do you figure that?'

'They elected me, didn't they? They keep electing me.'[7]

Jim Thompson, *Pop 1280*

Nick Corey, the high sheriff of Potts County (population 1,280), knows himself pretty well. Possibly too well: he's figured that the kind of person he is is just the kind of person that the people want as a sheriff, and so there's no reason for him to change, despite the fact that he is cowardly, lazy, dishonest and, it turns out, somewhat psychotic.

So there is a third fundamental ethical question that we may pose: what sort of person should I be? This question underpinned the ethics of the Ancient Greeks,[8] and although it fell out of favour for many years it has returned as a question that we must consider. This question is related to the first – how should I live? – insofar as the choices that I make determine what sort of person I am and what sort of character I have. My choices determine who I am in two senses. First my actions reveal what sort of person I am. It is by my actions that my character can be judged, so that if I claim to be generous, but in reality I am tight-fisted, then it is my acts not my words that betray my true character. Secondly, my character is determined by my actions in the sense that they cause me to become a particular sort of person. By acting in certain ways I develop habitual ways of behaving, what we might call DISPOSITIONS. And in this way my choices shape the person I become.

However, the question 'what kind of person should I be?' is different in emphasis from 'what should I do?' It is not concerned so much with particular, time-constrained, decisions and actions. Rather it asks us to consider our whole lives and how we wish to grow into that life. It is a question of personal development and education – the retraining, if necessary, of the habits and dispositions that we have accrued. For the Ancient Greeks it was also a question of flourishing – of becoming the sort of person who is best able to thrive and fulfil our potential as a human being.

experimenting with ideas

1 Not all uses of 'should' or 'ought' are moral uses. For each of the following claims decide which of them are examples of moral assertions, and which are non-moral.

a) The State should not be allowed to imprison terrorists without trial.

b) Banksy should not spray graffiti (no matter how witty) on Buckingham Palace.

c) Moira ought to wear paler lipstick.

d) Claire should not have had an abortion.

e) You should never believe something unless you have enough evidence for it.

f) I should try to be more assertive.

g) Wayne should have passed the ball earlier.

h) Jade should sort her life out before it's too late.

i) Scientists shouldn't be allowed to experiment on guinea pigs.

j) People in London ought to smile more.

k) The tabloids should double-check their facts before they write such headlines.

l) You should read all the novels suggested at the end of this book.

m) Justin should not be fooling around with other women.

n) You ought to show more respect to older people.

o) Alan should not have invested all his money in an ostrich farm.

p) My parents should not get divorced.

q) Moral philosophers should get down from their ivory towers.

r) You should abbreviate 'it is' as 'it's' and not 'its'.

s) If there is a place in our lives for just one bit of philosophy, then it ought to be that part of philosophy which addresses moral questions.

2 Are any of the claims ambiguous (i.e. they could be interpreted in either a moral or a non-moral sense) depending on the context? What contexts would make them moral claims?

3 What do you think is special about the moral sense of 'should' as opposed to the non-moral sense?

The questions that we have raised above, 'what should I do?', 'what should we do?', 'what sort of person should I be?' are important ones. If there is a place in our lives for just one bit of philosophy, then it ought surely to be that part of philosophy which addresses these questions. And that area of philosophy is called 'moral philosophy' or 'ethics'. (Note that for most philosophers the terms 'moral' and 'ethical' are pretty much interchangeable and we shall treat them in this way too.[9])

In the activity above you saw how there is both a moral and a non-moral use of 'should', but obviously what we're concerned with here, and throughout the book, is the moral sense of 'should'. We return throughout the book to the subtle distinction between certain moral and non-moral uses of terms like 'should', 'good', 'obligation' and IMPERATIVE. But it is worth saying briefly here that the non-moral sense of 'should' generally refers to something that it is in my interests to do, so that I might achieve certain other (non-moral) goals, such as staying healthy, keeping my life ticking along, having a laugh, making enough money to live well, etc. This non-moral use of 'should' is often referred to as its *prudential* use – because it is prudent, or sensible, to think carefully and take certain steps so that we might personally achieve all our goals in life. However, as is usually the case in philosophy, things aren't so simple that we can simply dismiss prudential goals as 'non-moral' goals. We shall see in Chapter 2 that some thinkers (ethical egoists) believe that there is little distinction between prudential and moral 'shoulds'.

In the rest of this chapter we shall sketch in more detail what ethics involves: we look at the origins of moral philosophy in the Western philosophical tradition, we try to identify what types of action fall within the scope of ethics and finally we outline three different levels of moral philosophy.

Philosophy and morality

Morality refers to the rules and codes that we live our lives by – morality tells us how we *should* live and act and develop as humans. Moral debates dominate the media: stories about the private lives of politicians, euthanasia, the atrocities of war, concerns about the environment, drugs and abortion cover the front pages of the national press every day. Such contemporary issues are a staple of daytime television and PSHE or citizenship courses in school and, while it may seem that we are encouraged to air our views, merely airing them doesn't really get us anywhere. All too often discussions do not move beyond the level of 'This is my opinion, what's yours?' Where there is disagreement between two people there is the tendency on the one hand to say 'hey, well it's okay to disagree, it's all subjective anyway' or on the other hand for the discussion to disintegrate into a quarrel in which neither side is prepared to listen to the other. Neither of these approaches is particularly satisfactory. It's as if moral discussions are a kind of 'therapy' with the mere expression of a view being enough to give it value. Sometimes a more cool and critical approach to ethical thinking is needed in order to move a discussion on, to assess a moral position, or to change people's behaviour. Moral philosophy, or ethics, is able to provide such an approach.

Philosophy involves the attempt to think critically about the issues that puzzle us about the world, and to reflect on the things that make us wonder. For thousands of years philosophers have questioned people's ordinary ideas about life, the universe and everything, and the best thinkers have done this by throwing a critical spotlight onto those ideas: What are they based on? What assumptions or hidden prejudices do they conceal? Are they contradictory? The goal of philosophers has mainly been to provide a more robust account of the world than is found in common sense. Moral philosophy is no different and so its concern is to reflect critically on the three questions we outlined above: what should I do?, what should we do? and what sort of person should I be?

In broader terms, the questions that moral philosophy poses take many forms, from the very general, such as *How ought we to live? What makes our actions RIGHT or wrong?* or *What does it mean to call actions right or wrong?*, to the particular, such as *Do other animals have any moral* RIGHTS? *What is morally wrong with scientists cloning humans?* or *Is it ever permissible to kill someone who is in a permanent vegetative state by ending their treatment?* It was in Ancient Greece that the Western tradition began its first systematic attempts to find answers to questions like these. So in the next section we will begin our exploration of these questions, and of the many different types of response to them, by looking at their origin some two and a half thousand years ago in Greece.

The origins of Western ethics

We can trace moral philosophy back two or three thousand years, to the flourishing of the disparate civilisation of Ancient Greece. It is worth noting that Ancient Greece was not one country, as we now think of it, but consisted of dozens of separate city-states, most commonly a major town and its surrounding countryside – each probably no bigger than Milton Keynes or Basildon. These city-states (in Greek called *polis*, which is where our word 'political' stems from) were nations in their own right, with their own laws, army, government, culture, etc.

The beginnings of philosophy in the Mediterranean are tied up with the beginnings of writing in the region. It is tough to hold and juggle lots of different ideas in your mind at once and to see how they relate. But when thoughts are written down it is much easier to spot connections and tensions between them, and so writing allows for a more systematic treatment of philosophical problems. Moreover, with written records each generation can build on or react to the discoveries and claims of previous generations.

The earliest writings (aside from 'IOUs' exchanged by farmers and merchants) capture the myths and heroes of their time: the *Epic of Gilgamesh* in Mesopotamia, and later the *Iliad* and *Odyssey* of Ancient Greece as transcribed by Homer somewhere between 900 and 800 BC. Homer's epic account of the Trojan wars was part of a rich oral tradition and many of the episodes he recounted remain familiar today, such as the story of the wooden horse, or of Odysseus' encounter with the Cyclops. However, when reading these verses we discover not just the dramatic struggles of heroes, but also a nostalgic picture of the ideals that Homer's society aspired to: its morals, its VIRTUES and its values. This is why we might say that moral philosophy in the West sprang from the work of Homer, as here for the first time we have a thinker who is describing a consistent ethical system and prescribing a way of life: to be heroic.

In order to see just how far removed the Ancient Greeks' conception of ethics is from our own, consider the following situation taken from Homer's *Iliad*:

> Hector kills Achilles' best friend, Petrochalus, in battle. Achilles, in his anger, goes out to kill Hector and then drags Hector's body round and round Petrochalus' tomb. At night he leaves it out to be mutilated by dogs. Achilles does this until little remains of the body. The gods are horrified and hold a council at which Apollo, the sworn enemy of Achilles, says 'Let him be made aware of our anger, even though he is good.'[10]

ACTIVITY How can Apollo still refer to Achilles as 'good' (in Greek *agathon*) after what he has just done? Think of three possible reasons that explain why Achilles is good.

For Homer and his fellow Ancients, one of the highest forms of praise was to describe someone as *agathon*, usually translated as 'good' but having a meaning closer to our term 'noble'. Being noble meant being heroic, being a warrior, being at the top of the Greek social system and being healthy, wealthy, handsome and strong. So in the warrior societies of Ancient Greece there was nothing better than possessing all the necessary attributes to make you *agathon* (good). Achilles (according to legend, the son of an immortal nymph) possessed these qualities in spades – he had it all, and for centuries was a heroic icon for the Greeks. Thus for the Greeks of Homer's time the foundations of morality lay in the kind of person you were and the types of virtues you possessed, in particular nobility, courage and physical prowess. This approach to morality – that it is determined by character and virtue – is still present in the ethical theories of Socrates, Plato and Aristotle.

Greek ethics in crisis

By the sixth century BC there was an ethical crisis in Greek societies, and many Greek thinkers abandoned the idea that their own city-state's conception of 'good' was the sole and correct conception. Alasdair MacIntyre[11] identifies two reasons why there was a collapse in the moral certainty of the Greeks between 900 and 500 BC. The first of these was the discovery and investigation of other civilisations, and the second the transformation that Greek society underwent during these years.

First, as merchant city-states such as Athens grew, their sailors encountered other Mediterranean civilisations with very different conceptions of what was good. The Phoenicians, the Babylonians, the Egyptians, etc. all had their own sophisticated cultures, and their conceptions of morality were not necessarily based on ideas about character, virtue or function in society. The Greeks became fascinated by such cultures, and MacIntyre argues that this discovery led them to question the absolute truth of their own moral concepts. Why the Greeks did this, whereas other cultures didn't, is a matter of speculation. One popular theory is that the Greek city-states did not operate under a rigid and hierarchical religious system (as was the case in Ancient Egypt), and because of this relative tolerance they were in a position to question their own moral cultures without persecution – at least up to a point, as Socrates found out when he was executed by the Athenian state in 399 BC because of what it saw as his subversive teachings.

Secondly, MacIntyre suggests that as the city-states such as Athens, Sparta and Miletus expanded in size so the traditional hierarchies of the *polis* began to disintegrate. In Homer's time city-states were small, everyone knew their place and their social role and Homer's strict moral order made sense. However, as the population increased and traders could become as wealthy as aristocrats, many citizens found that they could move up and down the social scale, irrespective of their ancestry or nobility. Other citizens found themselves doing several different jobs throughout their life, none of which could be identified with a specific social role. So as individuals' functions became less clear, it became increasingly difficult to determine how to live a virtuous life.

The Sophists

By 500 BC the moral conservatives (those who harked back to Homer's day as a golden age of morality) were in a minority and unpopular. Into this moral vacuum stepped a number of wandering sages, who preached their own perspective on morality. They argued that all morality was relative: that ultimately there is no such thing as good; that morality is all subjective; and that what is good for you may not be good for me. In other words, they argued for moral RELATIVISM: the view that what is right and wrong varies from place to place, time to time and person to person. Such a relativist position was famously captured by the Sophist Protagoras who argued that 'man is the measure of all things',[12] which Plato interpreted as meaning that 'each thing is to me as it appears to me, and is to you as it appears to you' (*Theaetetus* 152A). We return to relativism on page 168 below. Ethical relativism means that there is no such thing as good 'in itself'; rather if an action seems good to me and bad to you that is the end of the matter. There is no objective basis for us to discover the truth.

These sages became known as 'wise men' or Sophists (from the Greek *sophia* meaning wisdom) and, for a small fee, they offered instruction in how to lead the best possible life, whatever *polis* you chose to live in. Now, many Sophists travelled extensively around the Eastern Mediterranean and had seen for themselves that the moral codes and systems of law differed widely in different societies. They stressed that what mattered was not striving after some non-existent notion of goodness, but knowing how to get ahead in the particular society in which you lived. In Greek society this would mean taking an active and successful part in political life, being a skilful speaker in the public assemblies, and, more generally, conforming in your lifestyle to the accepted notions of what was right and just. So many of the Sophists claimed they were experts in teaching what we now call sophistry: winning ARGUMENTS and persuading people of your position no matter what the truth might be, since for them 'truth' was a fluid concept.

It was the Sophists' particular brand of scepticism about morality that inspired Socrates to prove these cynics wrong, and the work of Socrates was built on first by Plato then by Aristotle and led to the creation of moral philosophy.

Socrates, Plato and Aristotle

Socrates 469–399 BC

↓

taught

Plato 427–347 BC

↓

taught

Aristotle 384–322 BC

It is difficult to separate clearly the views of Socrates and Plato because Socrates left no writings, and most of what we know about Socrates' beliefs and methods we know through the work of his pupil Plato. Plato's dialogues figured Socrates as the main protagonist, and, in the early dialogues at least, Socrates is represented as primarily concerned to uncover the ignorance of his contemporaries with regard to moral matters, as well as to resist the moral relativism implicit in their views. While he agrees with the Sophists that virtue is teachable, he does not regard it as a simple matter of social convention. Rather he argues that all humans share a common understanding of what is morally good, which is innate and natural.

Because there is no direct record of what Socrates believed we do not really know how Socrates thought it was possible to attain moral knowledge. But his pupil, Plato, had very definite views on the nature of genuine moral understanding. It lay in the apprehension of the world of 'forms' – a realm of perfect ideas of which the physical world is just a poor imitation. In particular Plato identified moral knowledge with a grasp of the highest of all the forms: the Form of the Good. Only with knowledge of the Good could we come to be truly virtuous, and lead a life that truly flourished. Moreover, someone who has encountered the Form of the Good is instantly motivated to pursue it – such is the compulsive power of the good.

Plato's response to the moral relativism of the Sophists is a compelling and forceful one. Not only does he describe how moral knowledge is possible, what it might be like and what effects it might have on us, but he also attacks the whole approach of the Sophists, accusing it of being incoherent, wrong-headed and damaging to those they taught. In contrast to the Sophists' view of learning as simply a means of achieving personal goals and power, Plato established philosophical reasoning as the route to genuine knowledge of objective and universal moral truths as well as to living the morally good life.

Plato's own pupil, Aristotle, built on his moral philosophy but from a very different perspective (see pages 91–99). Aristotle embraced the power of philosophy to discover universal truths, even about morality, but he rejected Plato's claims that these could be found in some mysterious ideal world, the world of Forms. For Aristotle, what we could know about morality could be discovered here in this world, by studying the way people live and behave. Such study suggested to Aristotle that Plato had to be wrong when he said that if we had moral knowledge we would feel compelled to be good. For Aristotle, such a view seemed to fly in the face of the facts of human nature. After all, human beings are often weak-willed, selfish and lazy, and so simply knowing what is the right course of action is not sufficient to make us do it.

So Aristotle's approach to morality, although still systematic and rigorously philosophical, is much more practical and empirical than Plato's. We can find out how to be virtuous by examining the facts of human nature. By inquiring into what kind of creature we are, we can determine what our function or purpose should be. By asking what sorts of characteristics people generally aspire to we can discover how to develop our character for the better. And by asking how virtuous people tend to behave we will learn how we should behave ourselves. Finally, Aristotle is concerned to ask what place philosophical, and practical, reasoning have in a fulfilled life in order to determine how best we should spend our time.

Whatever their differences, Socrates, Plato and Aristotle placed philosophical reflection at the centre of our moral existence. Frustrated by the spin-doctoring and relativism of the Sophists they each responded with the same message: don't blindly follow traditional or populist thinking; consider what you believe carefully; deal with inconsistencies in your beliefs; engage in dialogue with others and be open to their criticisms; aspire to find truths that go beyond your own time and place. This set the tone for the next two and a half thousand years of moral philosophy in the West. Europe has changed beyond recognition since Aristotle's time with the rise and fall of empires, the ebb and flow of religious influence, and passing of artistic, scientific and industrial revolutions. But throughout these upheavals philosophers have kept true to the critical spirit of the Ancient Greeks in their reflections on morality. This, for better or for worse, has been the legacy of those three giants of the ancient world.

What makes an action 'moral'?

Sometimes we think of 'moral' as meaning 'morally good'. But when philosophers use the term 'moral' they usually take it to refer to an action which comes within the scope of morality, i.e. an action which is morally significant either in a positive way (because it is good or right) or in a negative way (because the action is bad or wrong).

We have already seen how some concepts have both a moral and a non-moral sense. For example, the term 'should' has a prudential use (you shouldn't throw money down the drain) and a moral use (you shouldn't kick people when they're down). But what are we referring to when we say it has a 'moral' use, in other words what sorts of thing is morality all about anyway? One way we can go about answering this question is to consider what sorts of thing make an action a moral one, as opposed to a morally neutral one.

Many, if not most, of the actions we perform in life, such as putting on a raincoat, sharpening a pencil or counting apples, are not in themselves either good or bad acts. Such actions are, we might say, morally neutral or non-moral. By contrast, stealing from libraries, punching people or helping the disadvantaged are considered morally significant actions (the first two are generally judged to be bad, and the third good). But what makes an act enter the moral arena? In other words, what features of actions, such as stealing or being charitable, make us judge them to be good or bad, right or wrong?

Even if we have never reflected on such a question, we all seem to have our own gut-feelings about which actions are morally significant, and will from time to time pass moral JUDGEMENT on the actions of ourselves and others, by labelling them right or wrong, good or bad, and praising and laying blame on the people who perform them. (We shall look at moral judgements in more detail below, on page 19.) So it seems that we must have at least an implicit understanding of what it is that makes an action moral and what distinguishes it from non-moral acts.

One way of becoming clearer about how we draw this distinction would be to search for the criteria that we use in order to identify moral actions. This approach to clarifying a concept is common practice in philosophy. It involves trying to uncover the rules we use to make the distinction, or the features we search for when judging an action to be moral. A good way to start doing this is to reflect on what is going on when making such judgements, as you will do in the next activity.

experimenting with ideas

Read through the following situations, and for each one decide whether it is **a)** good, **b)** bad or **c)** morally neutral. (You should judge the situations on the information given and according to your own moral intuitions.)

1 A deer is caught in a forest fire caused by a freak lightning strike and is burnt to death.

2 A killer whale toys with a seal that it has half killed – batting it into the air with its tail and catching it with its teeth. It takes twenty minutes before the seal finally dies. The whale leaves it to rot on the ocean floor.

3 You deliberately step on someone's toe in a lift but pretend it was an accident.

4 You accidentally poison your neighbour's dog.

5 You beat your friend in an ant-killing competition (with a winning combination of bleach and boiling water).

6 You persistently bullied a classmate at school.

7 A rich billionaire builds herself a space rocket and leaves Earth forever. For the rest of her life none of her actions ever affects another living thing. Could any of her future actions be good or bad (**a** or **b**) or will they all be morally neutral (**c**)?

8 You successfully pass the ball to members of your team 15 times in a 1–1 draw at a friendly local hockey match.

9 An orphanage is set up to help victims in a war-torn country.

10 A builder shouts 'Nice legs!' to a person walking past.

11 You stop to help a blind man cross the road but fail to notice the unstoppable juggernaut that injures you both.

12 An evil scientist releases a new bio-chemical into the water supply of a large city intending to kill millions. However, this agent, when diluted, turns out to be a harmless cure for cancer and countless lives are saved.

Now make a note of all those actions that you decided were morally neutral. You may find it helpful to draw up a table as follows and to list some of the features that moral actions/morally neutral actions have in common. What is it that makes an action morally neutral? You will probably find that it's more than just one thing. On the other side, what features of an action make it morally significant (either good or bad)?

Moral action	Morally neutral action

A moral act involves an agent

Situations 1 and 2 in the activity above raise the question of who must initiate an act in order for it to count as a moral act. (Remember that when we refer to a 'moral act' we are not talking about a morally good act, but an action which is morally significant, i.e. which may be judged to be either good or bad, right or wrong.) Your intuitions may suggest that if something is a 'natural event' or an action performed by an animal then it is morally neutral – it doesn't appear on our moral radars. The question is, why do our intuitions tell us this? How are actions performed by humans different from actions performed by animals or from events that occur in the natural world? Many philosophers would say that a moral action is one that has been freely and thoughtfully chosen. It seems as if natural events and the actions of animals are morally neutral, because there is no choice involved. In other words, events caused by nature or animals do not stem from any AGENCY, meaning the capacity to reflect and decide what to do. We might wish to say that only humans can be moral AGENTS. Or we might argue that any creature, human or not, that can freely and thoughtfully choose its actions will count as a moral agent.

We may also question whether all humans fall into the category of 'agent', for example whether young children or people with severe brain damage are capable of freely and thoughtfully chosen actions. In the novel *A Clockwork Orange*, Alex, a sociopathic gang-member, is put onto an experimental crime prevention programme by the government: he is to be conditioned to behave in an appropriately moral way. This conditioning means that, although he still wants to lie, steal and kill, he can't because of the physical sickness that envelops him when he tries to do these things. If he behaves in the opposite way (even though he has no natural inclination to do so) and is honest, respectful etc., then he feels a lot better. Once this conditioning is complete, Alex is put on display as the future of crime prevention; he is a 'clockwork orange', physically incapable of doing any harm. He now grovels in front of the man he wishes to slice up with **15** his knife. One observer questions the success of this experiment; to him Alex is no longer a moral agent:

> *'Choice ... He has no real choice, has he? Self-interest, fear of physical pain, drove him to that grotesque act of self-abasement. Its insincerity was clearly to be seen. He ceases to be a wrongdoer. He ceases also to be a creature capable of moral choice.'*[13]

A further issue arises with regards to situation 1 if you believe there is a God who created the universe. Some people have argued that if there really is an almighty creator then so-called 'natural disasters', such as earthquakes, droughts and the agonising deaths of deer in a forest fire, are all the result of a moral agent's (i.e. God's) decisions and should therefore count as moral acts.[14] The existence of pain and suffering that is caused by natural events presents a challenge for believers in God, and is part of the problem known as the Problem of Evil. We do not discuss this problem here, but we do in another book in this series, *Philosophy of Religion*.[15]

A moral act involves intention

Several of the situations (3, 4, 6, 11 and 12) in the above activity require us to consider the importance of an intention behind the action. You may have discounted situations 1 and 2 because there was no possibility of intention, as there was no moral agent. However, you may have felt that even where a moral agent was involved (as in 4) if there was no intention, for example if the action was accidental, then it counted as a morally neutral act. Your judgement of situations 11 and 12 might reveal how much weight you attach to intentions or motives when making moral judgements. Do you think that our motives are the most important, or sole, criterion for determining the rightness or wrongness of a moral action? In the next chapter (pages 30–47) we shall look at some ethical theories, known as deontological theories, which do make this claim. However, you may feel that actually some unintentional acts can also be moral, such as those done through negligence. So you might say of situation 4 that we all have responsibilities, or DUTIES, towards the welfare of animals in our local area and as such we have a responsibility not to leave poison out in the garden, in which case neglecting this responsibility, even accidentally, makes us morally culpable.

A moral act affects others

However, even the presence both of an agent and of clear intention may not be enough for you to say that an action is morally significant. Something else might be lacking. So, for example, situation 7 ticks both these boxes (yes there is an agent, and yes many of her future actions will be deliberate) but her future actions may still strike you as morally neutral. What you might say is missing is that her actions don't actually affect anyone. If you did believe that her actions could be good or bad then was it because you believed her actions were affecting others? Perhaps you even thought that her actions could affect her future self, for example if she decided to start smoking whilst in the capsule, then ten years down the line she got lung cancer and died a horrible death alone in space. Her future self would (morally) condemn her past self for making this foolish decision. So she can act now in a way that could be (morally) good or bad for her future self.[16]

So a moral action needs to involve an agent, and needs to be deliberate but it also needs to affect others (those we might call moral 'patients'). Situations 4 and 5 raise the question of how far the scope of 'others' extends: who is included in it (ants? dogs?) and who is excluded? Traditionally we might only have included humans within the range of who is to count as affected by a moral action. But in the past 200 years we have extended 'others' to include higher mammals, or other animals, or ecosystems, or the world as a whole. At the other extreme some philosophers, for example ETHICAL EGOISTS, have argued that it is only our self (and our future self) that we should be concerned about, and we should forget about other people (see page 49).

But does *every* intentional action caused by an agent and which has an effect on others count as a moral one (i.e. a morally significant one, whether good or bad)? Situation 8 meets all these criteria but you may still have thought of it as morally neutral. After all, you may think, these people are just playing a game, nothing rides on it and no one is significantly affected by it. So it seems that it's not enough for an action merely to affect others – for it to be moral then it needs to affect others in significant ways.

Situations 9, 10, 11 and 12 bring out our intuitions that a moral action is one that has harmful or beneficial consequences for others. But what is meant by 'harm' or 'benefit'? Harm may be physical, emotional or psychological, and it might also include depriving others of happiness. Benefits may also be physical or psychological; they may be positive, in that happiness is produced, or negative, in that pain or harm is prevented. On pages 47–87 we examine some of the main examples of consequentialist theories, i.e. those that claim moral judgements are made on the basis of the harmful or beneficial consequences of an action.

Summarising the points above we can suggest the following key criteria as a working definition of 'moral action'. A moral action is one which:

- is performed by *agents*, creatures that are capable of free choice.
- is the result of *intention*; the action was done on purpose with a particular motive.
- has *significant consequences* on others in respect of the *harm* or *benefits* it brings about. These others may be either other moral agents (such as humans) or 'moral patients' (any other creature who may be deserving of our moral consideration).

Ethics and our moral intuitions

The activity above teases out our intuitions about morality: what is included in our moral framework, and what is excluded. But why should philosophers care about our moral intuitions? After all, moral philosophers are the experts, having spent years considering ethical questions, and possessing an understanding of the many answers that have been given in the past. What could we ordinary folk contribute?

For the most part philosophers are, quite rightly, wary of using intuition as a reason for a belief or theory. Intuitions are neither based on sense experience (which would count as a basis for belief according to EMPIRICIST philosophers) nor do they come from reason (which would count as a basis for belief according to RATIONALIST philosophers). They seem rather mysterious, immune to analysis, and in general to be unphilosophical. However, in moral philosophy things are rather different: intuitions count for something. There are some philosophers, the INTUITIONISTS and MORAL SENSE THEORISTS, who believe that moral judgements rest purely on intuition. This extreme form of 'intuitionism' is unusual, and one that faces many problems; but, even so, many other moral philosophers (such as Aristotle, Hume, Mill) look to capture the ordinary moral beliefs of people within their theories.

What does a moral theory need to do? It must at least account for our current moral values and beliefs, and suggest how, individually or as a group, these ought to develop. So there is both a DESCRIPTIVE element and a PRESCRIPTIVE element. Any theory must begin somewhere and the starting point for moral theories (in the absence of God appearing, or the discovery of a moral law) is how people actually behave and the judgements they actually make. If a moral theory fails to account for our current behaviour and judgement (let's say it 'proves' that we ought to commit suicide) then we wouldn't really recognise it as a moral theory – it would be more like a kind of cult or obscure religious sect. This is how Adam Morton puts it:

> *(A) On the one hand a moral philosophy must be in accord with many, at least, of the moral opinions that we feel intensely. Ideally, it should connect them up together in a way that helps us to see the deeper values that underlie the things we care about.*
> *(B) A moral philosophy must help us to find our way through the moral problems that trouble us. It ought to help us to see more clearly what makes a problem difficult, and how we might find a solution for it.*[17]

We bear (A) in mind throughout this book, holding as one of the tests of a moral theory to be whether it conforms with or clashes against our moral intuitions. Where a theory obviously does clash with moral beliefs that have been held throughout human history (and we shall see in the next chapter that on occasions both CONSEQUENTIALIST ETHICS and DEONTOLOGICAL ETHICS do clash with our intuitions) then this may be an indication that something has gone wrong with the theory. This does not mean that our moral beliefs have philosophical immunity, and we would expect a moral theory to challenge us to reflect on our beliefs and judgements. We return to (B), the claim that moral philosophy should be able to help us improve our moral decision-making, right at the end of Chapter 4, on pages 219–231.

Ethics and moral judgements

We saw at the beginning of this chapter that our interest in doing moral philosophy may well be initiated by thinking about how we should live. We have also seen that we cannot get far in these thoughts without encountering moral judgements, and the activity on page 14 above required that we begin to make moral judgements. The term 'judgement' sounds very grand, the sort of thing that is left up to juries, magistrates and Law Lords. But it also sounds very interfering, in the sense of being 'judgemental', being opinionated or ready to condemn. But we make judgements all the time in our everyday lives: and a judgement in this sense means a decision we take, by weighing up reasons for (or against) this decision. So we might make a judgement about what to wear on a first date; about what mobile phone to buy; about where we're going to live for the next ten years; even about which checkout queue in the supermarket to step into.[18]

These judgements are often evaluative – they not only involve weighing up reasons, but they also involve making a decision about the value of something (for example, whether it's better to go to university or to get a job). A *moral* judgement involves a similar decision-making process and assessment of value. We are all familiar with the linguistic clues that tell us someone is making a moral judgement: for example, the use of words like good, bad, right, wrong, vicious, virtuous, blame, praise, despicable, saintly. We make moral judgements not only about people's actions and characters, but also about the decisions and policies of governments and businesses.

It is possible to think of moral judgements as the touchstone for three different levels of moral philosophy. So NORMATIVE ETHICS involves examining the systems behind the moral judgements we make, and whether that system is well founded, coherent, or consistent; META-ETHICS involves questioning the very meaning of moral judgements; whilst PRACTICAL ETHICS requires us to actually make moral judgements about issues that face us in real life.

Three levels of moral judgement

The three levels of ethics described above form the foundations for the rest of this book. In recent times moral philosophy has often been divided into these three levels, according to the degree of abstraction of the discussion. It is fairly easy to mix up these levels when engaging in a moral argument or to switch between them without realising it. So it is useful to familiarise ourselves with what these three levels are, and what issues and questions arise in each level.

Normative ethics involves asking what some philosophers call *first-order* moral questions, i.e. questions concerning what it is right to do, what is good or obligatory, how we ought to live and so forth. A normative theory of ethics provides action guides and a system for making moral judgements. We look at the three main normative positions (consequentialist ethics, deontological ethics and VIRTUE ETHICS) in Chapter 2.

Meta-ethics asks what is going on when someone engages in normative ethics. It asks *second-order* questions concerning the nature and meaning of moral judgements as such. So meta-ethics is not concerned with making and defending normative value judgements or with issuing any specific directives about how one ought to act. We address meta-ethics, the most abstract level of thinking about morality, in Chapter 3.

Practical or applied ethics is an application of normative theories to the actual world. Its concerns are those of investigating and resolving the tough issues and DILEMMAS that confront us in life – for example, what judgements would a consequentialist or deontologist make about animal welfare or abortion or euthanasia? Chapter 4 focuses on three specific issues in practical ethics, namely abortion, euthanasia and animal rights.

Figure 1.1 below shows the connection between these three levels of ethics. We've taken as an example DIVINE COMMAND ETHICS (dealt with in the next chapter) because it is easy to see the relationship between the three levels of divine command ethics. According to divine command theory an action is right if it complies with the commandments of God. So at a meta-ethical level we can see that the meaning of 'right' means 'God commands it'. At a normative level we have the rules and commandments that we have to follow. Below that, at a practical level, we have an example of a commandment put into practice (Should I kill a burglar? No, because God commands us not to kill). In the far left column is the 'level' of ethical theory; in the middle column is an example of a question that might be asked at that level. In the right-hand column are the answers to those questions that a divine command theorist might give.

■ **Figure 1.1**
The three levels of ethics within divine command theory

Level of ethics	Example question	Divine command theory
Meta-ethics	What is the meaning of Right?	'Right' means 'whatever God commands' 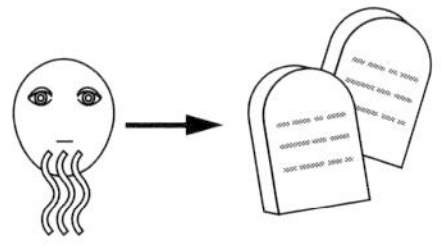
Normative ethics	What rules should we be following?	You should not kill You should not steal You should love your neighbour as yourself, etc. 
Practical ethics	Is it wrong to kill a burglar?	Killing burglars is wrong because we have been commanded not to kill. 

How this book matches AS/A2 Level Exam Specifications

This book can be used as a general introduction to the main ideas and arguments of moral philosophy within A Level Philosophy. However, as a textbook it also covers topics within a number of A Level exam specifications, as outlined below.

Chapter	Topic	AQA Philosophy	AQA Religious Studies	Edexcel Religious Studies	OCR Religious Studies
	➤ Deontology 1: divine command ethics	Yes	Yes	Yes	Yes
	➤ Deontology 2: Kantian ethics	Yes	Yes	Yes	Yes
Chapter 2	➤ Consequentialist ethics 1: egoism	Yes			
Normative ethics	➤ Consequentialist ethics 2: utilitarianism	Yes	Yes	Yes	
	➤ Virtue ethics	Yes	Yes		Yes
Chapter 3	➤ Realism/cognitivism	Yes		Yes	Yes
Meta-ethics	➤ Anti-realism/non-cognitivism	Yes		Yes	Yes
	➤ The ethics of killing	Yes			Yes
Chapter 4	➤ Abortion	Yes	Yes		Yes
Practical ethics	➤ Euthanasia	Yes	Yes		Yes
	➤ Animal rights	Yes	Yes		
	➤ The skills of ethical decision-making				Yes

Key points: Chapter 1

What you need to know about **philosophy and ethics**:

1 Moral philosophy, or ethics, is important because it addresses three fundamental and unavoidable questions: What should I do? What should we do? What sort of person should I be? But we need to distinguish between non-moral (or prudential) uses of 'should' and the moral use of 'should'. The prudential use of 'should' instructs us how to behave in order to achieve certain non-moral, practical goals. The moral use of 'should' tells us how to behave in order to reach moral goals, such as becoming a good person or doing the right thing.

2 We can trace Western moral philosophy back to the thinkers of Ancient Greece. The first significant writings, such as Homer's *Odyssey*, described a moral ideal based on nobility and heroism. However, these ideals were tested and questioned as the Greeks encountered other cultures with very different ideals. One solution to this challenge was to abandon the belief that there were any ideals, and this solution was adopted by the Sophists. The Sophists were wandering sages who taught people how to do well in public life, whatever the city or culture they lived in. They did not believe that there were any objective moral truths which remained the same across cultures.

3 Socrates' response to the Sophists was to question whether what they believed was coherent or consistent. Socrates inspired Plato to put careful, critical, philosophical reasoning at the heart of thinking about morality. Plato's philosophical approach led to his claim that there were moral truths, and that moral knowledge was possible if we were able to grasp the world of Forms. Aristotle, while disagreeing with Plato on his theory of Forms, also placed philosophical thinking at the heart of ethics. He believed that we could obtain moral knowledge by studying the world and people around us. By using philosophical reasoning to address moral questions these three philosophers, Socrates, Plato and Aristotle, established a legacy that set the tone for the rest of Western philosophy.

4 We might ask 'what is morality anyway?' One way of answering this question is to find out what distinguishes a moral action from a non-moral (or morally neutral) action. By classifying actions into 'moral' and 'non-moral' we find that those we tend to think of as moral satisfy at least the following conditions: 1) they are performed by agents (creatures capable of free choice); 2) they are deliberate

actions (they are not accidental); 3) they affect others in certain significant ways, most notably they are either harmful or beneficial to others.

5 Recently philosophers have identified different levels, or orders, of ethical issues and questions. First there is normative ethics, which proposes action guides and a system for making moral judgements. Secondly there is meta-ethics which reflects on the activities of ethical thinking generally and asks whether moral judgements are meaningful and what their meaning might be. Finally there is practical ethics which is an application of the theories of normative ethics to the problems we face in the real world.

2 Normative ethics

Introduction

If I choose to kill Brisseau, I am defining myself as a murderer ... By choosing my action, I choose it for all mankind. But what happens if everyone in the world behaved like me and came here and shot Brisseau? What a mess! Not to mention the commotion from the doorbell ringing all night. And of course we'd need valet parking. Ah ... how the mind boggles when it turns to ethical considerations![19]

Woody Allen

Woody Allen is right: our minds do boggle when it comes to ethics, and it's often more than we can take. We tend to get in a real state about moral issues that we care deeply about: our passion for a cause turns to anger at those who don't support it; we become threatened, as if a button has been pushed, when people disagree with our moral judgements; sometimes we abandon strongly held moral principles when we have to confront the issue in real life; we go on about the importance of being rational when it comes to morality, but when confronted with a dilemma we leave a decision to the last minute then do whatever 'feels right'.

Let's face it, most of us are in a mess when it comes to making moral decisions; and our actions are not always consistent, or congruent, with the moral principles that we say we have. In fact, what we say out loud about our moral beliefs is often not the best guide as to what our beliefs actually are. A much better guide is what we choose to do, how we act in the real world.

So how can we arrive at a set of moral beliefs that are consistent, are supported by firm reasons and reflect the way we actually act in the real world? One thing we can do is to assess the main moral systems that philosophers have constructed over the past two thousand years. Each of these systems strikes a chord with some intuition we have about morality, but each prioritises one element above all others (and defines and understands the other elements in terms of this one element). These systems, which prescribe how we should go about living and acting in the world, are known as normative ethics.

Normative ethics is the most traditional form of moral philosophy. At this level philosophers are working out and justifying the rules and codes that will tell us how we should live. 'Normative' implies the setting of norms, rules or action guides. So this level of ethics is also called 'prescriptive' which suggests guidance for action (as in a doctor's prescription for medicine), again a form of rule-setting. You can tell whether a statement is normative or prescriptive by looking for key words such as 'should' and 'ought'. Some philosophers, such as Plato and Aristotle, tend to be prescriptive about what kind of person we should be, while other philosophers, such as Augustine, Kant, Bentham and Mill, tend to be prescriptive about what kind of actions we should do; we can think of the former type of theory as 'agent-centred' and the latter approach as 'act-centred'.[20]

Different types of normative ethics

There are many different forms of normative theories, and Figure 2.1 illustrates some of the ways in which they can be classified.

■ **Figure 2.1**
Some ways of categorising normative ethical theories

Person	Motive	Action	Consequences

Focus on the person	Focus on motives conforming to certain rules	Focus on actions conforming to certain rules	Focus on the consequences of the action
Virtue theories	**Deontological theories**		**Consequentialist theories**
'Roles'	'Rules'		'Goals'
Prioritises what's virtuous	Prioritises what's right		Prioritises what's good
Agent-centred	**Action-centred**		

As you can see, normative ethical theories can be categorised in all sorts of different ways. One of the most common is to see them as falling into three basic types, according to whether they are based on: 1) certain principles or rules that exist prior to the action; 2) an assessment of the consequences of an action; or 3) the character of the person who performs the action. Those of the first type are called 'deontological' theories (from the Greek *dei* meaning 'one must') and we examine these on pages 30–47.[21] Theories of the second type are called 'consequentialist' or 'teleological' theories (from the Greek *telos* or 'end') and we look at these on pages 47–87 below. Theories of the third kind are termed virtue ethics, which we examine on pages 87–117.[22]

So a deontologist assesses the moral worth of a particular action, by looking to the action itself, and whether it conforms to certain principles or rules. The deontologist does not consider the consequences of an act to be morally primary, and these are put to one side when making moral judgements. The principles or rules of deontology may be ones governing our motives for an action (these may be called 'motivist' theories) or they may simply identify specific kinds of actions that are permitted and/or forbidden, for example, by the Ten Commandments (these may be called 'absolutist' theories).

A consequentialist, however, assesses the effects that the action has on my life and those of others. They wish to weigh up the impact, in terms of the benefits or damage that it brings to people's lives. These benefits may be identified differently according to the type of consequentialist you are. So some consequentialists see the value of an action to lie in the amount of happiness it brings to the individual, others see it as lying in the balance of pleasure over pain for everyone concerned.

Finally the virtue theorist is concerned with living a good life by cultivating an excellent (virtuous) character, rather than focusing on particular principles of action or their consequences. For the Ancient Greeks developing our character properly first meant determining what kind of role we were supposed to play, or what function we had, in society or as human beings in general. Working out what we are *for* (what role we have) enables us to identify those virtues necessary for excelling and flourishing as human beings.

These three kinds of ethical theory can conveniently be remembered by the rhyme 'Rules, Roles and Goals' referring to deontological (rules), virtue (roles), and consequentialist (goals) theories.

The Right and the Good

more difficult

Another way to classify normative theories is to identify what each theory sees as the most basic bearer of ethical value. Within deontological theories, the primary value is right action itself and an action's 'Rightness' carries with it the duty or compulsion for us to perform this action. For a consequentialist theory, the primary value is a good state of affairs (the 'Good'), although consequentialists differ on what precisely the Good is. For virtue theorists the value that is given primacy is a virtuous character, meaning a character which excels in all the appropriate ways (virtuous in the sense of 'virtuosity' or 'virtuoso', i.e. achieving an excellent proficiency in some skill or disposition).

Each value – what's right, what's good and what's virtuous – stems from our basic moral intuitions. We saw this in the activity on page 14 above: right motives, good outcomes, virtuous agents. For a normative theory to ignore any of them would be philosophical suicide; it would be an indication that the theory had failed to account for a large part of our moral lives. However, it is worth remembering that the most successful theories are able to accommodate the primary values of the other theories.

So, for example, within consequentialism a right action is defined in terms of the kind of action that tends to bring about the most positive outcomes. So for a consequentialist the 'Right' (i.e. the rules we should follow) can be understood in terms of maximising the 'Good' (i.e. bringing about the most beneficial outcome). We shall see that for some consequentialists specific rules which tend to bring about the best outcome (such as not killing innocent people) may even be treated a bit like obligations to do what is right, but this is justified on grounds of goodness (treating these rules as if they were obligations tends to bring about the best outcome). The same 'translation' of values is possible in the currency of deontological ethics, which gives primacy of value to certain right actions, particularly doing our duty. So according to a deontologist bringing about the Good is not fundamental, it is simply one duty among many (it is sometimes referred to as the duty of beneficence).

Some philosophers have maintained that it is a mistake to try to find one single value that underpins all others. Instead they argue that we should accept there is a plurality of values, none of them definable in terms of the others. This is an important point and we shall come back to this when we look at intuitionism in Chapter 3 and again when we turn to ethical decision-making in Chapter 4. We shall spend the rest of this chapter examining and assessing each of the three normative theories sketched above: deontological ethics, consequentialist ethics and virtue ethics.

Read through the following tale and then answer the questions below.

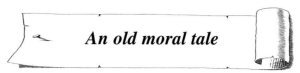

An old moral tale

Robin Hood sets off on one of his escapades to rob the Sheriff of Nottingham of his gold. He sees himself as an anarchic freedom-fighter struggling on behalf of the ordinary people against the yoke of the Norman overlords. However, for practical reasons (being an outlaw isn't cheap – arrows to be bought, merry men to be fed, etc.) Robin tends to keep most of the stolen gold for himself. Today, though, on his way back from the robbery, he's feeling pretty flush. He passes through an impoverished village, and on a whim tosses a few gold coins to the filthy peasants – money which to them is the difference between starvation and survival.

Later that week **Friar Tuck** is giving a sermon on how we should all strive to become more charitable. However, his sermon, which uses stories from the Bible, doesn't seem to be having any effect on his congregation. Someone shouts out 'what about Robin Hood?', and the Friar seizes on this as exactly the contemporary example needed to drive his point home. So the Friar (who is honest to a fault) proceeds to describe in great detail the generosity of Robin Hood and cites Robin's recent distribution of the stolen gold to the poor as a good example of charity.

Unfortunately for the Friar, the **Sheriff of Nottingham** was sitting at the back of the Church. He is a man bound by his obligations to the State, and is proud to be the keeper of law and order in his county. Whatever his personal feelings about the terrible poverty of the Saxons, he feels that he must act against criminals and terrorists like Robin Hood wherever they break the law. Acting on the information that Friar Tuck had let slip in his sermon, the Sheriff arrests Robin and casts him in shackles in Nottingham Dungeon.

Maid Marian is the Sheriff's fiancée but a Saxon herself. She can see that Robin (despite his character faults) is the only hope for the poor people of Nottingham. She knows that Robin's rare acts of charity give the Saxon peasants just enough extra income to help them fight off starvation. She decides she must free Robin, at all costs, and helps him to escape from prison. Robin's escape leads to a series of horrible reprisals against the Saxons, with the Sheriff's men burning several villages, leaving many villagers homeless and facing a harsh winter.

1 Rank the four characters according to who you feel made the best moral decision, from 1 (= best moral decision) to 4 (= worst moral decision).

2 Explain why you have ranked them in this way.

Now think back to the three primary moral values that we identified above (goodness, rightness and virtue).

3 For each of the three characters explain whether his/her actions displayed a commitment to a particular moral value. (For example, was he/she committed to achieving beneficial consequences, to maintaining a certain principle, or to promoting a virtue?)

4 Does the way you have ranked the characters in **1** reveal anything about your own commitment to a particular moral value – are you, instinctively, a consequentialist, a deontologist or a virtue ethicist? Explain.

Deontology: duties and rights

Da Mayor	*Always try to do the right thing.*
Mookie	*That's it?*
Da Mayor	*That's it.*
Mookie	*I got it.*[23]

In Spike Lee's film *Do The Right Thing*, Mookie, the main character, is advised to do the right thing. This seems a simple and sensible approach to life, but what does it entail? What do we have to do in order to do 'the right thing'? How do we find out what the right thing to do is? How do we know when we have done it?

We saw, above, how one approach to the question 'what should we do?' focuses on getting our actions right. In other words making sure that our actions are in accord with certain principles, rules or commands – irrespective of the possible benefits or harms they might bring as a consequence. This 'rightness of action' approach to ethics is called deontological ethics.

Deontological theories regard us as having certain duties or obligations that we must stick to. This approach goes right the way back, at least in the Western tradition, to the rules laid down in the first five books of the Bible, and most famously in the Ten Commandments.[24] Immanuel Kant (1724–1804) put forward a non-religious form of deontological ethics at the end of the eighteenth century, and this proved to be incredibly influential. It was later attacked by the British utilitarians (such as Jeremy Bentham and John Stuart Mill), but defended and revised in the twentieth century by the intuitionist philosophers H. A. Prichard and W. D. Ross.

In the past few hundred years a slightly different form of deontological ethics, the theory of rights, has emerged, which grew out of the increasing political and economic power of individual citizens within Europe and America. The concept of rights was introduced into Western thought in the late sixteenth century and popularised by the political philosophy of Hobbes, Locke and Rousseau. Talk of rights famously appears in the American Declaration of Independence, which claims that we have three rights to 'Life, Liberty and the pursuit of Happiness'. But a statement of rights also appears in the United Nations Declaration of Human Rights.[25] The concept of natural 'rights' is a heavily contested term, and in fact some philosophers (for example, Jeremy Bentham) thought that talk about such rights was nonsense.[26] The connection between individual rights and deontology is that when an individual claims a right they are asserting this as a principle which is to be protected come-what-may. Setting aside the issue of whether we have 'natural rights', the clearest way of understanding rights is to understand their connection to duties. It is often thought that if I have a duty to do something (for example, to help others), then others have a right to that thing (for example, a right to my help). Conversely, if I claim that I have a right to something (for example, a right to free speech), then others have a duty to enable me to do this (for example, a duty to allow for free speech). So rights and duties can be seen as two sides of the same coin.

In this section we shall concentrate only on the 'duty' side of the coin, and in particular two of the most influential forms of deontological theories: divine command and Kantian ethics.

Deontology 1: divine command ethics

The time came when God put Abraham to the test ... God said, 'Take your son Isaac, your only son, whom you love, and go to the land of Moriah. There you shall offer him as a sacrifice on one of the hills which I shall show you.'

Genesis 22:1–3

According to the divine command theory an action is right if God commands it. So when God commanded Abraham to kill his son Isaac as a sacrifice to God, then it was, by definition, the right thing to do.[27]

Many people have seen a strong analogy between morality and the conventional laws of the state. Moral principles or rules tell us what to do in much the same way as state laws do. However, there are also important differences. It often seems that our moral duties are more fundamental than any duty we have to the state's legal system. Our obligations to do the morally right thing are more deep-rooted than our legal obligations, and the two can come into conflict (consider prisoners of conscience, for example, who break a particular law because they believe that this law is immoral). Moral laws also differ from state laws in that they have no conventional human origin and are not written down. And, while there are criminal sanctions for breaking the law, there are no evident parallel sanctions for breaking a moral principle.

One way of explaining both the similarities and differences between morality and the law is to regard morality as a kind of legal system, but with a divine origin. In the Judaeo-Christian version of this view, the moral law is formulated for us by God and it is he who wields punishments for transgression. Within this tradition, the Ten Commandments represent our primary duties and forbidden activities which God would have us adhere to.

Part of the attractiveness of this view is that it explains where morals come from. After all, since moral laws are not written down, and there are no punishments for transgressing them, it is not at all clear why we should follow them or even if they are real. Put another way, what possible grounds could there be for the fact that we are bound by certain moral laws? What is to stop us from doing what we want for our own personal gain? Why do we feel reluctant to exploit others, given that self-interest seems to be the only sensible way to explain our behaviour? How come people get away with sinning? All these questions can be answered if we suppose there is a god who legislates for us. If we grant that there is such a thing as moral consciousness of shame and guilt, even when no human knows what I have done, then we must be ashamed before someone who is more than merely human. If moral conscience involves the experience of guilt this can be best explained by saying we are ashamed for having gone against the will of God.

Equating 'what is right' with 'what God wills' is often called the *divine command theory* or *theological voluntarism* ('theological' because it is related to God, and 'voluntarism' because it is determined by God's will). Supporters of this view claim that 'right' and 'wrong' mean, respectively, commanded and forbidden by God. So they hold that what makes an action right or wrong is that it is commanded or forbidden by God.

The Euthyphro Dilemma as a difficulty for divine command ethics

An apparent consequence of the divine command theory is that if God were to command cruelty, dishonesty or injustice then such things, because they were God's commands, would be obligatory. God could even command completely trivial things such as not stepping on the cracks in the pavement, and, if he did, then these would be our moral duty. But, so the objection runs, this is patently absurd, since it suggests that what is right and wrong is ultimately completely arbitrary.

There are two possible responses to this. On the one hand one can simply accept the objection and claim that any absurdity is only apparent. The reasons for God's choice may be beyond our understanding, but this is because of our limitations and doesn't make it capricious. God must in an important sense be beyond human morality and so what he commands may not conform to what we think of as right. Consider in this context God appearing to Abraham and commanding him to sacrifice his own son Isaac (Genesis 22: 1–13). What should Abraham do in such a situation?

In the Platonic dialogue the *Euthyphro*, Socrates raises this very problem. His interlocutor Euthyphro attempts to define 'holy' as 'whatever all the gods love'. In other words he attempts to define what is 'right', 'good' or 'virtuous' as what is approved of by the gods. In order to get Euthyphro to clarify his definition Socrates then asks whether he means that something is right because the gods command it, or that they command it because it is right.[28] The dilemma Euthyphro faces is to find a response to this question. He has to choose between the following options:

- EITHER *God's will is the source of morality* – whatever he commands is Good, in which case he can command us to do horrific things, which runs counter to our moral intuitions. (Plato then asks why we should worship a God who could command such horrific things.)
- OR *God's will is not the source of morality* – he is Good because he follows the moral law. In which case the moral law lies beyond God and we can by-pass God if we wish to be moral. (Plato then asks why we should worship a God who is bound by the same moral rules as ourselves.) Again this is a CONCLUSION unacceptable to many believers.

Eventually Euthyphro opts for the latter. Divine approval does not *make* an act right or wrong, and so ethical standards do not derive from a divine lawgiver. In this he is in the company of many philosophers who claim that we are able to determine what is right and wrong without appeal to God's commandments. One important implication of this, which cannot be avoided, is that we are able to judge God in the sense that we can recognise what is good and then turn to see if God conforms to it. If he does not, then we should be able to condemn him. John Stuart Mill expressed this view saying: 'I will call no being good, who is not what I mean when I apply that epithet to my fellow creatures, and if such a being can sentence me to hell for not so calling him, to hell I will go.'[29]

The Euthyphro Dilemma brings out another problem with divine command ethics. If 'good' just means 'whatever God commands' then it is pointless to wonder whether what God commands is good. (We shall see later, on page 145, that G. E. Moore had a problem with any such attempt to define 'good'.) It is like wondering whether bachelors are unmarried. For what God commands is good *by definition*. To find out that this is indeed so, one would have only to look in the dictionary, since it is a question about the meaning of words and *not* about the value of God's commandments. So if God's commands can meaningfully be called 'good' then the meaning of 'good' must be independent of God's will.

Further difficulties with divine command ethics

▶ criticism ◀   How are we to discover what God's will is? For example, how can we be sure that the laws revealed to Moses on Mount Sinai came from God? Even assuming that the Bible is the word of God it remains open to different interpretations so we must to some degree be ignorant of the demands being made of us. Plato makes an equivalent point in his dialogue the Euthyphro when he raises doubts about the stories told about the Greek gods and the fact that they appear to disagree about how humans ought to live.[30] In other words they make contradictory demands on us. Similarly, the existence of different religions with equal claim to our obedience may make us doubt that any of them can tell us definitively what God's will is.

The divine command theorist may not regard this as a fatal objection however, but rather as a practical difficulty that we inevitably face in our efforts to determine the moral law.

▶ criticism ◀   Another criticism is that the divine command theory must assume the existence of a benevolent (loving and good) God, and atheists will doubt this. If you are committed for independent reasons to atheism, then clearly divine command ethics will hold little attraction for you. One well-established reason for doubting the existence of a benevolent God is the Problem of Evil. This raises the question of why, if there is a benevolent and all-powerful God, there is so much pain and suffering in the world.

It is possible for someone who believes in God to meet this challenge. For example, a believer may maintain that pain and suffering is the result of human choices; or that it is, in some way, crucial to our development as human beings; or that it is a necessary by-product of having a universe governed by stable physical laws.[31]

▶ criticism ◀ If we equate morality with the will of God, then it follows that if there were no God than there would be no moral obligation. If we cease to believe in God, or worse if he were to cease to exist, then morality should, according to the divine command theorist, die along with him. (These are the terms in which Nietzsche represented the crisis in moral thinking facing humanity in the late nineteenth century with his proclamation of the death of God.) But we can in fact see that atheists, however misguided they may possibly be, are still capable of making moral judgements and still feel bound by moral obligation to others (many of the moral philosophers discussed in this book did not believe in God, yet held that we had moral obligations). This suggests that morality is not bound up with the will of God in the way that the divine command theorist thinks it is.

▶ criticism ◀ A further problem arises for the divine command theory when we consider that there are many situations that we face that God's commandments do not address. In the past fifty years, advances in biomedical technology have meant we can do things undreamt of by those who wrote the Bible. There are no commandments that deal with cloning, or the transplantation into humans of organs from other species, or genetic engineering. This means that there are large gaps in the moral law, as it is stands in the Bible. The divine command theorist has to improvise around those principles and guidelines that they have available to them, but sometimes this improvisation seems quite arbitrary.[32]

▶ criticism ◀ Another issue, and one which we shall be returning to, concerns our motivation to be moral: in this case the question of *why* we should do as God wills. The theologian may reply that we should do so because God will reward us if we do and punish us if we do not, if not in this life then in the next life. This reply may be meant only to motivate us to obey God, but if it is intended to justify the claim that we ought to obey God, then it presupposes a basic selfishness, for then the theologian is telling us that we ought to do what is in our own interest. This view is called 'egoism' and we will be discussing this theory below. For now, however, the point is simply that such self-interested behaviour is often regarded as the opposite of genuine moral behaviour, and so not a *moral* reason for obeying God's commandments.

We saw above that deontological theories consider doing what is right to be independent of the consequences of an action. So, for example, according to the divine command theorist it is *always* wrong to break the commandment not to kill even if such an act might save more lives. The conception of morality as a legal system doesn't take account of the consequences of actions in particular situations. Consequentialist considerations such as the possibility that killing might save a greater number of lives lead some theologians to accept that exceptional circumstances can justify killing. However, a strict divine command theorist would claim that if our moral intuitions tell us that occasionally we should disobey a command, then it is our intuitions that are fault, not the command.

Deontology 2: Kantian ethics

Kant

Two things fill the mind with ever new and increasing admiration and awe, the oftener and more steadily we reflect on them: the starry heavens above and the moral law within.[33]

By the end of the eighteenth century, philosophy in Europe had undergone a transformation. Intellectuals of that period, known as the Enlightenment, felt liberated from the restrictive ties to the Church that had characterised most of the Middle Ages, and which had even been felt by the father of modern philosophy, René Descartes (1591–1650). There was a confidence in human reason, boosted by the growing successes of 'natural philosophy' (what we now call science) in explaining the physical laws of the universe. The divine command theory no longer seemed to capture what people thought about morality. It seemed as if humanity was sufficiently 'enlightened' to realise that it had to determine its values for itself rather than expect them to be delivered by a higher authority.

Immanuel Kant (1724–1804) was sceptical of the optimistic claims made by some 'rationalist' philosophers about the extent to which human reason alone could grasp truths about the universe. He was also critical of the more pessimistic claims of the Scottish philosopher David Hume (1711–1777) that human reason could tell us nothing very interesting about the universe at all. Kant's project was to offer a 'critique' of reason: sketching its limits while showing that human reason could arrive at some truths about the universe after all. Part of this critique extended to practical reason, i.e. the application of reason to the question 'how should we live?'. Kant explained his ethical theory in two important works, *Groundwork of the Metaphysic of Morals* (1785) and the longer *Critique of Practical Reason* (1787).

Kant was a sincere Christian, but he did not believe that ethics could be founded on the commands of God. He believed that morality was independent of God's and everyone else's will. The moral law was part of the fabric of the universe, but it was something that each of us could discover through the use of our reason, rather than instructed in these laws in a paternalistic way.

Kant's ethical theory is deontological in that he believes a moral action is one which we are duty-bound to perform, and an action is only genuinely moral if it is prompted by a recognition of our duty. Thus, to the extent that I act for any other reason, for example out of self-interest, or even out of compassion, the act is not strictly a *moral* one. Kant argues that because people have different emotional reactions, these reactions cannot be significant in evaluating the moral worth of an act. For a rational determination of our duties will be dispassionate and so will determine the same duties for everyone. What this implies is that if I behave in a way which we would normally recognise as morally praiseworthy – for example, I regularly donate to charity – and if I do so simply because I have a terrible feeling of guilt and pity for the poor, this action is not properly speaking a *moral* act. Moreover, according to Kant, someone who, through the use of dispassionate reason, recognises her duty to help others in distress even though she has no compassion for her fellow human beings, is more praiseworthy than someone who would have helped others whether it were his duty or not, because of a compassion for others. For the former must act, as it were, against the grain of her inclinations.

Kant

....
All imperatives command either hypothetically or categorically.[34]
....

Kant points out that there are two senses of the word 'ought' (or, as Kant would say, two kinds of imperative – an imperative being an act we are impelled to do). One is a conditional or (in Kant's terminology) HYPOTHETICAL IMPERATIVE. An example of this use might be 'If you want your pudding, then you ought to eat your vegetables.' Note that this kind of 'ought' depends upon your having a certain goal or aim, namely getting some pudding. In other words, the ought is conditional upon a certain desire: if you want X then you ought to do Y. So if I don't want any pudding, then there is no earthly reason why I ought to eat my vegetables.

Children are constantly being given hypothetical imperatives of this sort, as they have to learn what is good for them, and what is or isn't morally and socially acceptable. To assist in this socialisation, parents use fairy stories and myths which speak of disobedient boys and girls not doing what they are told and suffering the consequences (traditionally this seems to involve being eaten by a wolf). A particularly terrifying set of hypothetical imperatives (aimed at satirising the whole morality tale genre, but terrifying nonetheless) can be found in the nineteenth century poems of *Struwwelpeter* (translated usually as 'Shockheaded Peter', because of the story of the monstrous freak, Peter, who refused to comb his hair!).[35] Here children find that if they don't want their thumbs chopped off by the psychotic Scissor-man then they ought not to suck them. They also discover that if they don't want to drown in the canal, then they ought not to walk around gazing at the sky. Another hypothetical imperative is found in the story of 'Augustus who would not have any soup'; and, as you might have guessed, the clear moral here is that if you don't want to die of starvation then you ought to eat up all your soup.

However, Kant isn't interested in this sort of conditional or hypothetical imperative. The imperatives that Kant thinks are central to morality are of another kind: the 'oughts' that are unconditional or (in Kant's terminology), *categorical*. An example might be 'You ought to respect your mother and father.' Note that this use is not dependent on any goals or aims you may have – the 'if you want X' bit of the imperative disappears, leaving only 'you ought to do Y'. These sorts of imperatives tell us that we have a certain obligation or duty regardless of any consequences. In this sense they are unconditional or categorical (they remain imperatives whether or not they help us to fulfil any particular desire). Now, it is this latter sort of ought which Kant regards as the only genuinely *moral* ought. That is to say, any action which we perform because we are trying to achieve some practical or personal end is not moral.

Read the following commands and answer the questions below.

a) I should do more sit-ups.
b) I ought to be more loyal to my friends.
c) I should pay more attention to my charming philosophy teacher.
d) I ought to buy flowers and grapes for my sick aunt.
e) I ought to start revising soon.
f) I ought to give more money to Children In Need.
g) I shouldn't lie as much as I do.
h) I ought not to kick my little brother on the shins.
i) I should get up earlier.
j) I should stop eating tuna fish.

1 Identify all those commands from the list above which are hypothetical imperatives. (For example, 'I should do more sit-ups' is a conditional or hypothetical imperative.)
2 For those you have identified as hypothetical imperatives, state the conditions they are dependent upon. (For example, 'I should do more sit-ups' could have the condition 'if I want to get rid of all this flab'.)

We have now seen the central idea behind Kant's approach to ethics, namely that in moral terms we are bound by categorical imperatives – these are our duties. However, we have yet to see how Kant thinks we can identify what our duties are, and we shall come back to this below. In the meantime it is worth expressing Kant's theory in more Kantian language.

An action done from duty has its moral worth, not in the purpose to be obtained by it, but in the maxim according with which it is decided upon.[36]

Kant

Kant suggests that we can think of there being a general principle of action or a *maxim* underlying the intention to perform any act. This is a rule of conduct, that is to say a reason why someone elects to act in a certain way or an expression of their motive to so act. But, to be moral, an act must have the appropriate maxim underlying it, namely (as we have seen) one which expresses our duty to perform the act. So my actions to help the homeless or to obey my parents, i.e. to be moral, must be grounded in a maxim such as 'Always help those in need (just because it is your duty)', or 'Always respect your father and mother (just because it is your

39

duty)', and not in a conditional one such as 'Always help those in need because then you'll get into heaven', or 'Always respect your mother and father because otherwise they will spend all your inheritance money'.

Kant

The moral worth of an action does not depend upon the results expected from it.[37]

As we have seen, the duties to which rational beings are bound are *categorical*, i.e. unconditional. For an act to be moral, our motive must be in accord with a principle which is absolute and applies whatever the consequences and however I happen to feel about it. Thus truly moral behaviour is motivated only by categorical imperatives. A categorical imperative will express a duty to do something irrespective of its effects. So it requires us 'categorically' or unconditionally to do something. Kant is arguing, in effect, that a truly moral act must be valuable in itself, irrespective of any consequences it may have. We shall see below that this approach is diametrically opposed to the consequentialist theories of Bentham and Mill.

Another way of expressing this point is that, so far as Kant is concerned, it is our motive which determines the moral worth of an act. The genuinely moral motive for action, i.e. a recognition of our duty, is what Kant terms the 'good will'. A good will is the only motive which is intrinsically or unconditionally good. That is to say, an act which proceeds from the good will is good in itself and not good in virtue of any consequences it has.

> *Heavy, Duty*
> *Heavy duty rock and roll*
> *Heavy duty*
> *Brings out the duty in my soul*[38]

Spinal Tap

Our duties, or the judgements of the good will, are determined by reason alone (and *not* by rock and roll, as Spinal Tap so confidently asserted). For Kant's intention is to demonstrate that we should act morally to the extent that we are rational, i.e. according to reason alone and not feeling. This, as we have seen, means that our moral obligations are not in any way determined by our SYMPATHY for others, our inclinations to happiness or any other purely psychological motive. For these types of motive to action only have value conditionally and not for their own sake. Moreover, for Kant, if we are swayed in our actions by emotions we are not acting freely. If we submit to the urgings of our feelings we are like slaves, simply doing the bidding of forces outside our control. And being a rational being means being able to deliberate autonomously about how to act, and not – as an animal does – simply follow our primitive impulses. Truly to be free, therefore, means acting purely according to the dictates of reason. To act out of a recognition of duty, motivated by the good will, is to exercise our freedom.

ACTIVITY   Which of the following actions are done from good will alone (i.e. without any motive of self-interest)?

1 Josie saves someone from drowning in order to impress the gorgeous lifeguard who she's been flirting with all summer.
2 Beth puts aside every Saturday to work in her local 'Making the World a Better Place' Youth Centre.
3 In the weeks running up to his birthday Marlon always makes an extra special effort helping out his parents, checking they're okay and whether they need anything, etc.
4 Mel decides that eating one more triple-choc cookie will make her sick, and so she puts the rest of the biscuits she 'borrowed' from her flatmate back into his cupboard.
5 Leonie gives Friends of the Earth £1 because she loves watching the coins whirl round and round the hole before falling into the charity box.
6 Samsia notices a large, unaccompanied rucksack by the door of a train, and asks the crowded carriage who the owner of it is.
7 Gary keeps his promise to show off his latest dance moves to his philosophy class, despite just having been promoted to Head of Department.

Since categorical imperatives are unconditionally binding, they are equally applicable to all rational beings. They must, in other words, be universal. It follows from this that the basic categorical imperative must be that:

Kant

I should never act in such a way that I could not will that my maxim should be a universal law.[39]

In other words we must always act in accordance with a maxim which is binding for everyone. This is the principle of UNIVERSALISABILITY, a version of the religious GOLDEN RULE to treat others as you would like them to treat you.[40] It means that you cannot make an exception of your own case when making moral judgements.

What Kant is saying here is that when we make a moral judgement about a particular act we seem implicitly to commit ourselves to saying that a similar act would be wrong in a similar situation. For example, if I argued today that it is wrong for me to eat beef it suggests (all things being equal) that it would also be wrong tomorrow. It also suggests that it would be wrong for anyone else to eat beef. Put the other way around, if I claim that it is wrong to eat beef today but that it is not wrong tomorrow, I am committed to there being some morally relevant difference between today and tomorrow. Or if I argue that it is wrong for me, but not for you, then I am committed to finding some relevant difference between my situation and yours. Note that the principle of universalisability implies that any moral reasoning must involve espousing rules or principles which bind us all.

Kant believes that the categorical imperative can help us to determine what these principles are. It will allow us to distinguish truly moral maxims from amoral or immoral ones. In one illustration Kant supposes that someone (person A) makes a promise but is ready to break it if this suits his purposes. A's maxim then may be expressed thus: 'When it suits my purposes I will make promises, intending also to break them if this suits my purposes.' But A cannot consistently will this maxim to be universally acted on, says Kant.

Kant

Could I say to myself that everyone makes a false promise when he is in difficulty from which he otherwise cannot escape? I immediately see that I could will the lie but not a universal law to lie. For with such a law [i.e. with such a maxim universally acted on] there would be no promises at all ... Thus my maxim would necessarily destroy itself as soon as it was made a universal law.[41]

The ideas of contradiction, inconsistency or 'self-defeating' are fundamental here. A duty is a maxim that can be made universal *without* any contradiction, inconsistency or it being self-defeating. For example, person A was following the maxim 'I can break promises when it suits me'; but what happens if everyone follows this maxim? Kant believes that if A's maxim were universalised then the very institution of promise-making would collapse, since there would be no genuine promises at all. So A's maxim is self-defeating since universalising it would undermine the possibility of making promises which the maxim presupposes. For this reason, according to Kant, we can recognise that this maxim is not moral and cannot be a duty.

Kant offers four illustrations of the types of duty that the categorical imperative entails.[42] The types of duty that Kant discusses are duties to ourselves and duties to others; and within each of these we find there are perfect duties (ones which have no exceptions) and imperfect duties (ones which may admit of exceptions). Each of the following examples shows how a particular maxim underpinning an action can (or cannot) be universalised, thus demonstrating whether or not that maxim is a duty.

1 *Perfect duty to ourselves.* Someone miserable is contemplating committing suicide, and Kant shows how the categorical imperative entails that the person has a duty not to commit suicide (no matter how miserable they are).
2 *Perfect duty to others.* Someone wants to borrow money on the promise that they'll pay it back, but they know that they will never be able to afford to pay it back within the agreed time limit of the loan. We have already seen that Kant believes the categorical imperative to show that making false promises cannot be universalised, it cannot be a duty and is morally wrong.
3 *Imperfect duty to ourselves.* Someone with natural talents lets them go to waste because they are lazy. Here Kant uses the categorical imperative to show that it is wrong for us to waste our natural talents – we must at least choose to develop some of them (this is why it is an imperfect duty, because we can choose to let some of our talents rust).
4 *Imperfect duty to others.* Someone who is doing pretty well in life is considering helping out other people. Kant shows that although it is possible to universalise the maxim '*don't help others*', it is not possible to 'will' this to happen – because we would not want to be in a situation where we need assistance and yet no one wants to help us.

Kant also expresses the categorical imperative using various other formulae alongside the principle of universalisability. One version is to say that others should be treated as *ends* in themselves and never as *means* to an end.[43] This entails that you should never simply use other people to further your own goals. Rather you ought always to respect other people's desires and goals. This is because a rational being does not have merely conditional worth, i.e. is not just worthwhile as a means to some end. Rather they are worthwhile for their own sake, or unconditionally. The Realm of Ends is an ideal community that Kant imagines in which everyone would treat one another as ends in themselves.

A summary of Kant's main theses

1 We have to determine what is right and wrong for ourselves by the application of reason, and not expect it to be delivered by any higher authority (such as God or the Church).

2 A moral action is one which proceeds from the proper motive, namely the 'good will' or a recognition of *duty*.

3 Duties are unconditional (or categorical) demands on our behaviour, for example 'You should give up your seat to the elderly and infirm.' They are unconditional or categorical because they do not depend on any conditions that need to be met: they are imperatives that apply to us all the time, whatever our personal desires and goals. In contrast, conditional (or hypothetical) demands depend on our having certain ends or goals in mind, for example 'If you want your pudding you should eat your vegetables'. If the conditions aren't met, for example if we don't like this particular pudding, then the command simply doesn't apply to us.

4 Our duties are determined by the use of reason alone. So any non-rational motive, such as an emotion or feeling of compassion, is not a moral motive. This is because reason alone is independent and autonomous.

5 Duties are determined by the attempt to universalise the maxim underlying an action.

6 If the maxim can be universalised without contradiction then it is a moral maxim and so a duty.

7 The ultimate duty is always to act in accordance with the categorical imperative, i.e. always to act in accordance with a maxim that you will everyone to act by.

8 A second version of the categorical imperative states that we should always treat others as ends in themselves and never as means to our ends.

9 The Realm of Ends is the ideal moral community in which everyone treats everyone else as ends in themselves.

Using only Kant's categorical imperative you must decide what would be the right course of action in each of the following situations. Note that, for the purposes of this activity, you are offered only two possible courses of action. To calculate what is right and wrong you must:

a) determine what the maxim is underpinning each course of action,

b) determine whether it is possible to universalise this maxim without contradiction or inconsistency,

c) work out which maxims can and can't be universalised. You will now know which course of action is right and which is wrong.

1 You promise to take your nephew (Little Johnny) to the park to play on Saturday. But on Wednesday your friend calls up with two tickets for a Cup Final/top West End musical/Richard Dawkins lecture. Little Johnny is away camping until Saturday morning.

   a) Do you break your promise?

   b) Do you keep your promise?

2 You are helping out your Auntie by taking her dog, Rooney, for a

walk to the newsagents. Suddenly the dog's fur catches fire, from the flick of someone's cigarette butt. Rooney is in pain, but there is no water available, only two pints of cold milk on No. 32's doorstep.

a) Do you steal the milk?

b) Do you leave the milk?

3 Your friend who recently developed an eating disorder asks you if her bottom looks lumpy in her new tight trousers. It does.

a) Do you lie?

b) Do you tell the truth?

4 You are standing on the roof of a building, hauling a piano up to the third floor. Suddenly you hear gunshots. A man directly below the piano is shooting at a passing parade of local dignitaries.

a) Do you drop the piano and kill him?

b) Do you let him carry on shooting?

5 With your partner away working a two-year stint on an oil rig, your very attractive yet terminally ill neighbour confesses undying love for you and asks for one romantic night together before the illness finally takes its toll. You cannot contact your partner.

a) Are you unfaithful?

b) Do you remain faithful?

Some criticisms of Kant's theory

A major difficulty for Kant's theory is that it seems that not every universal maxim is a moral one. It could be trivial or amoral. And this shows that not every maxim that passes his test of universalisability is a duty. The problem is that Kant does not tell us precisely how we are to distinguish moral duties from absurd imperatives, for surely there is nothing to stop me from universalising the maxim 'never step on the cracks in the pavement'. It is certainly not *inconsistent* to will that everyone do so. Similarly, it is not clear how Kant could distinguish moral obligations from social etiquette. I could easily will that everyone eats with a knife and fork and be outraged at the thought that some adults use their hands or just spoons. It is not hard to imagine my consistently regarding bad table manners as the height of depravity, for here there is no contradiction. But in so doing surely I would betray nothing more than my own bigotry. There are other, apparently innocent, examples of maxims which cannot be universalised and hence, on Kant's account, must be morally wrong. For example, 'using contraception when having sex' is a maxim that someone might have if they don't want children. But it cannot be universalised, because there would soon be no human species, and hence it appears to be morally wrong. This seems very counter-intuitive to most of us, and indicates that something is problematic within Kant's theory. **45**

Moreover it is also not clear that Kant's principle rules out certain *immoral* maxims, such as the maxim of never helping anyone. For surely there is nothing inconsistent with my willing this to be acted on by everyone. It may be that Kant can defend himself against this criticism by pointing to one of the alternative formulations of the categorical imperative, the one that says we should treat people as ends-in-themselves, and never solely as a means to an end. So, using this version of the categorical imperative, Kant might argue that never helping anyone at all involves treating others as means (because we all need a community in which to grow, be educated and survive) and not as ends in themselves (people who have needs just like us).

A second important objection is that Kant's approach provides no concrete advice as to how to behave. While providing a framework, it provides no substantive help in making moral decisions when we are faced with moral dilemmas. This is particularly telling when Kant comes to apply the categorical imperative to everyday life. The categorical imperative goes some way in this direction but if we encounter conflicts between different duties, it appears there is no way for us to choose. We shall see in the next chapter (page 150) how W. D. Ross tried to resolve this problem by claiming that duties were PRIMA FACIE and it is left to us to decide in a particular situation which duty is our actual duty.

There are aspects of Kant's theory that fall clearly outside of our 'moral intuitions', i.e. with what we are pre-theoretically inclined to say. Kant uses Plato's example from the *Republic* of the madman who wants to reclaim a lent weapon, say an axe, in order to show that we have a duty not to lie, no matter what the circumstances.[44] You are probably familiar with the example: you've borrowed an axe from an acquaintance to chop down a tree, and one night he knocks on your door, looking and sounding like he wants to murder someone, and he demands his axe back. Plato uses this example to show that an account of morality which requires us to return the axe in these circumstances must be a flawed account. Kant, however, drawing on a similar example (although in his example the madman already has the axe and simply wants to know whether the intended victim is in your house), thinks that we still have a duty to tell the truth to the madman, even though we suspect this will lead to a murder. Plato seems to be right here, and Kant's use of the example brings out a problematic inflexibility in his position. Again this example, and others like it, might be resolved by adopting the strategy that W. D. Ross suggests.

We shall see below that one of the criticisms of

UTILITARIANISM is that it encourages a cold and calculative approach to ethics – but Kant seems equally guilty of this by demanding that we put aside our feelings for the fellow suffering of others. In fact Kant's claim that emotions are irrelevant, and that the only appropriate motive for a moral action is a sense of duty, seems to be at odds with our intuition that certain emotions have a moral dimension, such as guilt and sympathy, or pride and jealousy. Don't we regard the possession of such emotions itself as morally praise- (or blame-) worthy?

Moreover we may doubt whether it is even possible for us to set aside the interests, concerns and desires that make us individuals, and to think of ourselves, as Kant wants us to, as purely rational autonomous beings engaged in universal law-making. Bernard Williams argues that the impartial position that Kant wishes us to adopt may be possible for factual considerations, but not for practical, moral deliberations.[45] For example, if I ask 'I wonder whether strontium is a metal?' it is possible to remove the personal 'I' from this question, and seek an answer that is independent of my own perspective on the world. This kind of deliberation means that it is possible for anyone to take up my question and be given the same answer; there is what Williams calls a 'unity of interest' in the answer. This is because deliberation about facts is not essentially personal, but is an attempt to reach an impersonal position (where we all agree that these are the facts). In contrast, Williams maintains that practical deliberation is essentially personal and it does make a difference whether it is me, or someone else (for example, the madman's mother, his intended victim, the victim's life insurer or the madman himself) asking the question 'Should I give this man his axe back?' We cannot and should not strive for the same impersonal position as in the factual case. With moral deliberations there is no longer a 'unity of interest', and a different person, with a different set of desires and interests, who is now standing in my shoes, might seek a different answer. The position from which we ask this practical question is a personal position, and the answer will affect us very much. Williams argues that Kant is wrong and that we cannot adopt an impersonal perspective (the perspective of the categorical imperative), because by doing so we lose our place in the world, our interests and any sense of self.

Consequentialist theories

In Stanley Kubrick's film *Dr Strangelove*, the rogue General Ripper orders a squadron of B52 bombers to carry out a pre-emptive nuclear strike on Russia. It turns out that the Russians have in place a nuclear 'Doomsday Machine' which will annihilate the United States should Russia ever be attacked. The B52 bombers cannot be recalled, and it looks inevitable that the Russian Doomsday Machine will be triggered, wiping out the entire population of America. General Turgidson suggests to the President that they can only destroy the Doomsday Machine by launching all their nuclear warheads into Russia.

General Turgidson	*Mr President, we are rapidly approaching a moment of truth … Now truth is not always a pleasant thing, but it is necessary now to make a choice. To choose between two admittedly regrettable, but nevertheless distinguishable post-war environments – one where you got twenty million people killed, and the other where you got one hundred and fifty million people killed.*
President Muffley	*You're talking about mass murder, General, not war.*
Turgidson	*Mr President, I'm not saying we wouldn't get our hair mussed – but no more than ten to twenty million people killed, tops.*
Muffley	*I will not go down in history as a mass murderer.*
Turgidson	*Perhaps it might be better, Mr President, if you concerned yourself more about the American people than your image in the history books.*[46]

Dr Strangelove

General Turgidson is adopting a clear consequentialist approach to this situation: he is asking the President to weigh up the outcome of two courses of action, and simply to choose the action that produces the best possible outcome. This pragmatic approach is in stark contrast to the strict adherence to principles that a deontologist demands. For Kant we have a duty not to kill, and if not killing results in the deaths of a further hundred million people, then we have still done the right thing by not killing anyone ourselves.

As we saw at the beginning of this chapter, consequentialist ethical theories assess the moral worth of an act, not on the basis of the motive behind it, but on the basis of the *consequences* it has. If, for deontological theories, it is wrong to steal because we have a duty to respect others' property, for a consequentialist, stealing must be judged on an evaluation of the effects it produces. In its pure form this would mean that individual acts are to be judged according to their actual consequences, but consequentialists may also make reference to the results of classes of actions, or to foreseeable or probable results, as we shall see.

There are two main forms of consequentialist ethics. The first, which we refer to as 'ethical egoism', considers an action to be good if it brings about the best possible outcome for me as an individual (or in your case, for you as an individual). The second, sometimes called 'ethical universalism' but most commonly known as utilitarianism, considers an action to be good if it brings about the best possible outcome for everyone in general.

Consequentialist ethics 1: ethical egoism

Callicles appears as one of the interlocutors in Plato's dialogue the *Gorgias*, where he mounts one of the most potent challenges to the ethical views of Socrates–Plato (views we examine below on pages 89–100). For Callicles the answer to the question 'how should I live?' is this: you should break free of the constraints of conventional morality and you should be as 'immoral' as you need to be, seeking only what is good for you, whatever the consequences for others. 'The truth, Socrates, is this way: luxury and excess and freedom, if it is well supplied, this is virtue and happiness; those other things, those ornaments, those agreements of men … those are rubbish, worth nothing.'[47] This positioning of self-interest at the heart of what we should do is known as ethical egoism.

Ethical egoism holds that I should always do what will promote my own greatest good: that an act or rule of action is right if and only if it promotes the greatest balance of good over evil for me compared with any alternative. The ethical egoist, however, need not be like Callicles and act in a manner we would ordinarily call 'egotistical', 'narcissistic' or 'selfish'. Whether I am selfish will depend on whether I think such behaviour to be in my interest. I may judge modesty and consideration for others to be the best long-term policy. I may, in other words recognise the need to co-operate with others, and to act in a way which is traditionally regarded as moral in order to serve my own best interests. For example, I may judge it an unwise policy to lie, cheat and steal, for this will doubtless lead to my being distrusted and disliked, and to my having to forego the benefits of society. An egoist who reasons in this way, and acts where necessary in a selfless way, is said to be an 'enlightened' egoist.

One influential moral theorist who adopts an enlightened egoist position is the seventeenth-century English philosopher Thomas Hobbes (1588–1679). In his great work *Leviathan* (1651) he develops an account of the origins of morality. He imagines a 'state of nature', the condition of mankind prior to any social organisation. In this state each of us pursues what benefits our selves without qualms. No one can expect anyone else to do anything other than whatever maximises their own self-interest. This state would consist in a kind of 'war of every man against every man'. There would be none of the advantages of civilisation because all of us would live in 'continual fear and danger of violent death, and the life of man, solitary, poor, nasty, brutish, and short'.[48]

Given the fact that the state of nature is bad for everyone, Hobbes reckons it is rational for everyone to want to escape it. Since the only escape consists in following rules which require co-operation between people – a kind of social contract – it is rational for us to agree to follow such rules so long as we can rely on others to do so too. So it is actually desirable for an egoist to conform to moral behaviour (and to sign up to the social contract) in order to avoid being harmed by other egoists.

Psychological egoism

Ian McEwan's novel *Enduring Love* begins in the Chiltern Hills with a man clinging to a hot-air balloon shouting for help. Inside the basket of the balloon is a child. Five strangers come sprinting to help, to grab the ropes and bring the balloon and child back down to earth. But a sudden gust of wind takes the balloon up into the air, with the five men still hanging from the ropes. If every member of this makeshift crew holds on then their weight might be enough to bring the balloon back down – but the higher they go up the more chance they'll die from the fall. Should they trust the others to hang on, or should they save themselves and let go?

> *I do not know, nor have I discovered, who let go first ... What is certain is that if we had not broken ranks, our collective weight would have brought the balloon to earth a few seconds later as the gust subsided. Hanging above the Chilterns escarpment our crew enacted morality's ancient, irresolvable dilemma: us, or me. Someone said me, and there was nothing to be gained by saying us.*[49]
>
> Ian McEwan, *Enduring Love*

Without a Hobbesian contract to bind the group together they resorted to self-interest. Once one of them had let go it became more dangerous for the others to hang on, and so one by one they released the ropes and dropped safely to the ground. Until only one man was left, desperately hanging on, drifting upwards with the balloon until he fell to a horrific death. For all but one of these men, self-interest won out over helping the group, with tragic consequences. The claim that humans are primarily motivated by self-interest is known as psychological egoism.

It is important to distinguish psychological egoism from ethical egoism. Psychological egoism is the view that human beings are by nature self-interested creatures. In other words, we are so constituted that we are primarily (or exclusively) concerned to maximise our own personal advantage. It is, in other words, a factual claim about human psychology. Ethical egoism, on the other hand, is the claim that we *should* prioritise self-interest above other goals, we *should* aim to maximise what is good for us as individuals. This means that the 'prudential should' (i.e. that which we ought to do in order to achieve our goals) coincides with the 'moral should' (i.e. that which we ought to do for its own sake).

Now, psychological egoism is often closely linked to the ethical variety. For one of the principal arguments in support of *ethical* egoism is a psychological one. The argument is that if the principal motivation for human behaviour is the pursuit of self-interest, then we must be justified in continuing in that pursuit. Indeed if it is natural for humans to seek their own benefit, then each of us has a right, even a duty, to do so. Moreover, if psychological egoism is true, it is simply flying in the face of the facts to search for some other principle governing moral behaviour.

The argument of the enlightened egoist, that to act in my own self-interest is not ultimately to act at variance with the ordinary dictates of morality, is given support from 'game theory' and the Prisoner's Dilemma.

The Prisoner's Dilemma

This game should be played against an opponent: a friend, classmates or online at http://www.iterated-prisoners-dilemma.net/ Basically it is a card game in which you try to get as a high a score as possible. You have two cards in your hands, a red one and a black one; so does your opponent. Now it is only the colour, and not the number, of the card that is relevant in this game. You conceal these cards from your opponent, then select one and put it face down on a table. Your opponent does the same. You then each turn over your card to reveal its colour. This is repeated five times before you add up the score. You then move on to play another opponent. The scoring system (which will determine which cards you decide to play) is as follows:

If you both play black then you both get 3 points. If you play red and your opponent plays black, then you get 5 points and your opponent loses 2. Obviously if you play black, and your opponent plays red, then you lose the 2 points, while your opponent gets 5 points, However, if you both play red then you get zero and your opponent gets zero.

This can be summarised in the table overleaf.

(Note that the first number represents the number of points you get, the second number represents the number of points your opponent gets. So <5, –2> means you get 5 points and she loses 2.)

	She plays red	**She plays black**
You play red	<0, 0>	<5, –2>
You play black	<–2, 5>	<3, 3>

The Prisoner's Dilemma and self-interest

The game is based on a well-known scenario used in game theory called the Prisoner's Dilemma. Two people are arrested and held in separate cells by the police. The police do not have enough evidence to convict both, and so they make each prisoner the same deal: either the prisoner stays quiet, and trusts his friend not to betray him, or he betrays his friend, not caring what happens to her. The choices and outcomes are roughly the same as in this game, i.e. the betrayal is the more tempting option (there is the opportunity to go free), and staying quiet requires trust that the other prisoner will stay quiet. So, in the activity above, the selfless/selfish courses of action that confront the prisoners are represented as follows:

a selfish action = playing the red card
a selfless action = playing the black card

This activity can be used to illustrate how our innate self-interest may lead in the long-term to altruistic (selfless) behaviour. If the game has been understood and played properly then one thing that you will have realised is that the red card is the potentially higher scoring card:

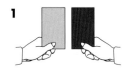

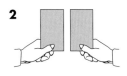

1 Selfish card v. selfless card – the selfish card wins and the selfless card loses.

Moreover the selfish (red) card also offers less risk as you can never actually lose points; the worst possibility is that you will score zero, but then your opponent will score zero too:

2 Selfish card v. selfish card – no one wins.

So, seen in terms of the outcome of each round, it seems more rational (and in our self-interest) to play the red card.[50]

The black card on the other hand is the riskier one because it relies on trust – you have to hope that your opponent will play black, and not sting you with a red. But where there is this mutual trust then there is also a reward:

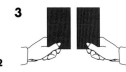

3 Selfless card v. selfless card – both win.

Students who play only red cards are thinking solely about themselves; those who play black are considering the overall outcome of the game for both themselves and for their opponent.

In the activity above, playing red all the time will eventually lead to failure. This can be shown by considering what would happen if this game is played many times ('iterated') among the same group of players. The more you play other friends, the more you learn to trust and co-operate with black-card players and penalise red-card players. Black-card players will start to do well, red-card players will start to suffer: either they will continue scoring zero or they will learn to play black. Taking this game as an analogy for society, it is possible to infer that, even in a state of nature, i.e. without any formal government or laws, we have the genesis of altruism (selflessness): you scratch my back and I'll scratch yours. So why should we be moral? Because in the long run being selfless (playing black) will bring us more benefits than selfishness.

So the origins of morality need not lie in some universal moral law, or in the commandments of God, as deontological theorists suggest. The origins could simply lie in our own self-interest, namely the realisation that, in social groups, altruistic behaviour is more beneficial to the individual. Evolutionary biologists have, in the last 30 years, started to suggest that altruism may be explained because it leads to greater evolutionary success for some creatures. This seems strange as these biologists also propose that we are all out to look after ourselves. This tension between our 'selfish genes' and our altruistic behaviour can be explained if strong altruistic instincts in an animal lead to its having more offspring than creatures who lack those instincts. Richard Dawkins is one thinker who takes such a line.[51]

experimenting with ideas

Below are some examples of how you might reason in a self-interested way (like the people clinging onto the balloon in Ian McEwan's novel).

1 You are pushing a car up a hill with four other people and you think 'I could just pretend to be pushing, only three people are needed for this job', and so you stop pushing.
2 You go to the supermarket to buy some washing powder and buy the own-brand budget powder, because it is slightly cheaper than the environmentally friendly stuff.
3 Every Friday night you go out with friends for a drink. The idea is that everyone buys a round, but you have never bought a round and don't intend to – after all there are always plenty of other people who offer to buy rounds before you.

4 You want to listen to the latest CD by your favourite artists, but you don't want to actually buy it. Instead you borrow a CD from a friend and burn a copy for yourself.

5 It is the weekend before an important exam. You know that, because the exam room is so small, you'll be able to look at the work of the people sitting next to you and copy their answers. So you decide that you won't do any revision and that you'll cheat in the exam.

Now, for each situation:

a) Describe what would happen if everyone acted in this way.

b) Describe whether the consequences of a) would damage what was in your interest.

c) What are the chances of everyone behaving in this way?

d) Having considered your answers to a), b) and c) would you say that it is *still* in your self-interest to behave in this way?

e) What would Kant have said we ought to do, and why?

You might ask how thinking about courses of action in this way differs from Kant's principle of universalisability. The activity invites you to consider 'what would happen if everyone did this', and it seems as if Kant is asking us to do the same thing: so why don't we just consider Kant to be a consequentialist? The answer is that Kant's categorical imperative does not ask us to consider the consequences of each action, as if they were to actually happen. When he asks us to universalise an action, it is not the outcome that we should be interested in, but the 'logic' of whether such a universalisation is possible. For Kant where a universalised maxim leads to a contradiction, an inconsistency or is self-defeating then that maxim cannot be a duty. On the other hand, when a consequentialist invites us to consider the golden rule they are asking us to think about what the consequences would be 'if everyone behaved like this' (as Woody Allen asked on page 25). From the point of view of ethical egoism, sometimes we come to see that we would be worse off if everyone behaved like this, and we need to calculate the chances of everyone actually behaving like this. And, where they are high, then we may need to moderate our behaviour. However, we may conclude that the chances of other people behaving in a selfish way are low, and that we'd be better off just sticking to our selfish guns.

Some difficulties with egoism

► criticism ◄ The standard objection to the move from psychological egoism to ethical egoism is that you cannot logically infer an *ethical* conclusion from a *factual* PREMISE about psychology (we discuss this in more detail when we consider the IS/OUGHT question on page 138). Even if the egoist is correct in his analysis of human nature it need not follow that we are morally obliged to act in our own self-interest.

In defence of the egoist, however, he may not be attempting to argue in this way. Rather the contention may simply be that it is unrealistic to propose that we ought to behave in a way other than for our own gain since we can do nothing else. If 'ought' implies 'can' – if we cannot be morally obliged to do what we cannot possibly do – then we cannot be morally obliged to be anything other than egoists. Thus the argument is reasonable if its analysis of human nature is correct.

► criticism ◄   But is it correct? Are we capable of caring about anything other than our own welfare? Surely people do all kinds of actions which are motivated by concern for others, and not for their own satisfaction. Consider here the actions of a parent raising their child, or of soldiers who are prepared to die to defend their countrymen, or the many charity workers who devote their lives to caring for the poor. To deny that people act altruistically is just to fly in the face of the facts. We shall see below (page 107) that David Hume believed that our sympathetic concern for others was at least as strong a feeling as self-interest.

To this criticism the egoist may retort that such apparently altruistic acts are ultimately egoistical in motive, as the Prisoner's Dilemma can show. Perhaps we only give to charity in order to persuade others we are generous, and only look after our children so that they will look after us in our old age and so on. Even though we may think we are being altruistic, in reality there is always a selfish – if unconscious – motive underlying the action. Perhaps the real reason people work for charity is for their own happiness. Perhaps the only reason people give up their seat on the bus is that it gives them a warm glow of self-satisfaction. (This explanation for altruism also occurs to Valmont in *Dangerous Liaisons*, below on page 108.)

► criticism ◄   One response to this is to point out that, even if we do get satisfaction from helping others, for example, this doesn't show that we do it *because* of this satisfaction. Just because it makes me feel good to help others, by itself this doesn't show that I only do it in order to feel good. For it may be that I feel good because I've done a good thing. In other words, the psychological egoist can be accused of confusing the object of someone's desire with the satisfaction that results from obtaining it.

► criticism ◄ The psychological egoist also faces another difficulty if they insist that all motives must ultimately be egoistical. If every apparently altruistic act is ultimately a disguised egoistic one the egoist position threatens to degenerate into an empty or *ad hoc* claim. This is because the theory becomes irrefutable. Nothing will count as evidence against it. For any apparently altruistic act a selfish motive is posited. But if nothing can count against it, then the theory doesn't explain anything. For if in reality there are no altruistic acts then there is no longer any contrast to be drawn between altruistic and egoistic behaviour. If all acts are selfish then there is no difference between a selfish and an unselfish act. But if there is no such contrast, then the concept of a selfish act loses its meaning. It simply becomes synonymous with 'motivated'; for the very concept of a selfish act trades on the concept of an unselfish one.

► criticism ◄ Ethical egoism has been accused of being self-contradictory. If, following Kant, we attempt to universalise the egoist's maxim into a universal law we find that it cannot be to an individual's advantage that all others should pursue their own advantage. So a Kantian would claim that it throws up an inconsistency. This appeal to the universalisability principle is made at the end of Joseph Heller's novel *Catch-22* as an argument against the hero's (Yossarian's) decision to become an ethical egoist:

> *'Don't talk to me about fighting to save my country. I've been fighting all along to save my country … The country's not in danger any more, but I am … From now on I'm only thinking of me.'*
>
> *Major Danby replied indulgently, with a superior smile, 'But Yossarian, suppose everyone felt that way.'*
>
> *'Then I'd certainly be a damn fool to feel any other way, wouldn't I?'*[52]

Joseph Heller, *Catch-22*

However, the Kantian argument does not show that ethical egoism is *logically* self-contradictory, for it is in no difficulty if what is to one person's advantage coincides with what is to the advantage of everyone. Someone might argue that the greatest good for all will be served only if we all pursue our own self-interest. If this is so, we can consistently will the egoistic maxim to be universally acted upon. The *laissez-faire* economics of Adam Smith (1723–1790) might be thought to imply just such a position. In the free market place, the unfettered pursuit of profit actually produces the greatest good for all. If we all pursue the profit motive we all get richer. So Smith's claim would be that there is not real conflict of different egoistic wills, for it is precisely competition which encourages economic growth, and makes us all better off. While this has some plausibility in the economic sphere, it is less plausible for social relations in general. For surely, if we all live without any concern for others, conflicts of interest will inevitably arise.

▶ criticism ◀ Finally, ethical egoism also seems unable to account for that aspect of our moral life that involves giving moral advice. In Sartre's lecture *Existentialism and Humanism* he describes how one of his pupils came to him with a moral dilemma, and asked him for guidance.[53] Now, if ethical egoism is true, then Sartre would have to advise his pupil to do what suits him (i.e. Sartre) best since this, according to ethical egoism, must be the right thing to do (for Sartre). Yet clearly Sartre's pupil is not particularly concerned with what suits Sartre and any such advice would be unhelpful and beside the point. (Actually, Sartre is unhelpful, but for very different reasons![54]) So an ethical egoist has difficulty in explaining why we would ask others for advice and in accounting for what is going on when we do ask someone for advice.

Consequentialist ethics 2: utilitarianism

> *Their eyes were drawn to the majestic buildings of Slough Crematorium. 'Phosphorus recovery' exclaimed Henry … 'Now they recover over ninety-eight percent of it. More than a kilo and a half per adult corpse.' … Henry spoke with happy pride, rejoicing in the achievement as though it had been his own. 'Fine to think we can go on being socially useful even after we're dead … Making plants grow.'*[55]
>
> Aldous Huxley, *Brave New World*

The brave new world of Huxley's novel is one where individuality has been sacrificed for the sake of the common good. There are no wars, there is no conflict, no family strife, no crime, no pain or suffering at all really. Everyone is happy and, like Henry, everyone is totally sold on the idea of social UTILITY. People are also brought up to believe that indulgence in sensual pleasures is what we should be striving for: there is no such thing as monogamy, and free-love is the social norm; new technologies have been used to develop amazing new games and entertainments; the cinemas are no longer just sight and sound but are 'feelies' with audiences tasting, smelling and feeling all that is on the screen; and if you ever want a break from it all then you can use your free prescription of the drug *soma* which transports you to another psychedelic world without any harmful side-effects whatsoever. Sound tempting? Since it maximises pleasure for the majority, such a society may seem the utopian ideal we should be aiming to create. Unfortunately there are certain dystopian costs. No one has any freedom, there is a strict social class system from which you cannot move, you are indoctrinated from the moment you are 'decanted' (no one is born, everyone is grown in a factory), there is no history, no art, no literature, no philosophy and no possibility of rebelling against the system.

Consequentialist theories are most often HEDONISTIC. That is to say that they identify the highest good with pleasure, and so a morally good act is defined as one which brings about the greatest amount of pleasure. Nonetheless, as we shall see, it is possible for a consequentialist to identify the good with other goals, such as power, knowledge, self-realisation, perfection, equality, justice, in which case a morally good act will be whatever brings these about.

We have already seen how ethical egoism can take a hedonistic form when it proposes that each individual should be striving to maximise pleasure for himself or herself. However the most popular and influential form of hedonistic consequentialism within the English-speaking tradition extends the value of pleasure to all of humanity. This 'ethical universalism' is generally referred to as utilitarianism, and despite the clunky name the theory is very simple, as we shall see. The term 'utilitarianism' stems from the idea of utility, meaning social utility or welfare, or 'good of society' (rather than 'utility' in the sense of useful or functional). The 'social utility' that utilitarianism is referring to is the optimisation of pleasure over pain for everyone.

The classic exponents of utilitarianism were Jeremy Bentham (1748–1832), John Stuart Mill (1806–1873) and Henry Sidgwick (1838–1900). We shall look first at Bentham's theory and then at Mill's refinement of it, before assessing some criticisms of the theory.

Bentham's utilitarianism

Bentham

Nature has placed mankind under the governance of two sovereign masters, pain and pleasure. It is for them alone to point out what we ought to do, as well as to determine what we shall do.[56]

Jeremy Bentham was a member of a group of thinkers (known as the British philosophical radicals) who wished to transform the British legal, parliamentary and penal systems. Bentham was a close friend of James Mill, and together they established the theory that they called utilitarianism. James Mill's son, John Stuart Mill, was brought up as a strict utilitarian, and went on to become the most famous proponent of the theory. Out of all the moral theories we examine, utilitarianism has probably had the most impact on policy-makers and governments. This is because of its ostensibly quantifiable nature, and in Bentham's work we find an explicit attempt to construct a method of calculating the morality of an action (the 'utility calculus') by quantifying outcomes.

Bentham saw himself as the successor of David Hume, who claimed that morality was grounded in utility and sympathy. (We shall look in more detail at Hume's theory in the 'Virtue ethics' section below on pages 105–111.) However, Bentham went beyond Hume by arguing that utility was the sole principle that we ought to live and judge others by. In his seminal utilitarian work *An Introduction to the Principle of Morals* (1780), Bentham aimed to explain the principle of utilitarianism and show its application to legal and penal reform.

Bentham begins this book with an apparently straightforward fact about the psychology of human beings: that we aim to secure pleasure and avoid pain. This claim is now known as psychological HEDONISM (hedonism comes from the Greek work *hedone* which means 'pleasure'). From this psychological principle Bentham goes on to draw a moral principle, which he called the utility principle, but which was later known as the greatest happiness principle. Utility in this context simply describes the worth of an action as is determined by the amount of pleasure and pain an action brings about. Bentham defines utility as:

> *that property of an object that tends to produce benefit, advantage, pleasure, good or happiness ... or ... to prevent the happening of mischief, pain, evil or unhappiness.*[57]

According to Bentham's reasoning, if psychological hedonism is true, and our actions are aimed at pleasure and avoiding pain, then the only reasonable moral theory is one that seeks to make such actions as consistent and effective as possible. In other words we must follow a moral system that invokes us to maximise happiness and minimise pain (for both the individual and the sum of individuals in a community). This is the 'utility principle'. We might summarise this by saying that psychological hedonism implies ethical hedonism.

■ The utility calculus

Bentham offers us a guide as to how we are supposed to apply the principle of utility, in other words how we are supposed to measure the amount of pleasure and pain an action brings and so maximise happiness. Bentham termed the 'hedonic calculus' (also known as the utility calculus) that method of calculating, measuring and weighing up the pleasure/pain of individual actions. What is crucial in Bentham's calculus is that the pains and pleasures of each individual are to be taken equally; no one is more important than anyone else. As Bentham says 'each to count for one and none for more than one'. For Kant, it is rational agents alone who are to be included in the moral arena, who we have duties to, who we cannot treat simply as means to an end; in other words, human beings. When wondering who should be included in our moral calculations, Bentham disagrees: 'The question is not, Can they reason? nor, Can they talk? but, *Can they suffer?*'[58] So, for Bentham, any animal, human or non-human, that can feel pleasure or pain should be included in our measurement of the consequences. We shall return to this point when we look at animal rights in Chapter 4.

■ **Figure 2.2**
Bentham's utility calculus

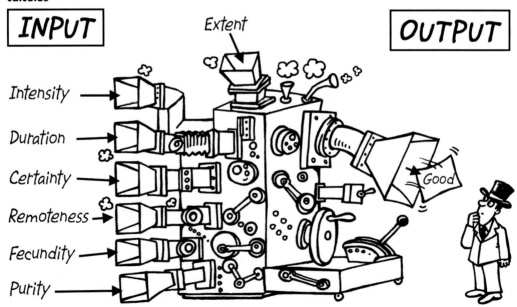

One of the advantages that utilitarians claim for their theory is that, unlike other normative moral theories (for example, Kant's), theirs can be easily applied to our day-to-day actions. To apply the utility principle we simply weigh up the amount of pleasure and pain an action might create and then select the action which brings the most amount of pleasure over pain. Easy, really, when you know how. Below is Bentham's suggested utility calculus, i.e. the steps for measuring the pleasure and pain that result from an action:

Step 1 Determine the amount of pleasure and pain brought to the person most directly affected by your action. To do this, Bentham gives us four things to measure:

    1 The *intensity* of the pleasure/pain
    2 The *duration* of the pleasure/pain
    3 The *certainty* of the pleasure/pain
    4 The *remoteness* of the pleasure/pain.

Step 2 Examine the effects of this pleasure or pain, including:

    5 The *fecundity* of the pleasure/pain
    6 The *purity* of the pleasure/pain.

By 'fecundity' Bentham is talking about the tendency of that pleasure to produce other pleasures (fecundity means fertility, or tendency to reproduce). By 'purity' Bentham means the tendency of the pleasure to produce *only* pleasure, and the tendency of pain to produce *only* pain.)

Step 3 This step comes only when we are considering the effects on other individuals:

    7 The *extent* of the pleasure/pain.

In other words, the number of people affected by the action.

Step 4 You then calculate the total utility by using 1–7 to count up the amount of pleasure units an action causes, and the amount of pain units an action brings.

Step 5 If you have a range of actions available to you then you must repeat Steps 1–4 for all these actions, and choose the action which brings the most pleasure over pain.

So Bentham's moral theory seems simple. We should strive to maximise pleasure and minimise pain for everyone in society. This means weighing up the quantities of pain and pleasure for each course of action, and choosing that course which brings about the optimum amount of pleasure.

▶ criticism ◀ Bentham's utility calculus, although it considers many dimensions of pleasure, ignores the quality of the pleasures and pains that are being measured. He once famously wrote that pushpin (a game played in pubs at the time) was as good as poetry, and therefore that both should be treated equally in the utility calculus.[59] Our fear might be that if legislators took a Benthamite approach, then society would degenerate into one described in Huxley's *Brave New World*, with everyone addicted to a harmless pleasure drug called *soma*. Such a society, where the overall amount of pleasure has been maximised, would, after all, appear to be the utilitarian's ideal. However, Bentham's 'lowest common denominator' approach to utility, which treats all pleasures as of equal value, worried his student, John Stuart Mill. Mill felt that the theory needed refining and he wrote a book entitled *Utilitarianism* in which he defended and developed the theory. We shall look at this in the next section.

Act utilitarianism

Bentham's version of utilitarianism is a form of 'act' utilitarianism. It holds that we should appeal directly to the 'principle of utility' in order to judge what is right in any particular situation. In other words, we must ask what effect *this* act will have in *this* situation. We must calculate the effects of each action on its own merits. So, while an act utilitarian may consider maxims such as 'never tell lies' as useful guides to producing the greatest balance of happiness, what ultimately matters is the effect of telling the truth in this particular case. Act utilitarianism of the kind Bentham proposes is susceptible to a certain number of problems which we shall now look at.

▶ criticism ◀ Firstly, we can object that we need to have general rules of some kind, maxims that can be universalised, if we are to have a meaningful moral theory at all. We have seen Kant argue that it is part of the very *meaning* of moral judgements that they be universalisable into general laws of conduct. In other words it is not moral to make exceptions just because of particular circumstances. We shall return to this point when we come to look at prescriptivism in the next chapter.

► criticism ◄ A second difficulty can be illustrated as follows. Consider a situation in which two acts, A and B, can be calculated to produce exactly the same quotient of happiness, yet A involves breaking a promise and B does not. For the act utilitarian there would be nothing to choose between the two acts and they would be equally good, and yet surely anyone not already committed to act utilitarianism would say that A is wrong and B is right. The point here is that an act can be made right or wrong by facts other than the amount of good or evil it produces, for example because it involves breaking a promise, or telling a lie. Such examples suggest that a purely consequentialist theory cannot be correct and that some injection of deontology is required.

► criticism ◄ Finally, it it is often objected that utilitarianism treats all conscious PERSONS capable of experiencing pleasure and pain as equally important to us in making our moral choices. However, there is a strong tendency in our ordinary moral understanding to regard our obligations to others as differing depending on who the others are. The obvious example is to contrast our moral attitude to our own family members and strangers. Surely, a mother whose child is about to be run over has a special duty to save it and would be justified in ignoring the plight of others also at risk, whereas Bentham says that she should be solely concerned with the happiness of humanity as a whole, and not the happiness of her loved ones.

experimenting with ideas

Consider the decisions made in the following situations and answer the questions below.

1 A group of philosophers have been exploring caves on the coast (possibly trying to find Plato's cave). As they are leaving, the philosopher who is leading the group, a man with absurdly broad shoulders, gets stuck in the mouth of the cave. The sea is rising and the group know that at high tide the cave will be submerged and they will all drown. The only way that they will avoid drowning is if they use dynamite to remove the man stuck in the cave's mouth. There are no other options. So they blow him up and escape.

2 The Emperor of Rome commissions the building of a massive Colosseum: an arena for blood sports. This action does not weigh on his conscience because he reasons that the 20,000 people in the crowd will derive a huge amount of enjoyment from watching the spectacle of a handful of Christians being eaten by lions.

3 One hundred years ago in America nearly everyone (men and women alike) found it offensive for women to drive cars. As a result, in the state of New Dakota the federal government passed a law that forbade women from driving cars.

4 You borrow a DVD player from a rich friend promising to give it back. A few months later she has forgotten she even lent it to you, yet you use it all the time, so you decide that you'll keep it.

5 A serial killer is on the loose. Thousands of citizens are in a state of panic and fear, and they march on the Town Hall demanding that the killer be brought to justice. This mob is getting out of control, but local police and magistrates have no idea who the killer is. Eventually they select someone at random from the mob, a man with a known criminal record who is widely disliked. This man is quickly tried and found guilty, and the mob disperses feeling happy and secure again.

6 In the eighteenth century the writer Jonathan Swift offers to solve, at a single stroke, Ireland's two main problems: i) its overpopulation and ii) its lack of food. He suggests that children, as they are dying of under-nourishment anyway, should be cooked and eaten in order to provide 'delicious, nourishing and wholesome food'.[60] Now imagine that the British government fails to see the irony and turns his 'modest proposal' into actual policy, because it really did solve these two problems.

For each situation or policy:

a) Do you think that the utility principle justifies the decision taken?

b) Does the decision taken go against your own moral intuitions?

c) If so, explain why you believe the utilitarian decision is the wrong one.

▶ criticism ◀ Occasionally, act utilitarianism appears to recommend courses of action that go against our moral intuitions. Take the example of the innocent scapegoat. If we could demonstrate that in order to prevent massive harm (perhaps further rioting or a civil war) we must execute an innocent person, then it seems as if Bentham thinks we should kill that person. But this seems fundamentally unjust, and Bentham, as we have seen, is keen to ensure that there is justice in the penal system. It goes against all our intuitions to say that it is morally *good* to kill, torture, lie or deprive people of their freedom, even if it does lead to beneficial consequences for the majority.

Bentham might argue that we must consider not only the immediate pleasure brought to the majority but also the pains brought by the fear that we might one day be arrested and tried for a crime we didn't commit simply to placate the mob. But it is possible to adjust the example so that the crowd wouldn't know that an innocent person had been executed – say, if the police and judicial system were able to orchestrate a perfect cover up – and therefore that there would be no risk of generating any fear of future injustices.

► criticism ◄

What does honourable mean? ... Everything that is useful to humanity is honourable. I understand only one word, useful![61]

Dostoyevsky, *Crime and Punishment*

In *Crime and Punishment*, Dostoyevsky is concerned to highlight the dangers of utilitarian thinking. Here he caricatures the utilitarian attempt to reduce all moral principles to utility. And many philosophers would agree that insistence on utility as the sole value is simplistic. Our response to the examples above suggests that other things, such as personal virtues (honesty, integrity, etc.) or rights (e.g. to one's own life, or to equality of opportunity for men and women), are morally valuable in themselves and need to be taken into account, if not instead of, at least as well as, any utilitarian considerations. Bentham believed that utilitarianism could account for the way humans behave as moral agents, and the utility principle was supposed to do this. But we do not, in general, believe that it is a good thing to please the majority by punishing an innocent minority, nor that the pleasure of the majority outweighs the pains of a minority. In fact we do not seem to be driven solely by a desire for utility, but for other values too, such as justice, equality, compassion.

Utilitarians who came after Bentham found that some of these problems could be avoided by rejecting act utilitarianism. These 'rule utilitarians', such as Mill, came to argue that we should not break any rule of behaviour which has been shown to maximise happiness and minimise pain in the past. We shall look in more detail at rule utilitarianism after we examine Mill's refinement of utilitarian ethics.

Mill's modification of utilitarianism

John Stuart Mill (1806–1873) was not only a moral philosopher; he was also a social reformer, a Member of Parliament and, in his day, a logician of great eminence. As a child he was the subject of an experiment in education by James Mill and Jeremy Bentham, who taught him philosophy, the classics, economics, maths, etc. from a very young age. At the age of 20, Mill suffered a nervous breakdown (triggered by reading the romantic poetry of Wordsworth) from which he recovered with a renewed interest in not just the intellectual but also the emotional side of his life. In 1861 he published *Utilitarianism*, which continued the work carried out by his father and Bentham.

Mill agrees with Bentham that the 'one fundamental principle ... at the root of all morality' is the utility principle:

Mill

Utility, or the Greatest Happiness Principle, holds that actions are right in proportion as they tend to promote happiness, wrong as they tend to produce the reverse of happiness. By happiness is intended pleasure and the absence of pain; by unhappiness is intended pain, and the privation of pleasure.[62]

So Mill, like Bentham, is proposing hedonism as the foundation for his ethical theory. (Note that 'happiness' is to be understood in terms of pleasure, not in the more general terms of 'flourishing' as Plato and Aristotle would have it (see pages 90–91).) Now, we have seen when examining ethical egoism that the term 'hedonism' has certain unsavoury connotations – of indulgent, self-centred and pleasure-seeking behaviour – and Bentham's theory was accused of being the 'greatest animal happiness principle'. Mill acknowledged this as a possible criticism of utilitarianism when he wrote that 'the accusation supposes human beings to be capable of no pleasures except those of which swine are capable'.[63] He attempts to defend utilitarianism by modifying Bentham's simple model.

■ Higher and lower pleasures

Bentham saw all pleasures as equal, so the pleasure derived from reading a celebrity magazine, in Bentham's calculus, has the same quality as the pleasure derived from solving a complex philosophical problem. Mill tried to give a more sophisticated account by differentiating between the higher and lower pleasures that humans enjoyed.

Savour the following pleasures and then answer the questions below.

1 Drinking a warm mug of hot chocolate on a cold day.
2 Watching the sun set over the ocean.
3 Seeing your favourite film the way the director intended it to be seen.
4 Falling asleep in a comfortable bed.
5 Going clubbing on a Friday night.
6 Reading and understanding a piece of difficult philosophy.
7 Laughing till you can't breathe from watching a comedy on television.
8 Listening to a favourite track on the way back from college.
9 Having a thoughtful discussion with friends about how to change the world.
10 Finally scratching a hard-to-reach itch between your shoulder blades.

a) Which of the above pleasures do you think are 'higher' and which do you think are 'lower'?

b) Do you think everyone would agree with you?

c) Do you think that ten years ago or in ten years' time you would have answered a) differently?

Mill doesn't give a list of which pleasures fall into which category, higher or lower. But you might guess that Mill, being a well-educated philosopher, believes that 'higher' pleasures are mental or intellectual pleasures, and that 'lower' pleasures are bodily pleasures. And you would be right, as the following quote makes clear:

Mill

It is better to be a human being dissatisfied than a pig satisfied; better to be Socrates dissatisfied than a fool satisfied. And if the fool, or the pig, are of a different opinion, it is because they only know their own side of the question. The other party to the comparison knows both sides.[64]

In other words, if you enjoy the higher pleasures, such as philosophising, you are able to compare these to the lower pleasures which you also enjoy, such as drinking a cup of tea. But if you have no understanding of higher pleasures you cannot compare them to the lower ones and so cannot make a judgement about which are better. So it is not just a matter of subjective opinion in deciding which are superior.

Mill, in order to preserve a degree of objectivity in utilitarianism, needs to find a way of deciding which pleasures we should be striving for, higher or lower. His method is to draw on the pronouncements of 'competent judges', i.e. people who have had experience of both higher and lower pleasures. Mill believed there would be substantial agreement between these judges, but if there were not then we should stand by a majority decision.

▶ criticism ◀

The problem is that Mill, in trying to make Bentham's utilitarianism more sophisticated, has created enormous problems for himself. What makes utilitarianism so appealing is its simplicity and practicality: it tells us that we can calculate what actions we should take by weighing up the amount of pleasure (and pain) that different acts produce. However, once Mill introduces the notion of quality, of higher and lower pleasures, then the simplicity disappears. We are left wondering what this thing 'pleasure' supposedly is. Is it one thing, produced in the mind, or lots of different things, felt in our mind and our body? For example, in order to calculate funding priorities for a local council we now have to compare 'pleasure produced by reading books in a newly built library' with 'pleasure produced by going to the newly built gym'. And Mill seems to take it for granted that the library will win, because reading is a higher pleasure. The question is – how can we compare two very different kinds of things, such as reading and physical exercise? We can also add that Mill appears to beg the question by saying competent judges have experienced *both* higher and lower pleasures, while the rest of us have only experienced lower. But if the point is for competent judges to determine which are higher and which are lower, then why have the pleasures that we have experienced already been defined as lower?

Furthermore, if the higher and lower pleasures are so different then how can they be compared? In some situations it may appear obvious which is the more 'valuable' (higher) pleasure: should the BBC spend public money on buying a trashy new Australian soap opera, or should it spend money on a series addressing the problems of philosophy? But even where it seems obvious which is the higher and which is the lower pleasure, the question remains: what should we do, as good utilitarians, when the lower pleasure is felt by millions of people and the higher pleasures by only a select few? We are left wondering whether 'higher pleasures' really just means 'the things that Mill and his friends like to do'.

Mill's proof of utilitarianism

In Chapter 4 of *Utilitarianism* Mill asks 'Can utilitarianism be proved?' and he attempts to clarify the foundations underpinning his and Bentham's theory. This one short chapter has generated an enormous amount of controversy ever since.

Mill

Questions of ultimate ends are not amenable to direct proof ... [but] considerations may be presented capable of determining the intellect either to give or to withhold its assent to the doctrine; and this is equivalent to proof.[65]

So Mill is claiming that the ultimate principles of morality, like all first principles, cannot be proven, but that reasons can be given for believing these principles, particularly if these reasons are simple matters of fact. Mill's principle is that 'Happiness is desirable, and the only thing desirable, as an end.'[66] In other words happiness (or pleasure) is the good that we should be striving to reach, not just for us, but for everyone. So the question is, what simple matters of fact can Mill find to provide the foundations for utilitarianism? He proceeds by saying:

Mill

The only proof capable of being given that an object is visible, is that people actually see it. The only proof that a sound is audible, is that people hear it. ... The sole evidence that it is possible to produce that anything is desirable, is that people do actually desire it. No reason can be given why the general happiness is desirable, except that each person, so far as he believes it to be attainable, desires his own happiness. This, however, being a fact, we have not only all the proof which the case admits of, but all which it is possible to require, that happiness is a good: that each person's happiness is a good to that person, and the general happiness, therefore, a good to the aggregate of all persons.[67]

In order to clarify this it may be helpful to identify three important steps in Mill's proof. First, Mill argues that we need only show that people do desire something in order to show that this is desirable. Second, Mill proposes that it is their happiness that people desire and their happiness that is desirable. Third, Mill concludes that each of us desires happiness and that it is the happiness of everyone that is the goal of morality. We shall look at each step in turn, dealing with any criticisms of these steps as they arise.

◼ Step 1 of Mill's proof

To show that:

1) The only evidence that X is visible is that X can actually be seen.
2) The only evidence that X is audible is that X can actually be heard.
3) Similarly the only evidence that X is desirable is that X is actually desired.

The crucial claim here is the third PROPOSITION, i.e. that something (X) is desirable because people desire it. Mill uses the first two claims as analogies in order to support the third claim. In other words Mill is trying to persuade us that the property of being 'desirable' is *like* (i.e. analogous to) the properties of being 'visible' and 'audible'. However, we don't have to buy this analogy. We may wish to argue that desirability is crucially different from visibility or audibility.

► criticism ◄ At the time Henry Sidgwick, and later on G. E. Moore, leapt on this part of Mill's argument. Moore in particular had a field day with this claim:

Well, the fallacy in this step is so obvious that it is quite wonderful how Mill failed to see it.[68]

Moore

We would all agree that visible does mean 'able to be seen' and audible means 'able to be heard'. But 'desirable' does not mean 'able to be desired'; a point which becomes clear when we consider that not everyone's desires are desirable. It is possible to think of all manner of gross things that people happen, as a matter of fact, to desire; for example, there are some people in the world who desire to drink their own urine in the morning. But it is not the case that such a desire is desirable (urine tastes particularly bitter, it smells, it contains waste products from the body, and is too warm to be genuinely thirst-quenching). If we say something is desirable then we are recommending it as something that is 'fit to be desired', in that it is something that we *ought* to desire. We shall return to this point in the next chapter when we look at PRESCRIPTIVISM. So the FALLACY, or logical error, that Moore thinks he has discovered in Mill's argument is the mistake of identifying 'what is actually desired' with 'what ought to be desired' or, according to Moore, to identify what's desired with what's good. We shall return to this point below.

We can now see that the analogy with visibility and audibility doesn't hold. 'Visible' does not mean 'fit to be seen' and audible does not mean 'fit to be heard' (your swearing out loud while trying to understand this argument is audible, but it is not fit to be heard). So in this part of the argument Mill has not proved that just because X is, as a matter of fact, desired, it ought therefore to be desired.

However, perhaps Mill doesn't really need to *prove* that if X is desired then it is desirable. Mill is interested in what the ends of our actions are, in what sorts of things we consider to be good. He asks 'how is it possible to prove that health is good?', and the answer is that it isn't possible to prove this, but we don't need to prove this because we all know it to be good.[69] So it may be that when Mill says that the only evidence we need is to show that X is desirable (i.e. a goal worth striving for) he means that X is desired by lots of people, i.e. people as a matter of fact strive after this goal. And this is what Mill says: that no one would be convinced that something was a goal, unless it was already in practice a goal.

■ Step 2 of Mill's proof

To show that:

4) Each person desires their own happiness.

and therefore (from proposition 3 above):

5) Each person's happiness is desirable.

6) Each person's happiness is good.

Propositions 4 and 5 fill in the gaps that were present in proposition 3 above. They specify 'happiness' as the object (X) that is desired and desirable. This is what Sidgwick referred to as 'psychological hedonism' and, as with Bentham's theory, this is fundamental to Mill's utilitarianism. The concept of happiness has a long tradition within moral philosophy and, among the ancient Greeks, Plato and Aristotle held that happiness is what we should all be striving for. Aristotle was also explicit that no one would disagree with the claim that happiness is what we are all after. However, for Mill 'happiness' did not refer to the general 'flourishing' of your life (which is how Aristotle understood happiness) but to the securing of pleasure and the avoidance of pain. It is this that we strive for, and it is this that is the end, or goal, of our actions – what philosophers call the 'good'.

There are two related problems with Mill's move here: the fallacy identified by Moore above, and another one that stems from some remarks made by David Hume a century before. We should sketch both criticisms here, although we shall return to them again in Chapter 3 (pages 138–150).

▶ criticism ◀   Let us take Hume's point first. In a famous passage from his *Treatise of Human Nature*, Hume says that when reading the works of moralists we find that they often start out by talking about matters of fact and observation and then, all of a sudden, conclude that therefore we ought to be doing this and we ought not to be doing that.[70] Hume seems to be saying that an argument is guilty of a logical error where it draws a conclusion containing an 'ought' from premises which were purely factual. So, for example, the fact that humans can and do eat meat does not entail therefore that they ought to eat meat. Yet this seems to be exactly what Mill is doing in his 'proof' of utilitarianism. He is starting out by claiming that people happen to desire happiness, then he moves to say that therefore happiness is desirable and is a good; in other words that people *ought* to desire happiness. If Hume is right then Mill cannot so easily take the step from psychological hedonism (the factual, descriptive claim that humans seek happiness) to ethical hedonism (the moral, prescriptive claim that humans ought to seek happiness). However, Mill is well aware of the so-called IS/OUGHT GAP and he writes about it in his *System of Logic*, saying that 'a proposition of which the predicate is expressed by the words *ought* and *should be* is generically different from one which is expressed by *is* or *will be*.'[71] It seems odd that someone who so clearly understands

Hume's point should be guilty of making the mistake himself, and supporters of Mill have tried to show that he was innocent of the charge, although no consensus has been reached.[72]

▶ criticism ◀ Moore's point is somewhat different, and it turns on an analysis of the words involved in Mill's argument. Moore argues that certain terms, such as 'good' and 'right', are indefinable and hence cannot be defined in natural terms, i.e. in ways that refer to the physical world. Moore labels these special terms as 'non-natural'. (We look at Moore's reasons for making this claim in the next chapter on page 145.) Non-natural terms are simple, in that they cannot be defined or broken down any further into other terms. So any attempt to define these indefinable (and non-natural) concepts in naturalistic terms will be making a logical error. This is what Moore called the NATURALISTIC FALLACY.[73] Moore gives 'yellow' as an example of a simple, non-natural term. We would be guilty of the naturalistic fallacy if we defined 'yellow' by describing it as light waves vibrating at a certain frequency. 'Good' is another example of a non-natural term, and we would be equally guilty of the naturalistic fallacy if we defined 'good' in naturalistic terms such as 'whatever maximises the general happiness'. Of course this is exactly what Moore thinks Mill does in his proof of utilitarianism when Mill says that 'good' means 'desirable'.

But is Mill guilty of the naturalistic fallacy? Mary Warnock thinks not. She argues that Mill is not interested in defining what 'good' is, nor is he interested in defining what 'desirable' is. He does not, Warnock says, *define* desirable or good at all.[74] According to Warnock, Mill's project is primarily an empirical one: he is simply setting out for us what sorts of things are, as a matter of fact, considered good. Mill is trying to persuade us of the truth of utilitarianism by informing us that people already consider happiness to be good (and desirable). But that isn't to say (as Moore believes) that Mill therefore considers the 'good' to *mean* 'happiness' or 'pleasure' etc. If it turned out that people considered something else (say pain) to be fundamentally desirable, then it would be this thing, pain, that was the good.

■ Step 3 of Mill's proof

To move from:

6) Each person's happiness is good.

to

7) The general happiness is the ultimate good.

Mill is saying here that if happiness is good to you as an individual, then the general happiness is *good* to the aggregate of all people. It seems to be quite a leap from the fairly innocuous claim that we are each after our own happiness (you are after happiness for you, I am after happiness for me) to the claim that we are all committed to the happiness of everyone. From an empirical point of view, the second claim that we are committed to a common good just doesn't seem to be borne out by the facts. In a letter that Mill wrote in 1868, he is clear that he did not wish to argue that every individual considered the happiness of every other individual as good.[75] So what does Mill mean?

Mill seems to be saying that there is another, general, good that arises out of the sum of all our individual goods. This general good, Mill thinks, is the good for the 'aggregate' (i.e. sum) of each of us as individuals. So because each of us as individuals desires our own happiness, then the aggregate-of-all-of-us desires the general happiness as our ultimate good.

■ **Figure 2.3** *We desire happiness for all of us as the general good*

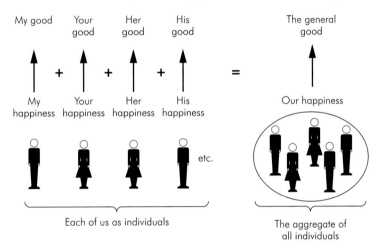

► criticism ◄ The problem here is that 'aggregate of people' is not the sort of thing that is capable of having desires or striving for the good. Society, which we might call the aggregate of people, doesn't literally have emotions, desires and feelings (although we might talk about this in a metaphorical sense). Sidgwick puts this criticism another way: 'an aggregate of actual desires, each directed towards a different part of the general happiness, does not constitute an actual desire for the general happiness existing in any individual'.[76] The point is the same: we cannot add up individual desires to generate a kind of 'super-desire' that each of us has, in addition to our own desires. To claim this is to commit the fallacy of composition. This is the fallacy of thinking that because there is some property common to each of the individuals within a group, this property must apply to the group as a whole. Bertrand

Russell (1872–1970) gives an absurd example of this: it is true that every member of the human species has a mother, but it is a fallacy to conclude from this that our species as a whole must have a mother.[77] In the same way it is true that each of us as an individual desires our own happiness, but it is a fallacy that the 'aggregate of individuals' desires happiness for that aggregate. So Mill cannot conclude, on the basis that we each think of happiness as our good, that we also think of the general happiness as the good.

Mill's 'proof' has many problems. It may well be that his proof isn't guilty of the leap from the descriptive claim (that we all consider happiness as the good) to the prescriptive claim (that we all ought to consider happiness as the good). It may also be that Mill doesn't commit the naturalistic fallacy, as Moore thought he had. But the step from 'I desire my happiness' to 'we desire everyone's happiness' seems to be a step too far. Were he to have been supported by the facts in this second claim (as he seems to be in his first claim) then we might still find the conclusion rings true. But, as we know too well, humans do not often care for the happiness of everyone else. Of course Mill, along with the other utilitarians, would claim that we *should* care for the general good, but he hasn't proved this.

Refer back to the situations given in the activity on page 44 above. (You promise to take your nephew to the park etc.)

Using only Mill's greatest happiness principle, you must decide what you should do in each of those situations. In order to calculate what is the best and worst course of action, you must calculate for each situation:

a) how much pain/harm each person involved would receive

b) how much pleasure/happiness each person would receive as a consequence of each course of action

c) which course of action brings about the most pleasure and least pain overall. You will now know which course you should take.

Rule utilitarianism

We saw above that Bentham's theory could be described as act utilitarianism, because it assessed the worth of particular acts on the basis of their particular effects. Mill's theory takes a somewhat different approach. Mill introduces the idea of 'secondary principles', in other words principles which we should adopt in order to guide our actions and which support the primary greatest happiness principle.[78] These secondary principles, or rules, are ones which experience has shown tend to produce the greatest happiness, and they should be adhered to, even though in particular cases breaking the rule might have better consequences. In another of his great works, *On Liberty* (1865), Mill lists some of these rules: for example, we shouldn't encroach on the rights of others, we shouldn't lie or deceive or cause injury to others.[79] By applying the greatest happiness principle to general rules rather than individual actions, Mill avoids many of the problems of act utilitarianism, while combining the best aspects of consequentialist and deontological theories. Mill, and utilitarians who advocate similar secondary rules, may be thought of as 'rule' utilitarians.[80]

One obvious advantage of rule utilitarianism is that it avoids the need to make complex calculations in order to take a moral decision. This is one of the key problems for act utilitarianism (due to ignorance, lack of time, personal bias, passion, carelessness, etc.). But the rule utilitarian can simply appeal to a rule.

Like deontology, rule utilitarianism emphasises the centrality of rules in morality and insists that we appeal to a maxim (such as that of truth-telling) rather than look to the consequences of a particular action. But unlike deontology it requires that we determine our rules by asking which will promote the greatest good for everyone. Rules are to be selected, revised and replaced on the basis of their utility, and so the principle of utility remains the ultimate standard. This means that for the rule utilitarian it is good to obey a rule to always tell the truth, or never to kill healthy patients, even though, in particular cases, telling the truth does not lead to the best consequences.

Rule utilitarianism can be defended on utilitarian grounds by saying that it is only by our acting for the most part according to rules, rather than attempting always to evaluate situations on their own merits, that the greatest good is served. (For example, the rule that we should *always* drive on the left-hand side of the road contributes to the greater good, even though on certain occasions it may seem more sensible to drive on the right.)

experimenting with ideas

In 1985 two mountaineers, Joe Simpson and Simon Yates, became the first people to climb the west face of Cerro Sarapo in the Peruvian Andes. On their way down, Joe fell and shattered his knee. His friend Simon helped lower him 3,000 feet down the mountain. But then Joe hurtled down into an abyss. He was hanging in free space, in a crevasse with no way back up, with Simon holding onto the rope at the other end. Soon they would both freeze to death. Simon held on for an hour and then started slipping down the mountain. One of the rules of mountaineering is that you never abandon a buddy. But

Simon knew if he didn't then they would both die – so as he was slipping Simon cut the rope and Joe fell into the void.[81]

1 How would an act utilitarian judge Simon's action? What reasons might they give for their judgement?

2 How would a rule utilitarian judge Simon's action? Again, what reasons might they give?

3 Do you think the judgements of the act and rule utilitarians would be different? Why?

Some problems with calculating utility

One of the main advantages of Bentham's and Mill's moral theory appears to be its practicality. It seems as if we can determine what is the morally best thing to do, using something like the simple method of calculation described in the activity on page 74 above. However, when we look more closely at this method of calculating pleasures and pains we see that it is beset with problems. These problems are possibly more damaging than Mill's failure to provide a proof for utilitarianism, as they hit home at utilitarianism's very usefulness!

▶ criticism ◀ We can set to one side Bentham's utility calculus as a bureaucrat's fantasy. It may be possible to think of ways to measure the certainty and duration of the pleasures/pains arising from a particular action (perhaps based on past experience). But Bentham does not explain, nor has anyone else since, how we're supposed to go about measuring things like the 'intensity' or 'remoteness' of the pleasure or pain. Should we issue a questionnaire to the people involved? ('On a scale of 1–10 how would you rate the pain of exam revision?') Perhaps we could develop some kind of biometric device to which people could be hooked up to calculate the intensity or remoteness of a sensation, but this seems like science fiction.

▶ criticism ◀ More fundamentally we may question whether there is any single experience (or *qualia*) called 'pleasure' that can actually be measured. Bentham is asking us to add up units of pleasure and pain for different choices and pick the one with the most units of pleasure and the least units of pain. But Aristotle suggests (in Book X of the *Ethics*) that the word 'pleasure' doesn't refer to one single sensation.[82] For Aristotle there are as many different pleasures as there are pleasurable activities, and these pleasures cannot be compared with one another. In technical terms, philosophers say they are 'incommensurable' – that is, they cannot be meaningfully compared or represented on the same scale of measurement – so the pleasures of tea-drinking are incommensurable with the pleasures of winning the lottery or the pleasures of paragliding. In fact Aristotle seemed to think that pleasure wasn't a sensation in itself, but something that 'perfected an activity'; in other words, it was a way of describing the intensification of the usual sensations of, for example, drinking a cup of tea, particularly when an action was done well. The point is that on this account there is no such thing as a single sensation 'pleasure' which we can measure in terms of a single unit, as Bentham suggests. Perhaps we could get round this difficulty by proposing some sort of 'exchange rate' between different types of pleasure, based possibly on the experiences of Mill's competent judges (doubtless there would need to be a whole government department devoted to this). But this is moving the theory far away from the simple guide to life that its proponents intended it to be.

1 Jean-Paul Sartre's short story, 'The Wall', is set during the Spanish Civil War. A man, Pablo, has been captured and he is asked, along with his comrades, if he knows the whereabouts of one of the rebel leaders, Ramon Gris. Pablo refuses to say. At dawn his comrades are led out one by one and are executed against the brick wall outside his cell. Pablo is brought back in for a final interview, and to bide time he lies to his captors and tells them that Ramon is hiding at the cemetery. He waits for them to find out that he's lying and execute him. They return to his cell but, instead of his being taken to the wall to be shot, he is released. He finds out later that Ramon had switched hiding places and *had* gone to the cemetery – Pablo's lie had led to the capture of a key rebel leader.[83]

   a) How would a utilitarian judge Pablo's lie? Was it a good act or a bad act?

   b) On what grounds would they say this?

   c) Do you agree with the utilitarian's judgement and reasons?

   d) Why? Why not?

2 You are walking alongside an Austrian river in January 1900, as the new century is beginning. You see a young boy, about 11 years old, fall into the river and you wade out and rescue him from drowning. This boy is called Adolf Hitler and he goes on to cause the deaths of millions and millions of innocent people.

   a) According to utilitarianism, was rescuing the boy a bad act?

   b) At what point did it become a bad act? Was it a bad act at the time of the rescue, or only later (perhaps when Hitler became Chancellor of Germany in January 1933)?

   c) Do you agree with the utilitarians on this point?

▶ criticism ◀ Further problems arise as we ask which consequences are relevant to our judgement of the moral worth of an act. All of the consequences? Or those that we can foresee? Or those that happen within a reasonable time limit? An act utilitarian like Bentham proposes that for each action (or policy) we're about to take we should work out how much pleasure and pain it's going to produce. The problem is that we cannot foresee what all the consequences of an act are going to be. So, once we have chosen the course of action that we think will be best, do unforeseen consequences affect the moral value of that action (as in Sartre's short story)? If they do, then moral judgements become much less certain. For example, would we have to withhold a judgement of an action until all the consequences have unfolded – even if this took years? We could resolve this question by making judgements that were 'date-stamped', for example, by saying that 'saving Adolf Hitler was good as the consequences stood on 31 January 1900'. If, years later, we reappraise the consequences on utilitarian grounds we could make this transparent by saying, for example, that 'saving Adolf Hitler in 1900 was good up until January 1933 then bad thereafter'. This all sounds very odd, and not what Bentham had in mind when he proposed the utility calculus as a practical means of determining the best course of action.

These particular problems are felt most by act utilitarians, i.e. utilitarians who think we should consider each action individually according to its utilitarian merits. However, it is not so much a problem for rule utilitarians (i.e. utilitarians who think that we should act according to certain rules, adherence to which will maximise happiness). We have seen that Mill introduced the notion of secondary principles (subsidiary to the main rule that we should maximise happiness), i.e. rules that have been tried and tested through the ages (such as the rule that murder is wrong). These rules exist because, in general, they maximise happiness and minimise pain.

Mill had pre-empted some of these criticisms. For example, he thought it was puzzling to attack utilitarianism on the grounds that 'there is not time, prior to the action, for calculating the effects of any line of conduct on the general happiness'.[84] For Mill, to criticise utilitarianism on this count is like saying 'a Christian has no time to decide how to act because she has no time to read the Bible before she does so'. Mill thinks we already have in place many of the paths and signposts that lead us to the general happiness. We have all the experience of our forefathers to help us decide, and in most cases we know very well the immediate consequences of our actions.

We have now looked at some of the practical problems with applying the utility principle and with calculating utility. But in the next two sections we look at a more fundamental problem with Bentham's and Mill's utilitarianism, one concerning its hedonistic foundations. Both Mill and Bentham maintained that the utility or greatest happiness principle could not be proved. So what is it based on? Ultimately Mill and Bentham ground the principle in the fundamental fact about human nature: that we seek pleasure and aim to avoid pain. We have referred to this as 'psychological hedonism', but the question is: are the claims of psychological hedonism correct? And, even if they are correct, what problems remain for ethical hedonism?

Criticisms of psychological hedonism

Aristotle attacked psychological hedonism on the grounds that humans had goals other than mere pleasure and that this is what distinguishes us from other animals – we are not simply pleasure-seeking beasts, like cows.[85] That is not to say that pleasure isn't a part of the good life, only that it arises when we engage in other activities that contribute to our good life (and which we pursue for their own sake, not for the pleasure that they bring). For example, I might go rock-climbing and get an intense feeling of satisfaction when I reach the top. But the satisfaction of having survived another climb wasn't why I did it (it's partly the process, the feeling that one false move might mean I fall, and partly my overcoming the fear that I might trap my arm under a fallen rock and have to saw it off with a pen-knife just to free myself). Aristotle argues that humans are not simplistic 'pleasure-seekers' but 'happiness-seekers'; and to explain behaviour in terms of the quest for human flourishing is far more alive to the riches and complexity of human desires.

Psychological hedonism faces a further, logical problem. If hedonism is true then we can define 'pleasure' as 'what we seek'. In which case the sentence 'we seek pleasure' is a tautology, i.e. it is true by definition and tells us nothing new about the world (another, rather dull, example of a tautology is the statement that 'bachelors are unmarried men'). According to a psychological hedonist 'we seek pleasure' simply means 'we seek what we seek'. But this isn't the case. If someone tells you that all they seek is pleasure then they are telling you something interesting about their personality; they aren't just expressing a truth about what it is to be a human. Committed pleasure-seekers are not just regular people, they are a particular type of person (possibly the type of person who might be a laugh on holiday for a couple of weeks, but who you wouldn't want hanging around your house during a crucial period of exam revision).

Furthermore, according to the formula 'pleasure = what we seek', the statement 'I do not seek pleasure' becomes a contradiction, something that is false by definition. According to the psychological hedonist the sentence 'we do not seek pleasure' means 'we do not seek what we seek', which of course is absurd. But there are people who clearly do not seek their own pleasure, who go out of their way to help others for no other reason than to help others. Martyrs (of both the religious and non-religious kind) are one extreme example of people who act in selfless, non-pleasure-seeking ways. Sacrificial behaviour, saintly acts, and even everyday altruistic acts, can also be seen to count against the view that all we seek is pleasure.

In Xanadu did Kubla Khan
A stately pleasure-dome decree.[86]

Samuel Coleridge, 'Kubla Khan'

Read the following scenario and then answer the questions below.

■ **Figure 2.4 The pleasure dome**

Scientists have developed an amazing new machine, which they call the pleasure dome. The pleasure dome is a virtual-reality machine that taps into your brain to generate sensations as vivid and real as the world you now inhabit. By stepping into the pleasure dome the scientists can guarantee that you will receive pleasures, of a variety of sorts, for the rest of your life. Your physical well-being is not threatened by your inactivity as your body is kept moving (as in a virtual world) by the machine, and, in all effects, your life expectancy in the pleasure dome is exactly what it is in this world. The only downside is that once you have stepped into the pleasure dome you cannot come back out, but then again, you won't want to. As the ads say: *'You Won't Ever Want to Leave: Welcome to the Pleasure Dome.'*

1 Given that the pleasure dome is completely safe, with no side-effects whatsoever, and no threat to your health, would you plug yourself in for the rest of your life?
2 Why/Why not?

The thought experiment in the activity above helps to bring out the intuition that we are not hedonists, and that psychological hedonism is false.[87] If pleasure were all that we desired then we would all want to plug ourselves into the pleasure dome for the rest of our lives. Similarly, if pleasure were the only good, then Huxley's vision of a *Brave New World* would be a utopian ideal. However, while the machine might bring us constant pleasure, many people would not want to plug themselves in, because they feel (like Aristotle) that they would be missing out on a vast amount of other things we desire, such as the sense of achievement after struggling to do something.

We might argue that the very idea of a 'pleasure dome' is an incoherent concept. This is because in order for us to experience pleasure we must have something to contrast it with. After a short period in the pleasure dome we would either no longer recognise what we felt as 'pleasure' or we would want out – we would want to seek pain or at least absence of pleasure in order to be able to experience pleasure again. This again suggests that what we really seek is a range of experiences, and not just pleasurable ones.

Criticisms of ethical hedonism

Ethical hedonism is the claim that pleasure, or happiness, is the good. We have seen above that some philosophers consider it fallacious to derive ethical hedonism from psychological hedonism. But the Ancient Greeks found a further problem with ethical hedonism, known as the 'paradox of hedonism'. This is the problem that it is counterproductive to live purely by aiming to maximise your own pleasure. The paradox is that the more we pursue the life of pleasure the more elusive it seems to be, for pleasures quickly perish and we are once again unsatisfied.

Plato argued against hedonism in a similar vein, offering us the following analogy in the *Gorgias* (see over). He asks us to consider the lives of two men, one who is temperate, i.e. who moderates his desires, and the other who is intemperate, i.e. who indulges his desires.

Consequentialist ethics 2: utilitarianism

81

Plato

Suppose for instance that each of two men has a lot of jars, and one has sound and full jars, one full of wine, another of honey, another of milk [etc.] And suppose the sources for each of these things are scarce and hard to find, provided only with much effort. Now when one man has filled up, he brings in no more, and doesn't care about them, but is at rest as far as they are concerned. The other man has ... vessels that are leaky and rotten, and he is forced to be always filling them day and night, or else he suffers the most extreme distresses. Now if this is how each man's life is, do you say that the intemperate man's life is happier than the temperate man's? [88]

For Plato the answer is clear. The hedonist is persistently striving to satisfy their desires, just as the man with leaky jars has to constantly fill them up. But the person who is able to control their desires is far better able to achieve real happiness. So utilitarians are missing the point – what we really desire is not pleasure, or even fleeting happiness, but permanent happiness (what the ancient Greeks called *eudaimonia*) and this is far more complex than utilitarians imagine.

The most famous hedonistic philosopher of the ancient world, Epicurus (*c.* 341–270 BC), tried to show how the paradox of hedonism could be avoided. In his *Letter to Menoeceus* he identifies the good with happiness and happiness with pleasure. But he regarded one's own happiness as best served by living in accordance with the traditional virtues of prudence, justice and temperance.

According to Epicurus it is not in our long-term benefit to pursue an immediate gratification of all our desires. For example, if we live the life of a glutton we gradually compromise our capacity to experience pleasure. For we become sick and fat. Similarly, if I always give way to my desire to drink beer because it brings me pleasure, in the longer term my pleasure will give way to a painful hangover, the loss of my job, and to a destitute and ultimately miserable life. Moreover, true pleasure is as much to do with what you are used to as with the intrinsic quality of what you consume. So if you become used to rich foods, jewellery and designer clothing, fast cars, a Jacuzzi, and so on, then you will not be able to continue to afford to service the increasingly expensive requirements of such a lifestyle. Once you are used to one luxury, the only way to get the same level of pleasure again is to consume something even more expensive, like a drug addict on the slippery slope to oblivion.

Because of considerations such as these, Epicurus argues that if we are truly to live the most pleasurable life possible we will need to think carefully about how we seek pleasure. He claims that someone who is used to eating only bread and water can gain as much pleasure from eating a dry biscuit as can be gained from eating fancy foods and fine wines by someone used to living the high life. So he recommends living a temperate, almost monastic, lifestyle. Plato comes to a similar conclusion, recommending to us in the *Gorgias* that 'instead of the insatiable and unrestrained life to choose the temperate life, adequately supplied and satisfied with whatever it has at any time'.[89]

Plato offers an additional attack upon ethical hedonism in the *Gorgias* by arguing that not all pleasures are good. For example, Socrates suggests to Callicles, who is adopting a hedonist position, that the pleasures of running away from battle are not good pleasures; and Callicles, mindful of how Greek society viewed cowards, agrees. Quite amusingly, Socrates also proposes that someone who gets pleasure from itching and scratching, and who does this all their life, is not actually living a good life, even though they are satisfying their desire to itch and scratch.[90] In which case not *all* pleasures are good, and we do not seek *all* pleasures, therefore ethical hedonism is wrong. John Stuart Mill's attempts to distinguish between higher and lower pleasures can be seen as a response to this type of criticism. But we have seen that this complicates the simple ideas of utilitarianism, and makes any calculation of 'pleasure' or 'happiness' almost impossible. We might wonder whether in fact it would be better to abandon hedonism altogether and adopt a more Platonic or Aristotelian approach to happiness and the good life; we shall come back to this possibility below.

Some modern adaptations of utilitarianism

Despite the many problems with Bentham's and Mill's versions of utilitarianism, the theory captures a powerful intuition: that morality is not just about following rigid rules and principles irrespective of the consequences (as Kantian deontology tells us). For many policy-makers, utilitarianism is the only moral theory in town: it doesn't depend on any metaphysical system (such as the belief in God); it is flexible (unlike Kantian ethics); and it seems to describe much of what we do mean by a morally good act (one that increases the amount of happiness and decreases the amount of pain in the world). It is a firmly humanistic and practical system, even if it isn't the whizz-bang moral calculating machine that its originators first thought.

Because of its power it has become influential in policy-making around the world. When economists and politicians try to determine policy they will, in general, perform a cost–benefit analysis on the different courses of action available to them. In other words they weigh up the costs and the benefits, to help them to decide what policy or decision will maximise the benefits. So utilitarianism is here to stay, if not in the moral arena, then certainly in the political 'shall we build a motorway through Stonehenge?' arena. Let us now look at some further developments of utilitarianism.

■ Positive and negative utilitarianism

Bentham's and Mill's version of utilitarianism regards the maximisation of general happiness as the sole principle – with emphasis on pleasure/happiness this has become known as 'positive' utilitarianism. However, for some utilitarians (so-called 'negative utilitarians' because they aim to reduce pain, not because of their miserable outlook on life) this emphasis is misplaced. Rather than strive to achieve the best balance of happiness over pain, negative utilitarians argue that we should be concerned with minimising extremes of pain. A world in which no one was particularly happy but in which no one suffered extreme pain would be better than one in which there were extremes of both but in which happiness outweighed the pain.

This modification to the theory might be able to deal with the example of the Romans' enjoyment outweighing the Christians' pain (above, page 63). And with the Hollywood producer who, by making a particularly gruesome serial killer movie, thereby entertains millions around the world. These 'entertainments' do not seem to be good in a moral sense (although people claim to be entertained by them), and the negative utilitarian, unlike their counterpart, is not committed to saying they are good (although they would be if it could be shown that watching serial-killer movies reduces the number of victims because they show us how to spot a killer in real life).

■ Strong and weak utilitarianism

Cast your minds back to rule utilitarianism, which proposes that we should adhere to certain rules, because a general observance of these rules will maximise happiness. An initial difficulty with this is that if it is clear that breaking a rule would produce greater happiness then it seems perverse – given that the rule is itself set up in terms of the principle of utility – not to break the rule on this occasion. And this may lead us from a strict or strong version of utilitarianism to a weak version. A strong utilitarian claims that we ought to keep to a rule no matter what the consequences may be of breaking it in a particular circumstance. The weak utilitarian, however, allows that there may be circumstances in which the net amount of pleasure or pain produced by a particular act needs to be taken into account and can override the advantages of keeping to the rule.

One further problem for the 'strong' utilitarian is that what they determine to be good may strike us as unjust. This is an issue for policy-makers and, given that both Bentham and Mill were concerned with policy, it is important to consider. Imagine that scientists have made it possible for one person to be sent into outer space with the means at her disposal for incredible and unlimited amounts of pleasure. This person in the capsule will definitely be alive for the next 10 million years, and will continue getting pleasure long after the rest of humanity has died out. Now a 'strong' utilitarian policy-maker might wonder whether to fund this amazing research project, or whether to spread the country's resources over millions of people, thus slightly improving the quality of our lives. If these two courses of action are calculated to produce the same net increase in happiness then strictly speaking the utilitarian cannot choose between them. However, there is clearly an unequal distribution of happiness between these two possibilities. It seems clear that in this case we should prefer the second option simply because it is fairer – because it distributes the happiness over a wider number of people rather than concentrating it in the lucky person in the space capsule. More realistically, a society which sustained an elite minority in great luxury while the majority lived in relative poverty might have more overall pleasure than one in which the resources were more equally distributed. But in such cases it seems to us that some notion of what is *just* overrides considerations of utility.

Ideal utilitarianism

In response to this problem of fairly distributing happiness some utilitarians have added other principles or values to the greatest happiness principle. Henry Sidgwick, for example, proposed an additional principle, the principle of justice, to ensure the greatest possible balance of good over evil and for this to be distributed as widely as possible. This means that some utilitarians have abandoned a strictly hedonistic position, and have recognised that there are other values (for example, justice) which take their place alongside happiness. G. E. Moore, despite his attacks on Mill's utilitarianism, was strongly influenced by Sidgwick's version of the theory, and Moore developed his own brand of utilitarianism that embraced several non-natural values. We know that Moore believed that it was a fallacy to define non-natural concepts in naturalistic terms, and the good could not be understood as 'happiness' or 'pleasure' or any other-worldly thing. Instead Moore believed that the 'good' and the other values were indefinable ideals that could be grasped only by our intuitions. This version of the theory became known as ideal utilitarianism,[91] and was associated with Moore, amongst others, because of his definition of 'ideal' as 'the best state of things conceivable' or the highest good.[92] Amongst Moore's list of these greatest goods were not just moral but also aesthetic and emotional values, in particular beauty and friendship, which was also apprehended by an intuition. Now unfortunately the inclusion of beauty as an absolute good does much to undermine Moore's theory, because different people regard very different things as beautiful, and there is no 'intuition' common to us all about what is beautiful. We examine Moore's theory in more detail in the next chapter (page 144).

Preference utilitarianism

The most recent popular adaptation of the theory (held by Peter Singer, amongst others[93]) is preference utilitarianism. It holds that an action should not be judged by its tendency to produce pleasure or diminish pain, as traditional utilitarians say. One reason why people have been inclined to object to the purely hedonistic version of the theory is that it doesn't take account of the different views that people will have as to what happiness is. After all, people may have very different ideas about how to live a fulfilling life, and it is often thought that people should be allowed to pursue what they take to be the best route so long as they don't interfere with any one else's own pursuit of happiness.[94] Now, preference utilitarianism is supposed to deal with this issue. Instead an action should be judged by the extent to which it conforms to the preferences of all those affected by the action and its consequences. In other words the morally good thing to do is whatever maximises the satisfaction of the preferences of all involved. So, if lying is wrong, it is wrong because it goes against the preference we have to know the truth. We shall see in more detail in the final chapter (page 186) what preference utilitarianism has to say against killing and how this differs from the hedonistic utilitarian account.

We must now pick up a thread that has been left trailing alongside our discussion of deontological and consequentialist ethics. This is the legacy of Plato and Aristotle on ethics: their critique of hedonism, their teleological approach and their emphasis on happiness and human reason. Their perspective on how we should live is a holistic one: we should consider our lives overall, and our goal should be to develop those characteristics that enable us to flourish. We turn, then, to virtue ethics.

Virtue ethics

> *I'm talkin' about friendship. I'm talkin' about character. I'm talkin' about – hell, Leo, I ain't embarrassed to use the word – I'm talkin' about ethics.*[95]
>
> Miller's Crossing

Character, that's what virtue ethics is all about: character. Virtue ethics is the name given to those moral theories that focus on the individual person, rather than an individual course of action. This difference in focus is an important one, and may appear to be at odds with our ordinary understanding of ethics. So it might help if we consider what deontological and consequentialist theories share, and then we can see how theories of virtue ethics differ.

It may seem as if the two types of normative theories we have already looked at, deontological and consequentialist, have nothing in common with one another. After all, deontological theories claim that the most important thing in morality is that certain actions are right – and we do what is right by following certain imperatives or commands. Consequentialist theories, in complete contrast to this, say that the most important thing in morality is trying to produce the best possible outcome – and so actions are good when they bring about the most beneficial consequences. Given these fundamental differences you might well ask what could possibly connect deontology and consequentialism?

ACTIVITY   Write down the main differences between consequentialist and deontological theories of ethics:

Consequentialist	Deontological

Take the example of some parents who steal a loaf of bread because their children are starving. The consequentialist and deontological theorist will disagree over the method by which this action should be judged. The consequentialist theorist would argue that the way to judge this action (as good or bad) is to examine its consequences. The deontological theorist would say that the way to judge this action (as right or wrong) is to assess whether it broke any pre-existing rules. Their disagreement seems to be a deep one, and it is not obvious what they could have in common.

But when you have a closer look at the differences between these two theories, you notice that they are specifically disagreeing over how to judge an action. So what they agree on is that it is the *action* that needs to be judged. Moreover they also agree that there is available to us a way of measuring or calculating whether or not an action is a good or right one. For consequentialists the formula is that we should do whichever action brings about the best consequences; for deontologists the formula is that we check to see whether performing this action breaks or adheres to certain rules.

But theories of virtue ethics approach morality by judging the person (the agent) who committed the act, rather than the action itself. Julia Annas describes virtue ethics as 'agent-centred' in contrast with deontological and consequentialist theories, which are 'act-centred'.[96] So within act-centred ethics our judgements are made first and foremost of specific acts: we judge them to be right or good. Agent-centred, or virtue, theories make judgements of character: of whether someone is a good or virtuous person. The kinds of questions that a virtue ethicist wishes to address are 'what makes a good person?', 'what sort of life should I be leading?' and 'how should I develop my character?'

ACTIVITY What is a virtue anyway?

1 Write down a list of characteristics (or personality traits) that people might say were 'virtues'.
2 Next to that list write down another list of characteristics that people might call 'vices'.
3 Is there anything that the characteristics you have called 'virtues' have in common?
4 Is there any obvious way in which they differ from the 'vices'?

One simple way of thinking about what virtue is is to think of a virtue as a disposition or character trait possessed by good people, i.e. by people we admire, value or praise. In contrast a vice is a disposition or characteristic possessed by bad or 'vicious' people, i.e. by people we condemn. What we mean when we are talking about a characteristic or a disposition or a trait is a *tendency to behave in a particular way,* so, for example, we say someone is kind (has a kind disposition) when they tend to be thoughtful and generous to others. The key idea here is that a disposition is not a one-off act (which utilitarians and Kantians seemed happy to pass judgement on) but a description of how someone has acted in the past, and how they'll probably act in the future. So virtue ethicists take a more holistic approach when making moral judgements; they consider not just the present action, but the past and the future actions of the agent. As we shall see, this means that virtue ethicists find it difficult to offer simple rules or guidelines about how we should live.

We shall now look at some examples of philosophers who have put forward virtue ethics as a normative theory. As we shall see, virtue ethics has had its supporters down the centuries (Plato, Aristotle, Aquinas, Hume) but it is only in the last forty years that it has been revived as a credible alternative to utilitarian and Kantian ethics.

Virtue ethics in Ancient Greece

The two founding fathers of Western philosophy, Plato and Aristotle, were both interested in finding an answer to the fundamental ethical question 'what sort of person should I be?' And they gave answers that centred on the development of virtues, although they differed in their understanding of what the specific virtues were and how we could acquire them.

Ethics for the Ancient Greeks rested on the relationship between certain key concepts. In order to understand the ethics of Plato and Aristotle, we need to understand these concepts, and how they connect with one another. They are:

- function – *ergon* (in Ancient Greek)
- virtue – *arete*
- happiness – EUDAIMONIA.

For many Ancient Greek philosophers, including Plato and Aristotle, the concept of being good was intimately connected with the idea of function, *ergon*: to be good meant fulfilling your function well. So for many centuries being a good person was linked to being good at whatever role you played in society. For example, if you were a farmer then you were good if you fulfilled your function well as a farmer. However, Aristotle believed that we had a function that went above and beyond the one prescribed for us by society. Aristotle thought that by understanding our function we would understand how we could be good, and this was the key to happiness.

The connection between something being good and its fulfilling its function is brought out in the activity below.

ACTIVITY   Consider each of the following pairs and answer the questions below.

1 A good can-opener; any old can-opener.
2 A good meal; an ordinary meal.
3 A good teacher; an average teacher.
4 A good computer game; a mediocre computer game.
5 A good person; a non-descript person.

a) What are the qualities and attributes that distinguish the good thing from the other, more ordinary, thing?
b) Which is better at fulfilling its function – the good thing or the more ordinary thing?
c) So, overall, what would Aristotle say made something good?
d) Imagine now that you were confronted with an unknown object 'Z' in a box – what method would Aristotle use to determine whether Z was a good object?

Now let us turn to the Greek word *arete*, which philosophers usually translate as 'virtue'. Unfortunately 'virtue' (derived from *virtu*, which was the Latin translation of *arete*) has certain connotations in modern times: it suggests a sort of Victorian prudishness, a goody-two-shoes or perhaps, even more narrowly, a kind of sexual purity. When thinking about virtue ethics it is important that we throw out these connections as they have nothing to do with 'virtue' in the philosophical sense. Remember that virtue has connotations of 'virtuosity' or 'virtuoso', in other words being brilliant or excellent in a particular area of life. In fact *arete* is better translated as 'excellence', but we shall follow the usual convention and refer to it as virtue. Now in the activity above you might have noticed that the good things had attributes or qualities that meant they were better able to fulfil their function – we can think of these qualities as virtues. So it is clear how virtue (in the sense of virtuosity) is connected to function and goodness for the Ancient Greeks: in order to be good you need to fulfil your function well; but in order to fulfil your function well you need to excel in the right ways – you need to possess virtues.

This brings us to the third key concept in Ancient Greek ethics: happiness, or *eudaimonia*. Plato and Aristotle believed that the ultimate goal in life was to reach *eudaimonia*, in other words to be happy. Now they did not mean this in a hedonistic sense; in other words, when they said that our goal was to be happy they did not mean we should aim to be walking around with a permanent smile on our face, or to satisfy all of our physical desires as much as possible. In fact we saw above (pages 79 and 82–83) that both Plato and

Aristotle consistently attacked hedonism as the goal or end of our actions. A rather better translation of *eudaimonia* is 'flourishing', in other words living well, achieving your goals, and generally doing well in life.

For those of us coming from an 'act-centred' perspective the first question we would want to ask is 'what does my struggle to be happy and to flourish have to do with ethics?'

Remember the first question we asked in this book was 'what should I do?' Now both Plato and Aristotle understood this question in its more global sense, applying it to our lives as a whole rather than just to individual actions. They were concerned with the question 'how should I live?', and their answer to this question is 'I should try to flourish'. On the face of it this seems a very selfish answer, and nothing to do with morality. However, both Plato and Aristotle defined *eudaimonia* in such a way that it was bound up with living what we would call a morally good life. Amongst the virtues that enabled us to flourish were those that enabled us to flourish within a community, particularly the virtue of justice. So my happiness is inseparable from the people and community I live with, and it is inconceivable to Plato and Aristotle that I could be happy by exploiting or hurting that community.

Although Plato and Aristotle share a common view on the connection between the virtues, happiness and morality, their ethical positions differ in some very important respects: firstly on their view of what our function is, secondly on the precise virtues we should develop and thirdly on what the ultimate good is. Let us now look at the different views that Plato and Aristotle had on these issues.

The differences between Plato's and Aristotle's theories

In Raphael's painting (Figure 2.5 overleaf) it is noticeable that Plato and Aristotle are pointing in very different directions, and these gestures indicate the direction they believe philosophy should be taking. Plato is pointing upwards to the sky; Aristotle's hand is stretched outwards, with his palm facing down. For Plato, philosophical wisdom and understanding lie away from this world, in the perfect, ideal world that is known as the world of the Forms. For Plato's pupil, Aristotle, the opposite is true and it is *this* world that provides us with wisdom and understanding. These differences underpin the differences between Plato and Aristotle's moral philosophy, as we shall now see.

■ What is our function?

Aristotle

It is evident that the statesman ought to have some acquaintance with psychology, just as a doctor who intends to treat an eye must have knowledge of the body as a whole.[97]

Our function, according to the Ancient Greeks, is determined by the kind of thing we are. So if we are a dog, then we have a doggy function, and our goals in life are very different from humans': to chase after balls, sleep a lot, guard our cave, eat as much as we can and have loads of offspring (actually they're not that different!). But what kind of thing is a human? For both Plato and Aristotle we are creatures with a soul (in Greek *psyche*, which is where we get our word 'psychology' from), as this is what makes us human. Our function as human beings is determined by the make-up of our souls. So if we want to understand our function we need to understand our soul. But, as might be expected, Plato and Aristotle differ as to the composition of the soul.

In his book the *Republic*, Plato argues that our souls consist of three parts: reason, spirit and desires.[98] In the

Phaedrus, Plato draws out the relationship between these three parts of the soul using the following analogy.

I divide the soul into three: two horses and a charioteer. One of the horses is good and the other bad.[99]

Plato

So our soul, according to Plato, has two powerful impulses, desire and spirit, and something that can control these impulses, namely our reason. We function well as human beings only when each part of our soul is functioning well, and performing to its optimum. Now this does not happen when one of the impulses (desire or spirit) is out of control. If desire (the bad horse) gets out of control then we become indulgent hedonists with no real sense of what is good for us overall. If spirit (the good horse) gets out of control then we become headstrong impulsive types, always leaping into things and making snap decisions; again this is no recipe for functioning well. For Plato what these impulses need is the firm government of reason, the charioteer, which can control and shape these impulses so that we can use them to attain what is good for us (see Figure 2.6). So the use of reason enables us to maintain a balanced and harmonious soul, which is absolutely essential for *eudaimonia* as we shall see.

■ **Figure 2.6 *Plato's three elements of the soul***

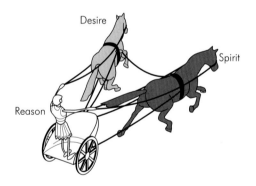

Aristotle was not only a philosopher but he was also one of the first biologists, someone who studied life in all its forms. He believed that everything in the world had a function, a purpose, and saw the world around him in those terms (this is called a TELEOLOGICAL perspective). Like Plato, Aristotle held that for humans our function is determined by our soul. However, he had a much more sophisticated, psychological view of the human soul. For Aristotle, it was a kind of 'blueprint' for a human being – the instructions for how we are going to develop in our lives. In Aristotle's book the *Ethics*, he describes the four parts of the soul: two non-rational parts (growth/nutrition being one, and desire/emotion being the other) and two rational parts (practical, day-to-day reasoning

■ Figure 2.7
*Aristotle's division of
the soul*

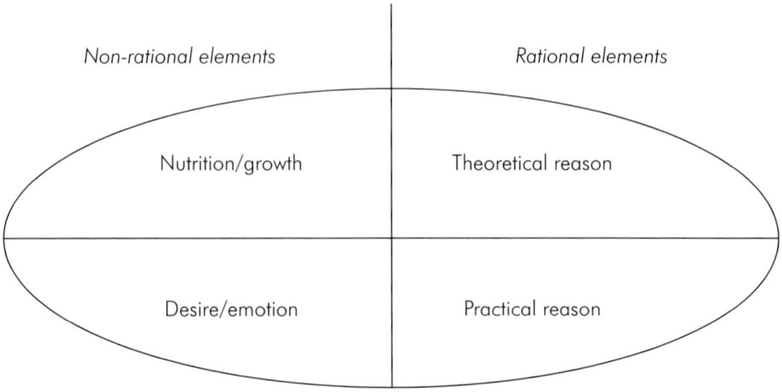

being one, and abstract, theoretical reasoning being the other).[100]

However, unlike Plato, Aristotle believed that each aspect of the soul (our psychological and physical make-up) could be subdivided into further parts that we could describe and analyse. We shall see below how this more sophisticated conception affected Aristotle's theory of virtue.

■ What virtues should we develop?

We saw in the activity above (page 90) how, in order to function well, something needs to possess all the necessary qualities (or virtues) that will enable it to do so. So, for example, for a can-opener to function well, it needs to be efficient, safe, sharp, ergonomic, etc. For both Plato and Aristotle, we function well as human beings through developing the virtues we need as human beings. Because their conceptions of what we are as human beings differ (they give different accounts of the human soul) we would expect their accounts of the virtues we need to differ.

We know that Plato divided the soul into three elements (reason, spirit and desire), and that these three competed and jostled with one another for control of the soul. In the *Republic*, Plato explains how virtue develops only if all the elements are in balance and 'each part of him is performing its proper function'.[101] For Plato this could happen only if reason was in control of all aspects of the soul. So spirit guided by reason carefully drives us to action; and desire, when tempered by reason, motivates us and enables us to live a healthy and satisfied life. So, for Plato, when reason is in control there are three virtues corresponding to each of the three parts of the soul:

■ reason – wisdom
■ spirit – courage
■ desire – temperance (or self-control).

Now when all these three virtues are in place then a fourth virtue emerges, namely justice – which is roughly equivalent in value to our own concept of 'moral goodness'. Justice is the most important virtue because it readies us for action:

When he [the just man] has bound these elements into a disciplined and harmonious whole ... he will be ready for action of any kind ... whether it is political or personal.[102]

Plato

Aristotle agrees with Plato that, in order to function well, we need to be virtuous (and excel) in all aspects of the soul, so we would expect to find in Aristotle's theory a virtue corresponding to each part of the soul. However, Aristotle believes that there are many virtues corresponding to the different parts, not just three as Plato maintained. In his book the *Ethics*, Aristotle analyses in great detail the many virtues, or excellences, that we need to possess if we are to function well as human beings. These include:

- excellences of character (controlling and shaping our desires and emotions)
- excellences of practical reasoning (having the skills to get what is good)
- excellences of theoretical reasoning (being good at philosophy, maths, etc.).

Within each of these general virtues, or excellences, there are other virtues. But, as with Plato, the crucial thing for Aristotle is that the rational part of the soul is in control, and this is the key to becoming virtuous.

Aristotle also went further than Plato in describing in detail what moral virtue (excellence of character) was and how we might acquire it. It was a type of characteristic, a personality trait, which we developed through practice, rather like learning to play the guitar. We were not born virtuous or excellent, but we became virtuous through developing good habits.

In the film *The Wizard of Oz* a young girl, Dorothy, encounters three creatures on her way to find the Wizard. Each of these companions is missing some virtue essential for happiness: the Scarecrow lacks wisdom, the Tin Man lacks feelings and the Cowardly Lion lacks courage. They misunderstand what these things are, and they believe that the Wizard of Oz, because of his powers, will be able to give them these qualities. When they finally confront the Wizard he can't do anything except give them tokens of virtue (an examination certificate, a clockwork heart, a medal). This was partly because the Wizard was a conman, and partly because virtue isn't something you can suddenly get; as Aristotle says, it is a habit that you develop. In the end, Dorothy's companions became virtuous by acting in a virtuous way: the Scarecrow had started to hatch plans, the Tin Man had started caring and the Cowardly Lion had begun to act bravely.

Aristotle argues that someone who is virtuous is someone who tends to avoid the extremes of over-reacting or failing to react in a particular situation. This means that when confronted with a situation we don't bottle up our emotions or drive for action (which would be deficient), but nor do we let our feelings come flooding out and completely over-react (which would be excessive). Instead we have to judge how far we should let a particular emotion affect us in this particular situation, and consider what would be the most appropriate thing to do in this situation. This description of the virtuous person is famously known as Aristotle's Doctrine of the Mean. 'Mean' here refers to 'middle', but Aristotle is not saying that we should be taking the 'middle way' in every situation, or acting moderately in every situation. Clearly there are some situations where a more (or less) emotional response is required, for example when protesting against extreme injustices. But what Aristotle does believe is that if you look at the behaviour of a virtuous person over their whole life then they will tend to avoid over-reacting or under-reacting (avoid excess or deficiency).[103]

Here are some specific examples of Aristotle's virtues:

'Moral virtues' or 'excellences of character'	'Intellectual virtues' or 'excellences of reason'
Courage, justice, honesty, dignity, pride, modesty, friendliness, temperance	Deliberation, understanding, cleverness, judgement, practical wisdom

So, for Aristotle, we become virtuous by becoming reflective, rational creatures and considering in each situation 'what is the right and appropriate thing to do here?' This means drawing on both moral and intellectual virtues. Now, deciding what is the right thing to do is a difficult judgement to make, but Aristotle believes that through moral education we are able to develop the wisdom that we need to make this judgement. Through hard experience, and by looking towards people we admire as role models, we can develop and fine-tune our decision-making capacities. Admittedly it is difficult to develop all these virtues, but Aristotle argues that it is only by doing so that we are able to reach the good and to flourish.

Write down what you would do when confronted by each of the following situations. Then answer the questions below.

1 At the end of your philosophy class you personally are asked to give a 10-minute presentation next week on some aspect of Aristotle.

2 After the class you have arranged to meet a friend, Alex, in a cafe. Jo, your girl/boyfriend, refuses to come along as s/he can't stand Alex. This means you have to walk to the cafe on your own. You walk down a deserted side street and you see a man lying face down on the pavement, his nose pressed into the concrete.

3 Your friend Alex is late arriving at the cafe and you nip to the toilet. On the floor of an empty cubicle you see a wallet.

4 You both order something to eat. Eventually Alex turns to you and says 'Why isn't Jo here? Doesn't s/he like me?'

5 When you finally receive your bill you both think you have been overcharged by a small amount, but neither of you remembers exactly how much everything cost.

Now, for each situation, consider the following.
a) What would be an over-reaction or an excessive response?
b) What would be an under-reaction or a deficient response?
c) What would be, all things considered, the reaction that was the right or appropriate one, neither excessive nor deficient?
d) Which of the categories above (a, b or c) does your own reaction fall into?

What is the good?

Aristotle

> *The good for man is an activity of the soul in accordance with virtue.*[104]

We now have an understanding of our function, and of the virtues we need to function well. For both Plato and Aristotle this knowledge will enable us to reach the good, the thing that we all strive for. Plato goes a stage further than this and argues that if we are not virtuous (for example, if we are hedonists) then we are actually damaging our soul and we shall suffer as a result.

So what is the good? According to many Ancient Greeks, the good is *eudaimonia*, i.e. to be happy, to flourish or to lead the good life. We saw above how Plato attacked hedonism, and Aristotle was equally damning of that theory. But what's the difference between happiness in the sense of *eudaimonia* and happiness as a hedonist might conceive of it? The difference can be brought out through an anecdote about the footballing genius, George Best. He loved to tell the tale of how, in the early 1970s, a room-service waiter came into his hotel room one morning. The footballer was in bed with one of the most beautiful women in the world, surrounded by thousands of pounds in cash that he'd won at the casino, drinking champagne from the bottle. The waiter looked at him, shook his head and said 'George … where did it all go wrong?' And it's true, something had gone wrong. From being hailed as the best footballer in the world, George Best had turned into an alcoholic playboy – he failed to fulfil his real potential. In a hedonistic sense he was happy, but in Platonic and Aristotelian terms he was not happy – he wasn't *eudaimon*, he was no longer flourishing.

For Plato we cannot understand what is good simply by analysing the actions of those we admire, or by looking to past heroes and how they behaved. Plato believed that this world was an imperfect copy of another more perfect world, and that everything in this world had a more perfect form in the other world. The world Plato is talking about is called the world of forms or ideals, and we grasp these perfect ideals with our intellect, not through our senses. Plato offers us a powerful analogy to help understand the difficulties of grasping the world of forms, as he describes the journey of a man from a world of shadows at the bottom of a cave (which he thought was the real world), up through the cave out into the blinding sunlight, which represents the world of forms. This journey, which we make through the tough and rigorous process of philosophising, eventually leads us to an understanding of the form of the good.

So, in order to really flourish, our reason needs first to be in control of our soul, and it must then turn us in the right direction: towards pursuing the right ends. We must use reason once again to make an intellectual journey towards understanding the form of the Good. Once you had grasped the Good, then for Plato it meant you could never go wrong in life, or do wrong, such was the power of this moral truth. For Plato, it is through understanding the form of the Good that we are finally able to flourish. However, this means that only a tiny minority of humans, namely a rare breed of philosopher, could ever be virtuous and ever be truly happy.

Unlike Plato, Aristotle did not believe in any mysterious world of forms and considered it to be an unrealistic and flawed philosophical view.[105] Aristotle argued that there was no single 'form' of the good, rather there were as many 'goods' as there were individual creatures, objects and situations. The good for humans does not lie in some other mystical dimension, as with Plato, but is within our grasp during our lifetime. Moreover, the rejection of Plato's theory also meant that the good did not have the same mystical compulsion for Aristotle as it did for Plato (remember that Plato believed that once we had grasped the Good then we could only do what was right). This led Aristotle to the rather more realistic view that we could know what was good, but fail to do it, because we were weak-willed.

For Aristotle what is good can be determined almost in a scientific way, by describing the kind of creature that we are, then identifying our function on the basis of this, then working out how we can excel at our function. We have been through these processes in the activity on page 90 above and for Aristotle it was as simple as that. But, we may still ask, what on earth does being good in a functional sense have to do with living a good life, in the sense of striving for the good and reaching *eudaimonia*?

Imagine you are a plant and you wish to flourish. Then, according to Aristotle's method, you must determine what your function is – let's say to grow, flower, reproduce, photosynthesise, etc. Now that you know what your function is as a plant, you follow Aristotle's advice by excelling (becoming virtuous) at your function. So you grow, flower, reproduce, etc. and become the brightest, bushiest plant in the forest. You are good (in a functional sense) at being a plant. But clearly you are also living the life of a good plant, you are striving for and reaching the good: you are flourishing.

Because Aristotle held a teleological view of the universe we could identify our good by identifying what we were *for* and then becoming good at that. So being virtuous, which means being functionally good (a good human being), also means that we reach the 'good' and so lead a fulfilling and flourishing life. This means striving to develop myself as a good person, striving to shape my desires so that they are good for me, and striving to achieve those goals I set and the ambitions I have. This sounds much more plausible than Plato's view, and, more importantly, all of us are able to do this, not just philosophers (as Plato believed).

A criticism of Plato's and Aristotle's theories

We shall return to some general problems with virtue ethics below. But here we shall address one specific problem faced by both Plato and Aristotle, namely that both their moral theories stand or fall on the success of their metaphysical theories.

Plato views the good as a perfect ideal that exists, literally, in the world of forms. Knowledge of how to be truly virtuous is only possible once we have knowledge of the form of the good. But, argues Plato, such is the power of the good that once we have seen it then it is impossible for us to do wrong.

Aristotle took issue with both Plato's claim that there is a single 'good' and with the claim that once you knew what was good you couldn't do wrong. Aristotle is pointing out a meta-ethical problem with Plato's theory. Plato thought that the term 'good' referred to a single attribute that was possessed by all good things. For Aristotle there was nothing substantive in common between, say, a good doctor and a good football team; there is no single universal quality called 'good' which they both share. Instead Aristotle argues that everything is good insofar as it meets the standards or criteria for that particular area of expertise: so a good doctor meets all the standards of being a doctor, a good football team meets all the standards for playing football as a team, etc. We would probably agree with Aristotle that Plato was wrong in thinking that 'good' refers to some single ideal, existing in another realm.

But there are also problems with Aristotle's metaphysical assumptions, namely with his teleological view of the universe. We know that Aristotle thought that everything had a function (everything was 'for' something), including humans. But Aristotle did not believe in a being who created the universe and thus created each thing inside the universe with a function in mind. We shall see below how St Thomas Aquinas (1224–1274) held this view as he believed in the existence of God, and so Aristotle's theory could be assimilated into a Christian framework. However, it is harder to assimilate Aristotle's theory into a modern scientific framework because we no longer believe that everything is *for* something, i.e. that everything has a purpose. If this is the case then we can't find out what humans are 'for' nor what our function is – we simply don't have one. It might still be true, however, that thinking of our lives in Aristotelian terms (striving to flourish by excelling in what we do) does bring us happiness, does make us virtuous and does make us moral. But this wouldn't be because we were being 'good humans' in the functional sense that Aristotle understood. We shall come back to this criticism when we look at problems with natural law ethics below.

Aquinas and natural law ethics

When Aristotle's writings were rediscovered in Western Europe in the thirteenth century it became clear to one philosopher, St Thomas Aquinas (1224–1274), that God was the key element missing from Aristotle. Aristotle, the pagan, had discovered the laws that governed the world we see, whilst Christianity offered the ultimate explanation for these laws. Aquinas made it his life work to reconcile Aristotle's philosophy with Christian theology, and in *Summa Theologica* (1273) he devotes much of his time to constructing a coherent, Christian, ethical system.

We have seen that Aristotle believed that everything in the world had a purpose, and things flourish when they excel in their purpose, when they are virtuous. For humans, this flourishing, or *eudaimonia*, is inseparably personal and moral. However, it seemed to Aquinas that Aristotle could not give a satisfactory explanation for his discoveries of the law of nature. This idea that everything is aimed at some goal suggests that there is a 'natural law' governing all living and non-living things. Everything is naturally and essentially constituted such that it strives to achieve its own peculiar goal.

But why had everything been created with a purpose, and why is moral goodness achieved by fulfilling that purpose? For Aquinas it was obvious that this natural law had been created by God, and that God had given humans a purpose through giving them a human 'nature'. Our goal as humans is to understand our nature, calculate what God wishes us to do, and then do this to our utmost ability. God, then, is the source of the natural law, and also the source of morality. So if the natural law has been created by God, then humans are *morally* bound to follow the natural law.

What Aquinas is able to do by using Aristotle's theory is to provide an explanation of why the universe and all things in it have a purpose. The answer is that they are *designed* with such a purpose in mind by a divine intelligence. In creating the universe God didn't throw it together any old how, rather he had a plan in mind. So everything within the universe serves a function within the divine plan. For this reason the universe exhibits a law-like order and rationale which we can discern by reasoning carefully about it. So if we think about what the divine purpose is for our lives we can determine how we ought to live. An important aspect of Aquinas' view of morals, just as it was for Aristotle's, is that the right way can be determined by reason, and the good life is one that is governed by reason. At the same time we should avoid those activities that are unnatural or which transgress the natural law.

Aquinas set about using his own reason to discover exactly what God had in mind for us. He concluded that the ultimate goal of human beings lies in the next world, in reaching God in heaven, but in this life we must also strive to follow God's natural law. So what are our purposes in this life according to Aquinas? In outline they are that:

- we should act virtuously – in the Bible, 1 Corinthians 13 lays out the three most important virtues – faith, hope and (Christian) love or *agape*

- we should avoid sin (failing to fulfil our purpose, i.e. engaging in activities that go against the natural law)
- we should live harmoniously in society, and have fruitful marriages
- we should seek to learn about the world using our reason
- we should worship God.

Aquinas thought that Aristotle's list of virtues was approximately correct, as we need to nurture all the characteristics that help us to live as human beings in a society. These may be called the 'natural virtues'. However, Aristotle's list needs to be supplemented by the 'supernatural' Christian virtues of 'faith, hope and charity'. These had been revealed to humanity in the Bible (1 Corinthians 13), and enabled us to reach our ultimate goal, which for Aquinas was 'blessedness' – eternal union with God. For Aquinas this strict morality meant that anybody who habitually goes against God's natural law, and against the virtues that are a product of this law, is a sinner and will be condemned by God.

The natural law approach to ethics has helped shape the position of the Catholic Church on many issues. A helpful way of understanding how it works in practice is to consider a few specific moral issues. Here are two examples of how Catholic thinkers have used natural law ethics to legislate on specific moral dilemmas.

First, when it comes to sexual morality, the natural law theorist asks first what the *purpose* behind the sexual act is. That is, she asks what the sexual act is designed for, or what it is supposed to achieve. The standard answer given by the Catholic Church is that it is for procreation. In other words the function of sex in God's plan is for human beings to reproduce. This can also be expressed as saying that it is in accordance with the natural law for us to have sexual relations for this purpose and only for this purpose. Now, it follows from this line of thought that any sexual activity which is *not* directed to the end of procreation is a transgression of the natural law and a perversion of God's intention, and is therefore morally wrong. By this line of reasoning, homosexuality and contraception (among other things) are to be condemned as sinful.

A second example, and one considered by Aquinas, is that of suicide. Aquinas argues that the natural state of human beings is to strive to keep themselves alive. Indeed, it is clear that a good deal of what we do is geared to this end. It follows that any action aimed at ending one's own life is a perversion of the natural course and therefore wrong.

Consider how a natural law theorist would deal with the following moral dilemmas.

1 Whether or not to have an abortion.
2 Whether or not to quicken the death of a terminally ill patient.
3 Whether or not to eat animals for food.
4 Whether or not to use animals for testing drugs.

Criticisms of natural law ethics

There are problems with the natural law theory, many of them revolving around the idea of what is 'natural'.

■ Natural law theory relies on a teleological view of the universe that is no longer commonly held

We have already seen that Aristotle's claim that everything has a function, and the examples he gives of the purposes of things, have been undermined by the success of modern science. For example, Aristotle believed that the reason why sunflowers turn to face the sun is because they are trying to get as much sun as possible to help them grow. Now, while in one sense this account is correct, modern science would regard this as only a manner of speaking, a kind of short-hand explanation. Sunflowers don't really *try* to do anything. They don't really have goals at all. They are just elaborate mechanical devices reacting to efficient causes. So a more complete explanation can be given which makes no reference to the purposes or goals of the plant. For example, it would refer to the mechanical causes of the movement such as the chemical changes in cells that lead to cell expansion or contraction. And similarly with human beings. Modern evolutionary biology explains the existence of human beings in terms which ultimately have to do with 'mechanical' explanations alone. We are the product of random mutation and environmental pressures, not of any divine plan.

■ It relies on a Christian theology

In Aquinas' version of the natural law theory God plays a crucial role. It is because the universe is created by God that it has a design and purpose. But if we have independent reasons for denying the existence of God, then we might well come to think that there is no design to the universe, and no purpose to humankind. This suggests that it is up to us how we live. We are not obliged, in other words, to conform in our behaviour to any pre-ordained plan or laws.

■ Natural law theory is reactionary

Natural law theory is well suited to a reactionary attitude to morality. What counts as 'natural' for the natural law theorist will normally reflect the status quo, or the way things have been up until now. For the way to work out what it is natural for people to do is to look and see what they do or have done. It follows that any argument which urges us to *change* our moral stance will tend to fall foul of a natural law argument. So, for example, the natural law theorist could well argue that, since women have traditionally reared children and stayed at home, it is *natural* for them to do so. And if it is natural then it is right. If you are inclined to believe that what human beings have done up until now may not be right then you have reason to reject natural law-style reasoning.

■ How do we work out what our function is simply by looking at nature?

It is very difficult to see how you can draw a convincing distinction between what is natural for human beings and what is not. Aquinas argues that suicide is unnatural. Hume famously responded in his essay *On Suicide* (1755) that if suicide is unnatural then it is even more unnatural to dam up a river. A river is far more powerful than a person, and more energy is required to pervert it from its natural course. But few would say that it is wrong to build a dam. Similarly, Hume argues, if it is wrong to interfere in the natural course of things, then if you see a slate blow loose from a roof and hurtle towards someone's head, it is surely wrong to shout out and warn them of the imminent danger. To be consistent, the natural law theorist has to say that it would be contrary to God's will to avert the impact of slate with skull. But this runs counter to what we expect a moral theory to prescribe and so the natural law theory loses credibility.

The more general conclusion of this line of thought is that human beings are always interfering in the natural course of things. Medicine, for example, is all about interfering with the natural course of diseases. Are we to say that all medicine is wrong? Paradoxically we might even say that it is natural for human beings to interfere with nature. But if we say this, where does this leave us with drawing a distinction between natural and unnatural activities?

David Hume and qualities

Hume

Public utility is the sole origin of justice, and ... reflections on the beneficial consequences of this virtue are the sole foundation of its merit.[106]

Because of claims like this, many philosophers, including Jeremy Bentham, have seen the British philosopher David Hume (1711–1776) as a sort of proto-utilitarian. However, a close reading of Hume puts him more in line with the agent-centred virtue ethics than with the act-centred approach of the utilitarians. Like Plato and Aristotle, Hume is interested in the virtues (or character traits) of a good person, and what the origins of these virtues are.

Hume's most famous book on morality, *Enquiry Concerning The Principles Of Morals* (1752), is more of an investigation into origins of moral judgements than a normative theory guiding how we should act. Hume's main concern throughout the *Enquiry* is to discover the principle underlying morality; in particular he wishes to understand on what basis we call some character traits 'virtuous' and other traits 'vicious'.

Before writing the *Enquiry* Hume had laid out his philosophical stall very clearly in his *Treatise of Human Nature* (1740). This work establishes his empiricist credentials but it also sets out his beliefs about the source of morality. Hume, a famous sceptic, was doubtful about the role that reason had in informing our moral decisions. Plato and Aristotle viewed reason as essential to morality in two aspects. First, 'practical' reason helps us to get what we want (as for example, when you plan your examination revision), so we use practical reason to select the means towards our ends (our goals). Second, reason at a more abstract and contemplative level enables us to find out what our goals should be (for example, what we need in order to flourish), so we can reason about ends as well as the means to those ends. However, Hume puts forward a convincing case that we *cannot* reason about ends, about the things we want, or what our goals are. We can only reason about means. This is because our ends, the things we want, are determined by our 'passions' which are non-rational motivators that we have no control over. For Hume it is a truth about human psychology that we begin with our passions (our wants and desires) and use reason to work out how to satisfy these passions. But we cannot work the other way round, i.e. we cannot use reason to shape our wants and desires, that's just not how our minds work. Two famous passages from the *Treatise* sum up Hume's position.

Hume

> Reason is ... the slave of the passions and can never pretend to any other office than to serve and obey them.[107]
>
> 'Tis not contrary to reason to prefer the destruction of the whole world to the scratching of my finger.[108]

The latter quote is particularly shocking, and not at all what we would expect to hear from a moral philosopher.[109] But all Hume is saying is that it is possible for my preferences to be primarily geared towards my own interests rather than towards the interests of the rest of the world. This is not to say that these desires are a good thing – only that they are not irrational desires, because according to Hume our preferences or desires come first and they cannot be derived from any sort of reasoning, such as a utilitarian calculation.

So, in contrast to the rational approach of the Ancient Greeks, Hume believes there to be a non-rational source of virtue. Because of his claims about the limits of reason as a motivator, Hume cannot link virtues to knowledge, as Plato does, nor can he tie them strictly to function and excellence, as Aristotle and Aquinas do. For Hume, we must build up our moral theory on the basis of the preferences, concerns and desires that human beings happen to hold in common, and particularly on those qualities that we find in people that we happen to approve of.

Hume

> Take any action allowed to be vicious: wilful murder for instance. Examine it in all lights and see if you can find that matter of fact or real existence, which you call vice ... In whichever way you take it, you find only certain passions, motives, volitions and thoughts ... Here is a matter of fact, but it is the object of feeling, not of reason. It lies in yourself, not in the object.[110]

Hume argues that when we make a moral judgement we are not talking about some feature of the world 'out there' that is good or right or virtuous. If we think carefully about the moral judgements we make then we discover that they are derived only from a feeling inside us. When someone does something kind, or generous or courageous, we have a general feeling of approval for such behaviour. So, for Hume, morality isn't really a (rational) judgement at all; it's more of a gut feeling, or, as Hume says, a 'perception in the mind' rather than a 'quality in the object': morality is in me, not 'out there'. We shall see in the next chapter the influence that this claim had on a group of philosophers known as the EMOTIVISTS (pages 157–158).

In the *Enquiry* Hume continues his investigation into ethics by seeking to discover, in a scientific way, the origins of morality. For Hume, morality is simply based on our (and everyone else's) reactions to people's behaviour, and it is these reactions that tell us whether someone is virtuous or not. Does this make morality a matter of personal opinion? Not according to Hume, because he believes that our moral reactions are all pretty similar, that we can all recognise virtuous actions when we see them, and that we have a common concern for other people. This conformity of response results from the innate capacity that each of us has to feel sympathy for one another. Sympathy lies at the heart of Hume's moral philosophy; he thinks of it as a kind of moral trigger that all of us (except perhaps psychopaths) possess.

Hume

Would any man, who is walking along, tread as willingly on another's gouty toes, whom he has no quarrel with, as on the hard flint and pavement?[111]

Sympathy is the connection we have with other people, and our appreciation of their pains and pleasures (nowadays we would use the word 'empathy'). Sympathy is what gives us altruistic desires, and makes it difficult for us to treat people as mere objects or as means. Hume is right, most of us just couldn't walk on someone lying on the ground as if they were another bit of pavement. However, he does recognise that our sympathy diminishes in proportion to the (emotional and physical) distance to us of the people concerned. So we may feel less concerned about an earthquake that happened thousands of miles away than about a car accident a friend was in. And Hume also recognises that sympathy competes with self-interest (another natural passion that we all share) as a motivator for action, although, for Hume, sympathy wins in most cases.

This tension between self-interest (or 'self-love' as Hume called it) and sympathy is brought out in Hume's discussion of the 'sensible knave' in the concluding paragraphs of the *Enquiry*. A knave is someone who is a bit of a scoundrel; a sensible knave is someone who disguises their selfishness: a cheat or a free rider who will try to get away with whatever he can. The sensible knave accepts, for example, that 'honesty is the best policy' but there are many exceptions, and the knave, who is motivated purely by self-interest, will take advantage of all those exceptions in order to get what he wants. In Laclos' book *Dangerous Liaisons* (1779) one of the main characters is a scheming and amoral aristocrat named Valmont – the kind of 'sensible knave' that Hume might have had in mind.

I summon the tax-collector, and yielding to my generous compassion pay him £56, for the lack of which sum [of money] five persons were to be reduced to living on straw and despair. You cannot imagine the shower of blessings this simple action brought down upon me from those present ... My eyes were moist with tears and inside I felt an unwonted but delicious emotion. I was astonished at the pleasure to be derived from doing good, and I am now tempted to think that what we call virtuous people have less claim to merit than we are led to believe.[112]

Laclos, *Dangerous Liaisons*

For the most part Valmont is a vicious and nasty piece of work; he has no interest in virtue and is driven only by hedonistic self-interest. Yet on the surface he displays all the virtues he needs to get by as a respected aristocrat – as on this occasion when he gives some money to the poor (and finds it astonishing that charity could be a source of pleasure – which suggests to him the amusing possibility that virtuous people are really just hedonists like him!). Such behaviour appears to be a problem for Hume's belief that sympathetic feelings win out over self-interested ones, because it seems that the rewards gained by a sensible knave like Valmont are greater than those gained by someone who is disposed to be selfless. But for Hume, as for Plato and Aristotle, these gains are merely apparent and such a person's lack of virtue will remain a barrier to their happiness. Such people

Hume

will discover that they themselves are the greatest dupes and have sacrificed the invaluable enjoyment of a character ... for the acquisition of worthless toys and gewgaws.[113]

Hume thought that there were basically two kinds of virtue, or qualities, based on the two sorts of positive responses we have to someone's behaviour. The first is a response to the usefulness of her behaviour, the pains and pleasures it generates, which Hume calls its utility. The second response is simply based on whether her behaviour pleases us, which Hume terms its agreeability. These qualities (of utility or agreeability) may either be extended to ourselves, or to other people. This is the principle that Hume believes governs morality: that we value those qualities which are 'useful or agreeable to the person himself or to others'.[114] Qualities that are neither useful nor agreeable to ourselves or others are not virtues. Hume gives as an example of such qualities the so-called 'monkish' virtues which are tainted by 'superstitious and false religion': such as celibacy, fasting, self-denial, silence, solitude, etc.[115] Below is a table of some examples of genuine virtues (or qualities), classified according to Hume's principle:

	To others	To ourselves
Qualities that have utility	Justice, benevolence, humanity, generosity, charity, gratitude, friendliness, honesty, fidelity, mercy, moderation	Industry, frugality, caution, willpower, wisdom, memory, economy, prudence, patience, judgement
Qualities that are agreeable	Good manners, wit, ingenuity, eloquence, affability, modesty, decency, politeness, cleanliness	Cheerfulness, magnanimity, courage, dignity, tranquillity, delicacy, serenity

ACTIVITY

1 Do you agree with Hume's classification of the virtues?

2 Do you think we still recognise and value all the virtues on this list? Why/Why not?

3 Are there any virtues that Plato and Aristotle acknowledge, but which Hume would miss out from his list?

4 Are there any virtues that you think could be added to this list?

Hume also makes a clear distinction between social virtues (which he also calls 'artificial virtues') and natural virtues. Natural virtues are ones that we all possess innately, perhaps as a result of our biological make-up (Hume was writing before Darwin and did not have a theory of how dispositions might be 'hardwired' through natural selection). Hume gives benevolence as an example of a natural virtue. Social virtues, on the other hand, are virtues that we gain through growing up and living in a community. Justice, the fair distribution and ownership of property, is an example of this type of virtue.[116] The social virtues act as essential moral glue for large societies, binding us together; this is because in a large society our natural sympathy towards fellow citizens diminishes as many more of them are strangers to us.

We said above that Hume is not a utilitarian. Yet Hume maintains that many of the most important virtues (especially justice) are approved of because of their utility value, i.e. their tendency to bring about benefits for other people. However, the emphasis that Hume places on utility does not make him a utilitarian because he is not claiming that we *ought* to maximise utility, but simply that humans *do* as a matter of fact approve of utility, and we applaud the behaviour of people who promote utility. Once again this is due to our feelings of sympathy that are aroused as we observe other people's conduct, and the pleasures or pains their behaviour causes.

Criticisms of Hume's ethics

The account of morality that Hume gives in the *Enquiry* is based on a kind of empirical investigative approach; he even says that he is adopting an 'experimental method'.[117] Hume thinks that by taking examples of qualities (virtues) that we all agree are valuable and then by analysing these qualities to see what they have in common we are engaging in a science of ethics. But is this really science? A science in its most basic form is generally thought to consist of gathering evidence and constructing hypotheses based on this evidence, then testing the hypothesis against new pieces of evidence. But the virtues that Hume has identified do not appear to be based on any concrete evidence in the sense that we now understand it (for example, qualitative research questionnaires from a sample of representative people). Perhaps if Hume were around today he would be conducting interviews as part of his research into the psychology of ethics, but you get the feeling that when he wrote the *Enquiry* he was making a slightly more personal selection of virtues.

Following from this Hume seems to think that we would in fact all agree that the qualities he picks out are universally valued. So, for Hume, morality is common to all humankind, and by definition a virtue is a quality approved of by everyone. But is this so? For many of these qualities (for example, chastity, sobriety, secrecy) Hume seems to be describing what he and his peers value, rather than virtues that are universally valued. If this is so then Hume's investigation is one that is limited to his own historical era and possibly his own social class.

Moreover Hume seems optimistic in thinking that vicious, non-virtuous people will always be disapproved of by the majority of people. You might say that the sensible knave is now the default position for many people. At the more extreme end of non-virtuousness, we need only look to the history of genocide in the past hundred years to find out how frequently vicious (i.e. non-virtuous) behaviour becomes normal amongst a majority, thus enabling a group to systematically kill those who fall outside of it.[118]

It appears as if Hume is already assuming what he is setting out to prove. Hume wishes to know what principle of morals we follow. In order to do this he examines qualities we all admire. His conclusion is that these qualities are all based on utility or agreeability. This is his principle of morals. But when faced with a counter-example (the 'monkish virtues' of poverty, chastity, humility and obedience) he dismisses them because they are not useful (and nor are they agreeable). However, if he is sincere in his empirical approach then he should try to understand *why* so many people do value these qualities. These qualities are counter-examples that go against his original principle of utility, and so either Hume must amend his principle, or say why they are not genuine counter-examples. Because he dismisses them outright, he must already be assuming that his principle is correct, even before his investigation has begun, which is hardly in the spirit of empiricism.

Contemporary virtue ethics

David Hume's legacy was not in reviving the virtue ethics of Plato and Aristotle, but in influencing the British utilitarians who took seriously Hume's message about the central role that utility plays in morality. In another direction Hume's scepticism inspired Kant to rethink his own epistemological and ethical views, which led in turn to Kant's deontological theory of ethics. It was only in the mid-twentieth century that philosophers such as Alasdair MacIntyre, Elizabeth Anscombe and P. T. Geach returned again to virtue ethics. Modern virtue ethicists have been able to see the shortcomings of Aristotle's, Aquinas' and Hume's theories – in particular the danger of proposing as virtues qualities that they may personally have valued, but which are not necessarily universally valued.

Anscombe and MacIntyre believe that ethical thinking has come adrift in modern times and that the strengths of Ancient Greek virtue ethics need to be revived. For both these philosophers we cannot make sense of the ethical theories we have now (in the main consequentialist and deontological approaches) unless we understand the history behind them. But, once we understand their history we shall see how strange they are. Consequentialism and deontological ethics employ concepts that no longer make sense, because the world in which the concepts were formed has changed. In particular the idea that we should follow a rule or a principle simply for its own sake (as Kant advocates with his categorical imperative) is a mistake, and according to Anscombe positively harmful![119] This is because the concept of 'obligation' has become removed from its original ties to our needs and desires as human beings living in a society. In ancient societies our concept of obligation arose out of the roles people played in society and because there was a very real sense in which fulfilling these obligations met their interests. But Anscombe and MacIntyre find hugely problematic the claim that there are somehow 'floating' rules and obligations which we are bound to obey, whether or not they are in anyone's interests.

Modern virtue ethicists have not found it easy to detach virtues from the idea of function, i.e. from the idea that humans are *for* something and that we should strive to be good at what we are for. Nonetheless MacIntyre believes that we shall be all the better for abandoning the hotchpotch of ethical theories now available to us, and returning to an Aristotelian type of ethic. But wishing for a return to these beliefs may not be possible so long as we consider humans to be purposeless.[120] P. T. Geach argued that it is possible to see humans as having a purpose, not in a biological sense, but in a social sense: when we come together to work on a project (which is frequently). So Geach claims that, in practical terms, we do have a purpose, namely one based on our projects with other human beings. Having established that it is possible to see humans in functional terms, Geach goes on to sketch the virtues that we would need to fulfil our function (as individuals bound together by some project). It turns out that many of these virtues – practical wisdom, courage, self-control, etc. – are the virtues that Plato and Aristotle identified two and a half thousand years ago. The problem is that completing these projects may not be 'good for us' in the way that Aristotle believed that fulfilling our function was good for us (because for Aristotle this enabled us to flourish). Some projects, for example those of Nazi Germany, did not enable anyone engaged in them to flourish or be virtuous.

Despite the difficulties (which other normative theories also face) in finding firm foundations for virtue ethics, a virtue approach has proved to be influential in modern moral philosophy. This is partly to do with what virtue ethics brings to the table, and partly to do with what the other theories omit. What both consequentialist and deontological theories seem to propose are rigid, almost mechanical ways of calculating ethical decisions. Where is the compassion in these theories? Where is the sympathy? Even utilitarianism, which claims to consider our feelings, does not actually require that we *care* about the people we are maximising happiness for – in fact utilitarian policy-makers and economists often do seem to regard people as units in a political game. In contrast, virtue ethics sees moral action as having a deeper connection with the agent than simply 'this is what I calculate now to be the right thing to do' – the agent must understand what they are doing, care about what they are doing, and wish to do the same again in the future. Virtue ethics requires us to think of our development as full human beings, and from this good and right actions flow.

In contemporary virtue ethics it is recognised that we bring judgements about virtues into our ordinary moral discussions whatever consequentialists and deontological theorists might say. So virtue ethics is filling in some of the gaps left by these two act-centred theories. Examples of virtues, of character traits, which are widely valued and promoted are: benevolence (trying to do good), compassion, generosity, kindness, honesty, being a good friend, conscientiousness, fairness, being responsible, courage, being altruistic. The list goes on. Similarly we widely condemn character traits that a virtue ethicist calls 'vices', for example: greed, disloyalty, callousness, spitefulness, cruelty, dishonesty, thoughtlessness, selfishness, arrogance, small-mindedness. These terms are part of our moral vocabulary.

So virtue ethics encourages us to try to develop our characters so that we become compassionate, generous, etc. But it also reminds us that these qualities contribute to the moral judgements we make, and they cannot be ignored. Take, for example, the rather absurd case of having to steal milk in order to put out a fire on the fur of a dog. The Kantian will approach this by assessing whether stealing is a rule that we can universalise, and if we cannot then the rule 'do not steal' must be rigidly adhered to. The utilitarian, on the other hand, will assess whether stealing the milk in this case will maximise happiness. But the virtue ethicist is astounded by these judgements, just as we would be. What is needed here is a sense of compassion towards the dog, the wisdom to make a quick judgement call about the efficacy of milk in putting out fire, the courage to steal the milk and then approach the flames, etc. It would be callous and vicious *not* to try to put out the fire with the milk, whatever the deontologists and utilitarians calculate with their fancy rules and systems. This is not to say that stealing is a virtue, just that in this case it was not unjust or dishonourable or dishonest to steal. Notice that the key phrase here is 'in this case'. The influence of Aristotle on modern virtue ethicists is clear. We should have a tendency or disposition towards honesty, but sometimes, in some circumstances, we have to make a judgement as to whether we must tell a lie in order, for example, to be more compassionate. So the virtue ethicist cannot give us strict rules about action, as the deontologist or consequentialist can. We must tailor our judgement to the particular circumstances that we face. But, as Aristotle would have said, although we may on this occasion decide to steal or be dishonest, over their whole lives a virtuous person does not steal and is honest (i.e. has a disposition for honesty).

Finally we should note that virtue ethics does not ignore the values of act-centred theorists; it just incorporates them within its theory of virtues. We saw that this capacity to assimilate and explain the values of other approaches was true for deontologists and consequentialists as well (the section headed 'The Right and the Good' above, page 28). A virtue ethicist would consider many of the duties identified by Kant to be essential virtues. So we should expect a virtuous person to have a tendency towards being honest, keeping promises, helping others, etc. But one thing that is missing from a Kantian account, according to the virtue ethicist, is flexibility. Having a disposition to be honest does not mean being honest in all situations, for example telling the mad axe murderer where his axe is. That sort of honesty is mechanical, robotic, almost thoughtless. Instead, a virtuous person would in general be honest, but they would also know when honesty might be inappropriate, foolish or catastrophic (as in the case of the axe murderer).

Similarly virtue ethics can explain how the values of consequentialism fit into their moral framework. Of course a virtuous person cares about the well-being of others (although Plato, Aristotle, Aquinas and Hume might all give different answers as to why they care). So a virtuous person thinks about the consequences of their actions on others as a matter of course: benevolence, courage, kindness, generosity, etc. are all virtues that are concerned with consequences. But again a virtuous person doesn't just mechanically calculate the consequences because, as we have seen (for example, on page 65 above), there are many situations where consequentialism ignores other fundamental values (rights and obligations) in its thirst to maximise happiness. So a virtuous person has a disposition to consider consequences and principles, whilst not being rigidly tied to either.[121]

experimenting with ideas

Refer back to the situations given in the activity on page 44 above. (You promise to take your nephew to the park, etc.)

Using only virtue ethics you must decide what to do in each of those situations. To determine the virtuous thing to do you should:

a) identify what virtues are involved in each course of action

b) identify what vices are involved in each course of action

c) decide which course of action is the most appropriate one to take in these particular circumstances (bearing in mind that your goal is to be virtuous).

Some further criticisms of virtue ethics

We have already touched on one of the main criticisms made of virtue ethics. In the case of Plato, Aristotle and Aquinas, their theories depend on certain metaphysical foundations (the theory of forms, a teleological universe, the existence of God), which, if undermined, also undermine their moral theories. We saw that contemporary virtue theorists are still addressing the problem of finding foundations for this type of ethics. But there are other problems that we must also highlight to give a rounded picture of virtue ethics.

■ Who decides what are virtues and what are vices?

One criticism that has been made of many virtue theorists (including Aristotle, Aquinas and Hume) is that they are simply describing the values of their social class and age, and their lists of virtues are somewhat arbitrary and even elitist. There just don't seem to be any accepted criteria for determining what is a genuine virtue and what isn't. Whatever the flaws in deontological and consequentialist ethics these theories at least provided firm guidelines, or rules, for determining what we should and shouldn't do. So, for example, the principle of universalisability and the utility principle gave us transparent criteria by which we could judge the rightness or goodness of an action. However, there are no such fixed principles in virtue ethics. In fact it seems as if deciding what is a virtue, such as friendliness, or a vice, such as rudeness, is a matter of personal opinion, perhaps a highly informed one (Aristotle was one of the most widely read and travelled intellects of his age) but an opinion nevertheless.

However, this isn't quite right. All virtue ethicists, in particular Plato and Aristotle, have provided reasons for their judgements as to whether a particular character trait is a virtue or a vice. Hume looked towards utility and agreeability to help him decide. Aristotle assessed character traits according to whether they contributed to our flourishing and to reaching *eudaimonia*. Whether or not we agree with the reasons they give depends in part on whether we buy into the rest of their theory. But in practical terms most of us do agree on what kinds of characteristics we would like to see in ourselves, our neighbours and colleagues, our children and fellow citizens.

■ Virtue ethics seems to be a very imprecise moral theory

Aristotle admitted that being virtuous was very difficult, and required all the subtlety and wisdom that we could muster:

To feel or act towards the right person to the right extent at the right time for the right reason in the right way – that is not easy.[122]

Aristotle

You might say that there is a fine line between 'subtlety' and 'vagueness' and that virtue ethics crosses this line. After all, if we compare virtue ethics to act-centred theories (consequentialism and deontology), we find that the latter two theories are able to provide us with some concrete rules about how we should act and make judgements. But virtue ethicists agree that 'it all depends on the situation' and 'we should use our own judgement' and 'we should look to virtuous people to see what is virtuous'. These comments smack of imprecision, and this is frustrating for those of us who look to moral philosophy to remove vagueness and to offer guidance about how we should live.

For the virtue ethicist there really are no hard-and-fast rules that will simplify the decisions we have to take and the moral judgements we have to make. The principles, rules and guidelines of deontological or consequentialist ethics are too good to be true, and there is no easy way of calculating right and wrong. Aristotle wrote in his *Ethics* that 'it is the mark of the trained mind never to expect more precision in the treatment of the subject than the nature of that subject permits'.[123] For Aristotle there is always going to be a certain looseness about moral decision- and judgement-making, because experience tells us that for every rule of thumb we prescribe (for example, it's good to be courageous) we shall find exceptions (for example, people whose lives have been destroyed by their courage). Life is complex, situations vary in subtle but significant ways, and no formula can accommodate these variations. It is up to us to make the judgement call, to reflect on this call, and absorb this experience into our character.

There is a sense in which virtue ethics is empowering; it tells us that we must take responsibility for moral judgements and actions and that we must develop our characters in order to be virtuous. It also tells us that morality is bound up with our whole lives, not just something that happens every now and then. So we must develop practical wisdom – the skills of decision-making – if we are to be virtuous, and this means thinking carefully about the situations we are in, as well as considering what other people (those mentors, role models or critical friends that we admire) would say or do. In the final section of Chapter 4 we look at some of the skills that might make us better moral decision-makers, and so more virtuous.

In this chapter we have looked at three normative theories that claimed to help us make moral judgements and determine how we should live: deontology, consequentialism and virtue ethics. In the next chapter we look at whether the moral judgements of normative ethics are actually meaningful and, if they are, what they mean. Following that investigation, in the final chapter we look in some detail about how normative ethics can be applied in the real world to some of the most serious dilemmas we face (abortion, euthanasia and animal rights). But before we move on to these other levels of moral philosophy, we shall end the chapter with a few thought-provoking but slightly more light-hearted situations to which you may apply the normative theories we've outlined above.

Read through the following eight scenarios. At the end of each scenario is a question which you should answer according to three different approaches:

a) as a Kantian

b) as a utilitarian

c) as a virtue ethicist.

Give reasons for your opinions and try to consider all the implications of your decisions. If your answer is 'It depends', then explain what it depends on and why.

1 You are a doctor working in a hospital. One day a healthy young man walks into reception and says that several members of his family are in danger of dying because they need organ transplants. One needs a heart, one needs a lung, two need kidneys and one needs a liver. He wants you to give him a painless but lethal injection, then take his organs and use them to save his relatives. If you don't he says that he will go to a back-street doctor who has agreed to 'have a go' at the operations for a small price. **Should you allow this youth to sacrifice his life in order to save his family?**

2 On his deathbed your father asks you to promise him that when he dies you will spread his ashes over the hallowed ground of Old Stratford, Ladchester City's football stadium. He has been a life-long supporter and you know how much it means to him so you promise you will. He dies a happy man and leaves you £10,000 in his will. You make some enquiries at the football club and Ladchester City agree to let you carry out your father's wish, but they explain that they charge £10,000 for this service. **Do you keep your promise?**

3 An empty train is fast approaching a junction. You are standing by the points. If you do nothing, the train will go straight on and will run over a baby who has crawled onto the line. If you alter the points, the train will be diverted and will run over a drunken old man who is lying on the track. **Do you divert the train?**

4 You pick up the telephone to make a local call. But the line is crossed and you overhear a conversation between two charity workers. From their conversation you gather that they have decided to break the law in a last-ditch effort to raise funds. They are planning an armed robbery on a large financial institution and will anonymously distribute the cash to a variety of charities. **Do you call the police?**

5 Your neighbour wins a lifetime's supply (about 10,000 cans) of your favourite beer in a crossword-type competition. As he is a teetotaller, he starts to use the beer (10 cans a day) to 'water' his garden, believing it will nourish his plants. You are rather green-fingered yourself and know that this is complete nonsense and will in fact damage the plants. One day he calls round saying that he is going on holiday for two months. He asks if you would keep watering his plants with the 600 cans of beer he leaves you. You promise faithfully that you will. **Do you keep the promise?**

6 A fiendish madman has kidnapped a group of people including yourself and taken you to a large disused barn. Alongside one wall of the barn are crates of explosives. As you are the only world-famous cricketer amongst the hostages, the kidnapper fastens one of your legs to a stake in front of the explosives. To your right he binds up a group of four top comedians; to your left he ties up four women at various stages of pregnancy; and straight ahead of you he chains four of the world's leading researchers into AIDS and cancer. Everyone is gagged. In front of you is an automatic bowling machine. Before leaving, the kidnapper hands you a cricket bat and tells you the following: 'In about half an hour the bowling machine will deliver a ball. The ball contains a grenade. If you do not hit the ball it will strike the explosives behind you and everyone will die. You must decide where to hit the ball – and thus who is saved and who is killed.'
There are only four possible choices. **Do you:**
a) play a cover-drive to the right, killing the comedians?
b) hook the ball to the left, killing the mothers-to-be?
c) push a straight bat onto the scientists, killing them?
d) leave the grenade to hit the explosives, thus killing everyone?

7 At a local barbecue your vegan neighbour takes a big bowlful of your pork, bean and bacon hot-pot. Not knowing what it is, she really enjoys it: 'The best food I have had since I was in New York – can I have the recipe?' She is already half-way through her bowl. **Do you stop her and tell her what she was eating?**

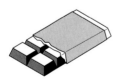

8 Thick fog descends on an outward bound expedition that you are leading. It forces you to set up camp, which is just as well because a blizzard fit to chill the devil starts an hour later. After two days in the storm, with no immediate prospect of rescue, your food runs out. Four hours later, you discover a small slab of chocolate. Divided among eight, the chocolate pieces would be minuscule, and you are the hungriest person there. **Do you eat the chocolate yourself?**

Key points: Chapter 2

What you need to know about **normative ethics**:

1 An ethical theory is *normative* if it offers guidance on how we should live, on how to make moral judgements and if it provides reasons for that guidance. So a normative theory might tell us which actions are right or wrong, what sorts of action are good or bad, or what sorts of people are virtuous or vicious. We may classify normative theories in many different ways: in terms of being act-centred or agent-centred; in terms of valuing what's right, what's good or what's virtuous; in terms of whether they are teleological or deontological. They are most commonly classified as deontological, consequentialist or virtue based.

2 Deontological theories claim that moral judgements should be made according to whether a course of action is 'right' or not. Whether an action is right is determined by whether it conforms to certain rules or principles. For some deontologists (known as divine command theorists) the origin of these rules and principles lies in the commands of God. Divine command theorists face the challenge of explaining whether God's commands are right just because they are made by God (in which case any of God's commands, even the command to kill your own child, could be right), or whether they are right because they conform to some other set of rules or principles (in which case we should attend to these principles rather than to God's commands).

3 Kant proposed another form of deontological ethics based on our existence as rational and autonomous agents. According to Kant a right action is one done from the proper sort of motive, namely duty, as only duty is unfettered by our desires and interests, only duty is free. Now duties are imperatives that we are bound to follow whatever the circumstances – they are unconditional or categorical. We can work out what our duties are by considering ourselves as rational beings placed alongside every other rational being – we must only do what it is rational for every other rational being to do. So, when faced with a course of action we must consider the rule, or maxim, that would motivate us to take that course of action. We must then ask ourselves whether it is possible to universalise that maxim, or whether it leads to contradiction or inconsistency. A maxim is revealed as a duty if it *can* be universalised. An initial difficulty with this theory is that all sorts of trivial acts (for example, tying my right shoelace before my left) can be universalised, but they

are not duties. More problematically Kant's view that duties are unconditional (i.e. must be followed whatever the circumstances) runs counter to our moral intuitions – we would consider it wrong to be honest to a mad axe murderer who wants to know where we've hidden his axe.

4 Consequentialist theories take outcomes, and not the actions themselves, as the proper basis for moral judgements – so they view morality primarily in terms of what is good (beneficial outcomes) rather than what is right (adherence to principles). Some consequentialists, known as ethical egoists, claim that the consequences we should be seeking are ones beneficial to us as individuals. This claim is often made on the basis of 'psychological egoism', the view that everything we do is motivated by self-interest and we are justified in pursuing it. Many people have questioned whether we are all self-interested; and even if we are can we build a moral theory on the basis of it?

5 Another form of consequentialism is 'ethical universalism', usually referred to as utilitarianism. This takes the good to be the good for everyone, not just (as in ethical egoism) the good for me. Most forms of utilitarianism are hedonistic, i.e. they take the good to be happiness or pleasure, and thus a good course of action is one that maximises happiness whilst minimising pain for the majority. Bentham provided a calculus that he believed could be used to calculate the utility of each course of action. One problem with this is that all pleasures are treated the same. Moreover this type of 'act utilitarianism' often runs counter to our moral intuitions – for example, we do not think it is good to punish a few innocent people in order to make thousands of others feel happy and secure. Mill refined Bentham's theory by arguing that we should differentiate between higher and lower pleasures. He also introduced 'secondary principles' or rules (such as 'it is wrong to punish innocent people'), which, if followed, would maximise utility and would make it easier for us to make decisions about what to do. Mill offered a 'proof' of utilitarianism, based on psychological hedonism – the fact that humans seek to maximise pleasure whilst minimising pain. But psychological hedonism has been under attack at least since Aristotle, and it is doubtful whether pleasure is the only thing we seek. Mill's proof, if it is one, is highly problematic and led G. E. Moore to proclaim that it was guilty of the naturalistic fallacy (i.e. of defining a non-natural term 'good' in naturalistic terms 'pleasure'). Recent philosophers have doubted whether Mill is guilty of this fallacy.

6 Virtue ethics focuses our attention on the character of the moral agent, and on the character traits, or virtues, that they possess. Both Plato and Aristotle viewed morality in terms of virtues, and they shared the view that being virtuous enabled us to flourish as human beings (achieve *eudaimonia*). Plato thought that knowledge of virtue could only come through knowledge of the world of forms. Aristotle disagreed and thought that we could be virtuous simply by understanding what our function was, and excelling in the appropriate ways. Aquinas took Aristotle's theory and incorporated it into a Christian framework; thus it was God who gave us, and everything else, its function and to be virtuous we must conform to this 'natural law'. Hume saw the foundation of virtue as lying in our response to the behaviour of other people. We felt approval either because their behaviour was useful (this struck a chord with our natural sympathy) or because it was agreeable. So morality, for Hume, is not based on reason but on our emotions, on the feelings that people's actions rouse in us. Virtue ethics has been revived in recent years because both consequentialism and deontology seem to oversimplify our moral judgements and seem to be too mechanistic. Virtue ethics stresses the fact that there is no simple rule to guide us in our judgements; it is up to us as virtuous people to take the appropriate course of action. It also stresses the fact that virtuous people care about what they are doing, they are not simply rule following, and they have demonstrated their care over their whole lives. However, people have accused virtue ethics of being too vague to be of any help in making moral judgements, and also of identifying as universal virtues that are valued only in a specific time, place or culture.

Meta-ethics

Introduction

Theft in Buna [the factory], punished by civil law, is authorised and encouraged by the SS; theft in the camp, severely repressed by the SS, is considered by the civilians as a normal exchange operation; theft among prisoners is generally punished, but the punishment strikes the thief and the victim with equal gravity. We now invite the reader to contemplate the possible meaning in Auschwitz of the words 'good' and 'evil', 'just' and 'unjust'; let everyone judge ... how much of our ordinary moral world could survive on this side of the barbed wire.[124]

Primo Levi

Primo Levi was one of the few people who survived Auschwitz, the largest slave-labour and extermination camp constructed by the Nazis. In this world of 'death and phantoms' Levi describes a process of complete dehumanisation, of bestial degradation. 'It is a man who kills, who creates or suffers injustice; it is no longer a man who, having lost all his restraint, shares his bed with a corpse ... [who] waits for his neighbour to die in order to take his piece of bread.'[125] Levi describes in horrific detail the way of life which emerged amongst the *Häftling* (prisoners), based on desperate survival from hour to hour. He challenges us to say how our moral concepts have any meaning or application in this hell on Earth.

Levi's question demands an answer: what is the meaning of moral judgements like 'good' and 'evil', 'just' and 'unjust'? Are moral judgements discoveries or decisions: discovered, like our unearthing of laws about the universe; or decided upon, like our construction of laws governing our society? Do they perhaps refer to something unchanging or eternal, or to some law-like aspect of the world (perhaps a kind of moral law akin to a law of physics)? In either of these cases we would expect moral judgements, and the meaning of moral terms, to be the same across cultural contexts, even in the hell of Auschwitz. If, on the other hand, moral judgements were inventions by human beings then we might expect differences in meaning across time and space, from culture to culture, even from person to person.

This question about the meaning of moral judgements is more abstract than the questions we've been looking at so far, about how we should live and what we ought to do. We have already needed, on several occasions, to take a more abstract approach – to ask about the meaning of words like 'good' and 'should' – in order to assist us in our understanding of normative ethics. Philosophers refer to this more abstract level of enquiry as meta-ethics.[126] Meta-ethics addresses fundamental questions about the status, meaning and origins of ethical terms, which many modern philosophers feel must be answered before the more practical issue of how we should live our lives can be addressed. Here are some important meta-ethical questions:

- Are moral judgements objective or subjective?
- Is morality discovered or is it invented?
- Are there any moral facts?
- What do moral concepts refer to (or mean)?
- Can moral terms (such as 'good') be defined by natural terms (such as 'happiness')?

For much of the twentieth century it seemed that questions such as these were the only real concern of moral philosophy. Even as late as the 1980s W. D. Hudson, who was writing a book surveying modern moral philosophy, felt able to pronounce in the opening lines that 'This book is not about what people ought to do. It is about what they are doing when they *talk* about what they ought to do.'[127] Hudson goes on to say that it is moralists who address the first issue, and moral philosophers who deal with the second. To put it another way, it is moralists who are interested in normative ethics and moral philosophers 'proper' who are interested in meta-ethics.[128]

Now this apparent dismissal of philosophers such as Kant and Mill as mere 'moralists' sounds odd to us, and it would certainly have sounded strange to these philosophers themselves (who did think of themselves as moral philosophers, and not as moralists).[129] We do not need to agree with Hudson on this point, but two things can be said in his defence. First, it is true that any moral philosopher engaged in normative ethics will, at some point, encounter meta-ethical issues about the meaning and origin of moral judgements. Secondly, it is fair to say that in the last century moral philosophy was dominated by meta-ethical issues and the two became virtually synonymous. But things have

changed now, and normative and practical ethics (Chapters 2
and 4 of this book) are once again also considered to be
'proper' subjects of moral philosophy. But in this chapter we
look at some of the unavoidable meta-ethical questions that
confront moral philosophers, and we shall do so by focusing
on the development of meta-ethics through the twentieth
century.

Ethics and the philosophy of language

In our discussion of virtues in the previous chapter, two
different views emerged about what 'virtue' referred to, i.e.
about what we were judging when we called something a
virtue. Aristotle thought of virtues as referring to particular
character traits: courage, self-control, practical wisdom, etc.
This seems like common sense: if I say that you are virtuous
then I am talking about your behaviour, the way you are
disposed to act. But Hume disagreed, arguing that our
judgement of someone's behaviour as virtuous did not spring
from their behaviour, but from *our feelings* about their
behaviour. So when I say that you are virtuous I am
expressing my feelings of approval about your behaviour; I am
not referring to anything intrinsic in your behaviour itself.
One way of putting this might be to say that for Aristotle our

■ **Figure 3.1** *The
differences between
Aristotle's and
Hume's view of what
a virtue such as
courage means*

term 'virtue' reflects something 'out there' (in people's behaviour), whereas for Hume 'virtue' reflects something 'in here' (the feelings of sympathy provoked by people's behaviour).

The question 'what does "virtue" mean?' is a meta-ethical question. This interest in the meaning of moral terms and judgements is a common concern of meta-ethics, and in the last century this concern became central to moral philosophy. In the early twentieth century some Anglo-American philosophers started to reflect on whether, over the centuries, philosophy had actually made any progress in answering philosophical questions. It occurred to some philosophers that perhaps the answers philosophers had proposed, and even the questions they had asked, might not mean anything. So these philosophers turned their attention to refining the most important tool that they had at their disposal, namely language. This change in focus away from substantive philosophical issues towards an investigation of language became known as the 'linguistic turn'. Moral philosophy was no exception to this switch in direction, and for the first half of the last century moral philosophers focused on the philosophy of language. These moral philosophers no longer made moral judgements, or gave us guidance on how to act; instead they wished to clarify what moral judgements meant and what moral terms like 'good' and 'right' referred to.

The differences we looked at above between Hume and Aristotle highlight one of the most important issues in the philosophy of language: do terms refer to something 'real' and 'out there' in the world, or are they something else altogether (for example, expressions of some personal feelings). The following activity aims to tease out some of your own intuitions about this issue, about whether a term refers to something real or not.

For each of issues 1–7 select the one option that best describes your beliefs. Then answer the additional questions A) and B) below.

1 Where are **rainbows**?
   a) In raindrops in the sky
   b) In cheesy songs
   c) In the minds of people who see them
   d) Nowhere.

2 Where does your **soul** reside?
   a) In a spiritual realm which we cannot speak of
   b) 'Only in my music, dude, only in my music'
   c) If what is meant by 'soul' is 'certain brain states' then it resides in your brain

d) Any answer to this question does not admit of meaningful, i.e. verifiable, truth-conditions and should therefore be dismissed as nonsense.

3 An **electron** is:

a) a tiny little particle that revolves around a neutron

b) I don't know – some kind of alien from Planet Electra?

c) a useful theoretical concept that helps us to understand certain features of the world

d) an invention designed to make arty students drop GCSE physics.

4 Love is:

a) a spiritual union of two souls

b) an invention to increase the sale of Valentine's cards and perfume

c) coming home to find your socks have been ironed and dinner on the table

d) caused by a hormonal imbalance in the brain.

5 Are post-boxes actually **red**?

a) Of course they are

b) Not round here, because they're all covered in graffiti

c) No, redness is a property of the mind – a mere perception

d) *You* might see them as red, but I see them as green.

6 People say that murder is **wrong** because:

a) it really is wrong to kill

b) they are deluded, the slaves of conventional morality

c) they have strong feelings of disapproval that need to be expressed

d) it's true by definition: what we mean by murder is 'wrongful killing' so of course wrongful killing is wrong.

7 This **book** on moral philosophy is:

a) a solid object that I can store away on my bookshelf

b) about moral philosophy

c) just a series of sensations (white, rectangular, etc.) bound together by my mind

d) full of fancy theories that mean nothing in real life.

8 Beauty is:

a) a perfect quality that we can all have knowledge of when we see it

b) the name of an exclusive new perfume from Paris

c) in the eye of the beholder

d) an evolutionary indication of health and potential child-rearing/bearing capacity.

Read through your answers again. For each of the words in **bold**:

A) do you think it refers to a property or an object that exists independently of us, out there in the world?

B) do you think it refers to something that is not independent of us, not real, and not 'out there' in the world?

If you answered **a)** for any of the questions then you are a 'realist' about the **word in bold**. Some philosophers might say that you have an 'ONTOLOGICAL commitment' to the existence of the property or object being talked about. In other words you believe that it actually exists independently of you, out there in the world. If you answered **c)** for any of the questions then you are an 'anti-realist' about the **word in bold**. We might say that you have no ontological commitment to the existence of the property or thing. In other words you do not believe it exists in the world, and the word refers to something else (for example, some property in our mind). If you generally answered **b)** then you may need to meet with your lecturer after the next class to have a little chat about your attitude. If you generally answered **d)** then you are a hardened cynic who needs to lighten up a bit.

Realism and anti-realism; cognitivism and non-cognitivism

more difficult

Meta-ethics raises the issue of REALISM and ANTI-REALISM by asking 'what does this term mean?' or, put more simply, 'what does this word refer to?' We have seen that if we believe a term (such as 'beauty') refers to something 'out there' in the world, then we are realists about that term: we believe it refers to something that exists independently of us, it is real. We have also seen that if we believe a term (such as 'wrong') doesn't refer to something out there in the world, then we are anti-realists. Anti-realists offer a non-realist explanation of what the term refers to.

To illustrate the distinction between realism and anti-realism let us look again at some of the terms given in the activity above. In the following table we show what a realist and an anti-realist might say about particular terms, and what they refer to.

Term	Realists might say this term refers to ...	Anti-realists might say this term refers to ...
Beauty	Beautiful things out there in the world	Our response to objects that we have been socially conditioned to call 'beautiful'
Red	The property of redness in the world	A mental image or idea of redness
Electron	A quantum object which has a negative electrical charge	A term which has a place in a complex theoretical system that usefully explains certain phenomena witnessed in laboratories
Wrong	The breaking of one of God's commandments	An expression of our disapproval at certain types of action

It's worth noting that realists do not necessarily agree on what the thing is that a term refers to. The same goes for anti-realists; there might be many different anti-realist accounts of what a term such as 'beauty' refers to (cultural conventions, an indication of potential child-rearing qualities, an inner feeling of desire, etc.). What anti-realist positions share is their rejection of realism, but there are at least three common forms of anti-realism. Anti-realists might reject a realist account because they believe that:

1 by using certain terms, e.g. good, no actual judgement is being made (for example, some anti-realists claim that moral terms are expressions of feeling, rather than judgements about people's behaviour)
   or
2 the judgements are based on terms that are mind-, or human-, dependent (for example, some anti-realists claim that judgements about the term 'beauty' are culturally specific and refer only to certain cultural conventions or signs)
   or
3 the judgements are simply false and there is nothing in the world, or in our minds, that the term refers to at all (for example, an anti-realist might claim that judgements about the colour of someone's aura is simply New Age nonsense).

There is some connection between the realist/anti-realist split and between the objective/subjective split. If you are a realist about, say, 'red' then you would claim that the judgements you make about post-boxes being red are *objective* judgements: the term 'red' refers to some mind-independent aspect of an object, in this case the colour of the post-box. We ordinarily consider scientific judgements and statements about 'matters of fact' to be objective judgements. (Although, in philosophy the objective status of these judgements has frequently been questioned.) If you are an anti-realist about 'red', then you would claim that judgements you make about red things are actually *subjective* judgements: they refer to some mind-dependent aspect of the subject, such as your feelings or sensations. Typical subjective judgements might be judgements of aesthetic value (whether this or that pop star is talented), or of emotional states (whether you are moved by a particular Hollywood weepie). One question that a moral philosopher would want to ask is 'are moral judgements subjective or objective?' or, to put it another way 'should we take a realist or anti-realist stance when it comes to moral terms such as "good" and "bad"?'

There is also a close connection between realist/anti-realist positions, which are ontological claims about what exists ('out there' or 'in here'), and cognitivist/non-cognitivist positions, which are semantic claims about whether moral judgements can be true or false or neither (and hence whether we can say we have 'knowledge' of moral values). Let's now look at COGNITIVISM and NON-COGNITIVISM.

Often when we express our beliefs (for example, about chairs, books or electrons) we are making claims about the world. These claims take the form of propositions or statements – we write them down or say them out loud. Now these propositions are capable of being either true or false, depending on whether they describe the world truly or falsely (in technical terms, genuine propositions have a TRUTH-VALUE). For example, if you sincerely state that

'The philosophy teacher is a brilliant woman with glasses'

then this statement tells us that what you believe is that the philosophy teacher is a brilliant woman with glasses. Now this statement may well be false (the teacher might be a brilliant woman but not wear glasses), but false sentences still make claims about the world (except they are false claims). A theory which says that statements and judgements express our (true or false) beliefs about the world is known as a *cognitivist* theory. Figure 3.2 pictures the way this might happen.

■ **Figure 3.2**
Within cognitivism a judgement expresses our beliefs about the world (truly or falsely)

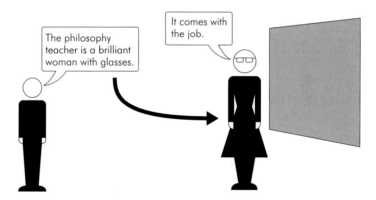

So cognitivism is the linguistic counterpart to realism. If you are a realist about something (chairs, electrons, the brilliance of lecturers) then you believe it really does exist independently of you. When you then talk about these things (chairs, electrons, brilliance) you are making statements that may be true or false, and you are expressing beliefs about the world that may also be true or false. This is cognitivism.

However, other philosophers have argued that there are many kinds of statements (for example, about souls, redness, beauty) which do not refer to the *world* at all. These types of claims are not capable of being true or false (they do not have any truth-value and are not genuine propositions). The name given to this position is non-cognitivism. There are many different non-cognitivist theories but they all reject the view that certain beliefs (about souls, redness or beauty) are propositional. Taking the example above ('the philosophy teacher is a brilliant woman with glasses') a non-cognitivist might say that the term 'brilliant' doesn't refer to any property in the lecturer, but may simply be an expression of approval – that this teacher is hitting all the right spots in you as a learner.

■ **Figure 3.3** *Within non-cognitivism a statement doesn't express a belief about the world and is neither true nor false*

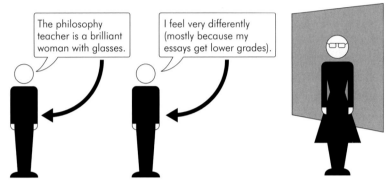

We can now see how non-cognitivism connects to anti-realism. If you are an anti-realist about a term like 'brilliant' then you do not believe there are any real properties in the world that 'brilliant' refers to. So a non-cognitivist would say that when you talk about someone being brilliant you are not expressing a belief about what's out there in the world, but you are expressing something else (such as a strong feeling of approval).

How does this discussion about realism/anti-realism and cognitivism/non-cognitivism relate to moral judgements? Let's tie this up now.

If you are a moral realist then you believe that moral terms such as 'good' or 'right' refer to objective properties that really do exist out there in the world. You might say that morality can be *discovered*. Because you believe that there are these 'moral facts' then when we make moral judgements we are referring to these facts. So moral judgements (such as 'it is good to be dishonest to mad axe murderers') are actually propositions – they attempt to describe the world – and hence are capable of being true or false. This is the cognitivist position.

On the other hand you may think that moral terms do not refer to anything 'real' in the world. In these cases you might say that morality is *decided* or *invented* by human beings. If you take this anti-realist position, then moral judgements cannot be propositions, they cannot be true or false, because they are not making claims about the world at all! This is non-cognitivism. Non-cognitivists look elsewhere to find what it is that moral judgements are doing (because they're clearly not talking about the world). But there are many different forms of non-cognitivism, for example you might say that moral judgements are expressions of personal feelings or that they are meaningless and empty.

■ Figure 3.4 An outline of the rest of this chapter

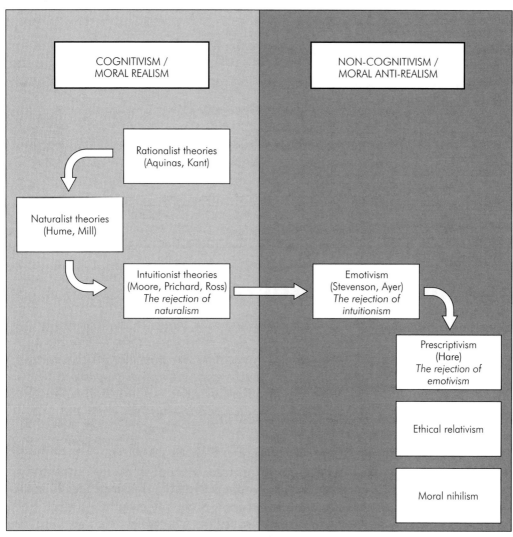

The philosophers we examine in this chapter disagree over whether there are moral facts or not; over whether morality is objective or subjective; over what moral statements mean, and over what we're doing when we make moral judgements. These were the concerns of moral philosophy for much of the twentieth century, and the story we have to tell about meta-ethics in this chapter broadly follows the development of meta-ethical positions from the eighteenth century to the present, while focusing mainly on the first half of the twentieth century. Figure 3.4 above gives a rough overview of that story, which also serves as an outline for the rest of this chapter.

Read through the following judgements and answer the questions below.

1 That new ring tone on your mobile is bad.
2 The morning BBC newsreader looks very fit.
3 Lying to the police is never wrong.
4 Atoms are made up of protons, neutrons and electrons.
5 The chair is bright red.
6 Your philosophy lecturer is tall.
7 It's good to fulfil your potential.
8 Everyone has a soul.
9 It was sad that her mum and dad split up.
10 The creator of the universe is all-loving.

For each judgement:

a) do you think it is objective or subjective?

b) do you think it is either true or false, i.e. it has a truth value (you are taking a cognitivist position on this statement)?

c) do you think it is neither true nor false, i.e. it has no truth value, but still expresses something (you are taking a non-cognitivist position on this statement)?

Cognitivism/moral realism

Since words are only names of things, it would be more convenient for all men to carry about them such things as were necessary to express the particular business they are to discourse on ... Another great advantage proposed by this invention was that it would serve as a universal language to be understood in all civilisations, whose goods and utensils are generally of the same kind.[130]

Jonathan Swift, *Gulliver's Travels*

Gulliver encounters this bizarre proposal on his travels to Lagado, where philosophers and scientists are engaged in all sorts of madcap schemes.[131] Some philosophers in the Academy of Lagado are realists who believe that all words are names of things. Their suggestion is that it would be easier, and put less strain on our lungs, if we were all to carry around large bags of objects and, whenever we wanted to have a conversation with someone, we would simply take the things we needed out of our bag and then point at them in the correct sequence, so that we might be understood.[132] So presumably these enlightened philosophers from Lagado would be able to make moral judgements by taking out of their bags the objects that the words 'good', 'bad' and 'wrong' etc. referred to (whatever those objects might be!).

We have seen that realism in moral philosophy is the view that ethical truths are mind independent. For a moral realist our ethical beliefs can be true or false and there exist moral facts which can be discovered (even if there aren't actually Lagadoan moral objects that can be carried around in bags!). Closely associated with realism in ethics is cognitivism, which is the idea that moral judgements can be known to be true or false because they refer to an objective moral reality. Because of this, cognivitists claim that human beings can acquire knowledge in ethics.

Another way of expressing the realist and cognitivist view is to say that moral judgements are actually rooted in facts, or in the nature of things. This can mean very different things depending on the kind of cognitivist you are. The ethical hedonist, for example, hopes to show that the moral good is in reality identical with what brings happiness or pleasure. Other philosophers believe that we can 'intuit' moral facts, possibly through some kind of special moral sense. Or you may hold, with Kant and the natural law theorists, that our reason enables us to discover the existence of objective moral laws. Or you may believe that moral judgements refer primarily to people's character traits, and that these virtues can be explained in empirical or naturalistic terms.

Each of the above approaches yields objective criteria for determining whether our moral judgements are true or false. Thus these realist foundations enable us to give reasons for our moral beliefs (based on the facts), and to have arguments with other people where we are genuinely disagreeing about a substantive issue (rather than simply expressing our likes and dislikes). Without these foundations the realist may fear that moral reasoning becomes empty and moral arguments become pointless (like two people arguing over which flavour of ice-cream tastes the nicest – there are no objective facts that can resolve this debate).

An important thing to note about realism is that it involves the claim that *ethical* judgements can be derived in some way from *factual* ones, be they empirical, or non-empirical. And this claim involves a certain difficulty. For it is often held (as we first saw with Hume, above on page 71) that it is fallacious to conclude on the basis of what *is* the case that certain things *ought* to be the case. Or, as it is sometimes put, we cannot derive an *ought* from an *is*. This is an important meta-ethical issue and one any realist has to deal with. We have discussed it before with respect to the argument from psychological egoism in support of ethical egoism (page 55), and we will be returning to it again below when we look again at Hume's law and the naturalistic fallacy.

Read through the following summaries of the normative theories that you have encountered then answer the questions below.

1 Plato thought that moral goodness (in the form of virtue) was understood and achieved only by grasping the form of the good.

2 Aristotle argued that moral goodness (in the form of virtue) could be understood and achieved by analysing human nature – what our purpose was – and then striving to fulfil that purpose.

3 Aquinas believed that moral goodness (in the form of virtue) consisted of understanding the natural law that governed our purpose, as given to us by God and as revealed through reason.

4 Divine command theorists held that the right moral action is dictated by the commands of God.

5 Hume argued that virtue was a sympathetic recognition of character traits which were either useful or agreeable.

6 Kant argued that moral rightness lay in duty, and that our duties could be discovered through the application of reason.

7 Mill held that moral goodness simply involved ensuring that our actions maximised happiness (the production of pleasure and the reduction of pain).

8 Ethical egoists believe that moral goodness is about doing what is most beneficial for ourselves, such as maximising our own happiness.

For each theory outlined above:

a) do you think this theory believes that moral judgements refer to certain moral facts that are 'out there' (objective)?

b) do you think, then, that this theory is a realist one?

c) if you do think this theory is realist, then what features of the world ('out there') is this theory talking about when it uses the terms 'right' or 'good' or 'virtuous'?

d) are these features of the world 'natural' or in some sense 'super-natural'?

We will now go on to look at three basic sorts of cognitivist or realist theory, which are rationalism, naturalism and intuitionism.

Rationalist theories

Hume

> *There has been a controversy started of late concerning the general foundations of morals; whether they be derived from reason or sentiment; whether we attain knowledge of them by chain of argument and induction, or by an immediate feeling and finer internal sense.*[133]

In the eighteenth century there was a controversy not just about the foundation of morals, but about the foundation of

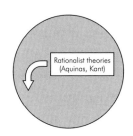

Rationalist theories
(Aquinas, Kant)

knowledge in general. Some philosophers (mainly on the continent) took the view that knowledge must be grounded in reason – they became known as rationalists. In contrast to this, other philosophers (mostly in Britain) took the opposing position, arguing that knowledge has to begin with our sense experience, and they were known as empiricists.[134]

We have already examined two philosophers who may be seen as having a broadly rationalist approach to ethics: Aquinas (from the thirteenth century) and Kant (from the eighteenth century). Both philosophers see reason as the foundation for moral beliefs and judgements. For rationalist thinkers, knowledge about the world in general (although not about God) is acquired through the application of reason, and moral knowledge is no exception. For both Aquinas and Kant, reason brings us an understanding of the moral law – a kind of eternal standard which our actions must comply with. They are realists because they believe in the objective reality of this moral law. It is not a law that is invented by humans (such as a sort of legal system), but rather is a law that is discovered (such as the laws of gravity and motion).

Kant argues that moral judgements such as 'it is wrong to break a promise' are necessarily true.[135] This means they are true no matter what the circumstances or conditions. He supports this contention by pointing to the difference between moral judgements and contingent judgements about human psychology (a statement is contingent if its truth or falsity depends upon certain conditions). So, for Kant, it is a contingent matter whether human beings are altruistic or egoistic – the truth of these claims might depend on our upbringing, our innate personalities, etc. But, it is not a contingent matter whether murder is wrong; this judgement doesn't change, whatever the conditions. Since matters of value cannot be verified or falsified by sense experience, the rationalist reasons that they must be given A PRIORI (i.e. prior to any further experience). Moral judgements, like other *a priori* judgements, appear to be either true or false independently of the way things happen to be. Also, like mathematical truths, moral judgements involve necessity (they *have* to be true) and universality (they are true for all times and places). To state that we have a duty not to break a promise implies that we have a necessary responsibility not to break a promise, not that we happen to have this responsibility at the moment. It also implies that everyone equally has the same responsibility, not only certain people in certain times and places.

The quote on page 134, which acknowledges the divide between rationalist and empiricist approaches to morality, was written by David Hume. Hume, an empiricist, fundamentally opposed the view that reason is the proper foundation for moral beliefs. Although Hume was writing before Kant, and was addressing his remarks to British philosophers of the rationalist school of ethics,[136] his account of the place of reason in morality undermines Kant's position. We have seen (on pages 105–106) that Hume believed reason to take secondary place to feelings when it comes to morality. Reason cannot determine the goals of morality, of what is good or right – these are supplied by our desires or feelings (what Hume calls our 'passions'). According to Hume, all reason can do is to assist and direct us in achieving these goals; reason is, in Hume's phrase, the 'slave of the passions'.

Now Hume's psychological account of the basis of moral judgements is an extreme one, and one that goes against the grain of moral philosophy ever since the time of Socrates. But even if we disagree with Hume's position, we may still want to admit that desire, feeling, sympathy, compassion, etc. have some place in our moral framework. For Kant and the other rationalists, this admittance of such contingent, non-rational elements would corrode and distort our moral knowledge.

Naturalist theories

Mill

The creed which accepts as the foundation of morals the Greatest Happiness Principle holds that actions are right in proportion as they tend to promote happiness, wrong as they tend to produce the reverse of happiness. By happiness is intended pleasure, and the absence of pain.[137]

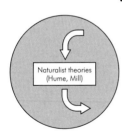

Naturalist theories
(Hume, Mill)

In the nineteenth century another form of moral realism was in the ascendancy. This was ethical NATURALISM (the term used by G. E. Moore, its greatest critic[138]). Unlike rationalism, naturalism is empiricist in inspiration. That is to say, it regards ethical concepts as derived from experience and not given to us by reason *a priori*. So the naturalist looks to the world in search of moral facts and values, hoping to show that moral judgements are really judgements about natural facts that we can discover. On the cognitivist side of the coin, this also means that our moral judgements express certain beliefs about the world, because they refer to some sort of fact, and hence they are capable of being true or false. For some critics of naturalism (most notably Moore, as we shall see below) what the naturalist is trying to do is to convert all our talk of morals into talk about something we can understand better, namely natural facts about the world and human beings. In this sense naturalism is a reductive doctrine. It says that moral values can be reduced to, or explained in terms of, something else. But we shall see later whether Moore is right on this matter.

In the activity on page 134, you might already have identified as naturalistic some of the moral theories we looked at in Chapter 2 (such as those put forward by Aristotle, Hume and Mill). These naturalistic theories all agree that we can analyse moral terms such as 'good' and explain them in other (naturalistic) terms – but they disagree on the precise explanation of these terms, i.e. there is no consensus as to what the 'natural' properties are that moral terms refer to.

The ethical egoist claims that moral values are explicable in terms of certain natural facts about human psychology, namely that we all pursue our own self-interest. The desire to look out for ourselves is a natural property; there's nothing mysterious or supernatural about it. If ethical egoism is correct, then moral judgements such as 'it is good to be dishonest to mad axe murderers' express either true or false beliefs about the world. (This judgement is true if, by being dishonest, you avoid being killed; it is false if the mad axe murderer has no intention of killing you but instead wishes to give you all his lottery winnings.)

The hedonistic utilitarian claims that moral judgements are simply judgements about how much pleasure (a natural fact), and for how many people, an action will produce. So on this view the moral judgement that 'it is good to be dishonest to mad axe murderers' can also turn out to be a true or false belief. It is true if it prevents the mad axe murderer from wreaking havoc in your neighbourhood, harming others and generally spreading an atmosphere of terror. It is false if the mad axe murderer wanted to turn himself in to the police because he realised he was a menace to society, and your dishonesty has now prevented him from doing this.

Theories of virtue ethics also fall into the category of 'naturalism', as virtues refer to natural facts about the way people behave (or, for Hume, about the way we all feel about the way people behave). For example, according to Aristotle our virtues are those character traits (a naturalistic concept) that enable us to flourish (another naturalistic concept), and the key to this lies in our capacity to reason (a further naturalistic concept). For Aristotle, there is nothing mysterious about ethics, we can work out what we should do on the basis of experience. So a moral judgement such as 'this mad axe murderer is callous and vicious' is true if he consistently hurts other people in extreme and pointless ways, but false if the anger that led to his wielding the axe was a single moment of madness in an otherwise calm and caring person.

Naturalism erodes the autonomy of ethics

If naturalism is correct then there are two important consequences, both of which have enthused or enraged philosophers and have generated their own cottage industry amongst academics. The first consequence is that ethics is not 'autonomous'. In other words, morality is not about some unique realm that we can't talk about, or can only discuss in poetic or metaphorical terms. Morality, according to naturalism, is just another aspect of this ordinary world. Naturalism might then be taken to imply that we can make observations about the ordinary world (about the pains or pleasure or amount of happiness that a particular action produces) and then, somehow, draw moral conclusions from these observations. So we can draw an ethical conclusion from factual (naturalistic) premises; in short, we can derive an 'ought' from an 'is'. We have already noted this 'is/ought' problem in Chapter 2 (on page 71) but we shall discuss it more fully below.

A second implication of naturalism concerns the meaning of moral terms. If ethics is not autonomous (if it is not a special, unique or distinct practice) then this suggests that we can define moral words in naturalistic terms. For example, a naturalist might say that 'good' ultimately boils down to 'maximising happiness'. It was this type of reduction of that irritated G. E. Moore and led to his claim that naturalism was guilty of a fallacy (the naturalistic fallacy). Again, we have already touched on this naturalistic fallacy above (page 72) and we shall return to it shortly in the context of G. E. Moore's intuitionist theory. First let us return to the is/ought question.

A problem for naturalism: the is/ought question

To pick up on an issue raised above, an important meta-ethical question is whether or not the naturalistic approach is fundamentally flawed. Many philosophers have insisted that an important distinction needs to be made between *matters of fact* and *matters of value*, between description and evaluation, between 'is' and 'ought'. Such philosophers go on to say that the distinction is such that we cannot argue from one to the other. Hume appears to have been the first philosopher to have made explicit this worry, and his idea has become known as 'HUME'S LAW'. There is a small paragraph buried in his *Treatise of Human Nature* that raises this point, and in the twentieth century this controversy fuelled many books and articles. Hume actually wrote the following:

Hume

> In every system of morality which I have hitherto met with,
> ... the author proceeds for some time in the ordinary way of
> reasoning, and establishes the being of a God, or makes
> observations concerning human affairs; when of a sudden I
> am surprised to find, that instead of ... is and is not, I meet
> with ... ought, or an ought not[. It] seems altogether
> inconceivable, how this new relation can be a deduction
> from others, which are entirely different from it.[139]

What Hume says in this passage is that we cannot infer
anything about what *ought* to be the case from any number of
facts about what *is* the case. But he complained that too many
moralists and philosophers ignore this simple principle. So this
passage seems to support the AUTONOMY OF ETHICS, the view
that moral judgements are completely different from other
sorts of judgements. Figure 3.5 shows the division between
the moral realm and the natural realm.

■ **Figure 3.5 *The
autonomy of ethics
suggests that
concepts in the
moral realm cannot
be derived from
concepts in the
natural realm***

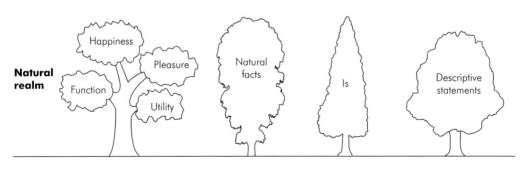

In the twentieth century many philosophers took Hume's law
to support their view that there is a fundamental distinction
between facts and values, and that moral judgements are
essentially different from factual propositions. So naturalism
appears to be in big trouble because it *does* seem to draw
evaluative conclusions (those in the moral realm) from non-
moral premises (taken from the natural realm).

But Hume's law, at least as stated by Hume, does not support any attack on naturalism. In fact Hume was himself a naturalist (he thought that our moral judgements were based ultimately on sympathy – a natural emotion). Hume is making a simple logical point. A deductively valid argument cannot slip into its conclusion any information that isn't already in its premises. So no matter how much factual information I provide you with about some state of affairs, you cannot legitimately conclude (on factual grounds alone) anything about what *ought* to be the case. This is because the 'ought', as Hume says, 'expresses some new relation or affirmation'. So Hume's claim is a simple claim about what can and can't legitimately be done when constructing an argument. We might restate Hume's law as this: *it is invalid to derive an evaluative conclusion (ought) from premises that are purely descriptive (is)*. It's worth noting that this goes for all valid deductive arguments, not just ones in moral philosophy: a conclusion must be based solely on what's in the premises, it can't suddenly smuggle new information in.

experimenting with ideas

Which of the following arguments do you think break Hume's law? (P = premise, C = conclusion)

1 P Everyone desires happiness.
  C Therefore happiness is desirable.
2 P God created us.
  C Therefore we ought to obey God.
3 P In order to flourish we must fulfil our function well.
  P Our function is to reason.
  C Therefore we ought to reason well.
4 P He is the captain.
  C Therefore he ought to fulfil his duties as a captain.
5 P Women are able to have children.
  C Therefore women ought to have children.
6 P It is wrong to cause pain.
  P An abortion causes a foetus pain.
  C Therefore it is wrong to have an abortion.
7 P You promised to pay back that £5.
  C Therefore you ought to pay back the £5.
8 P A man murdered his entire family in order to collect their life insurance.
  P The man was sane and knew exactly what he was doing.
  C Therefore the man ought to be punished.
9 P A man murdered his entire family in order to collect their life insurance.
  P The man was clinically insane.
  P We ought not to punish the clinically insane for their actions.
  C Therefore the man ought not to be punished.

10 P It is bedtime.
   C Therefore you ought to brush your teeth.

Hume is not saying that we should *never* appeal to matters of fact in order to justify our moral judgements. For example, I may want to argue that abortion is wrong (a moral judgement) by pointing out that a foetus can experience pain (a matter of fact). But, on Hume's law, if I wish to propose such an argument I cannot rely on facts alone. If the facts are to support the moral judgement then there must also be supporting premises which refer to some moral standards, in this case, for example, the additional premise that 'it is wrong to cause pain'.

To illustrate this idea consider the following very simple argument, put forward night after night by tired and irritable parents up and down the country: 'Clean your teeth', 'Why?' 'Because it's bedtime'. We can summarise this argument as follows:

P: It is bedtime.
C: So you ought to brush your teeth.

Although this is a prudential, not a moral, 'ought' (see page 6 above), the argument as it stands still violates Hume's law. The *fact* that it is bedtime cannot by itself give parents any reason to conclude that their children ought to brush their teeth. The premise merely states a fact, and so cannot force any value judgement upon you. It may well be bedtime, and yet not a good thing for you to brush your teeth (perhaps you've brushed them ten times already).

Nonetheless, the fact that it is bedtime clearly *could* be an important consideration in drawing a conclusion concerning what you ought to do (if you always go to bed without brushing your teeth, eventually they will fall out). But this, according to Hume, can only be because we are making certain assumptions in the argument which have not been made explicit. In this case, we may be assuming that it is a good thing for children to brush their teeth before sleeping (to avoid losing their teeth). So, to make the argument valid, we need to make this hidden assumption explicit:

P1: It is bedtime.
(P2: At bedtime you ought to brush your teeth.)
C: So you ought to brush your teeth.

This complete argument is now clearly valid. So Hume's point is not that facts are irrelevant to values and that we can never appeal to facts when drawing moral conclusions. Rather his point is that we need to make our values explicit when arguing, so that we can be clear about what the argument really is.

▶ criticism ◀

However, the American philosopher John Searle (1932–) has even questioned the claim that we cannot derive evaluative conclusions from descriptive premises.[140] Searle argued that there are exceptions to the claim that you cannot derive an ought from an is. Consider the following argument:

> P: You promised to pay me back my £5.
> C: So you ought to pay up.

Here the premise states a matter of fact: the fact that you made a promise to pay me back my money. And the conclusion makes a value judgement about what you ought to do. But this argument seems perfectly in order. The fact that you have made a promise seems clearly to imply that you ought to keep it, and so suggests that it is possible to bridge the is/ought gap. Searle is claiming that there are certain facts about human beings, for example that they have instituted a practice of promise keeping, which have implications for how they ought to act, and so perhaps some form of naturalism could be true after all.

How might Hume react to an example like this in defence of his law? One thing he might try is to find some hidden evaluative premise. Is there a hidden premise here so obvious that it seems not worth stating? In this case, the hidden premise might be that 'we ought to keep our promises'. If we were to add this we would make the argument valid and would not have moved from an ought to an is (because there was an ought buried in one of the premises). Another way of avoiding Searle's conclusion might be to point out that the meaning of 'promise' involves appeal to our moral obligations. So that if we fully explain the meaning of the premise it becomes 'You have made a *moral* undertaking to do something or other' and from this it seems unproblematic to conclude that you *ought* to undertake it. But here we have only moved from oughts to oughts. So it seems that any attempt to bridge the gap simply introduces values in the premises.

We should make one final comment on Hume's law. For some philosophers, Hume's law arises out of a particular historical context: one in which morality has come adrift from its roots. We saw at the end of Chapter 2 that Alasdair MacIntyre thought something had gone wrong with moral philosophy since the ancient Greeks, namely 'the disappearance of any connection between the precepts of morality and the facts of human nature'.[141] For MacIntyre the teleological perspective of Aristotle and the other ancient Greeks gave moral judgements their meaning. So in Aristotle's philosophy moral judgements were bound up with facts: to say someone is a farmer is also to understand what they would need to do to be a good farmer. Concepts such as 'farmer' or 'can-opener' or 'captain' are what MacIntyre calls functional concepts. In other words these concepts are defined in terms of the purpose or function that we expect them to serve. There is nothing mysterious about saying of a functional concept that it is 'good'; it's simple: a farmer fulfils his role, a good farmer fulfils his role well. The term 'good' does not refer to some mysterious other quality that the farmer has. So the distinction made between the moral and the non-moral 'realms' above (Figure 3.5) simply does not exist for Aristotle; ethics is not 'autonomous'. According to MacIntyre the loss of this teleological perspective has set moral philosophy adrift, and it has resulted in an impoverished set of moral beliefs, one of which is the belief that morality exists in a realm of its own: it is 'autonomous'.

Moral philosophy after naturalism

The discussion around the is/ought question is just one of the battles fought against naturalism at the beginning of the last century. The philosophers we are about to look at (G. E. Moore, A. J. Ayer, R. M. Hare and others) seemed to have what Mary Warnock calls an 'obsessive fear of naturalism'.[142] Their fear stems from the belief that ethics is autonomous, that it occupies a special place in logic (you can't derive an ought from an is) and in language (you can't define moral terms in non-moral terms), and that naturalism destroys this autonomy. It was G. E. Moore who led the way in this anti-naturalism: he believed that the proper concern of moral philosophy was conceptual analysis (meta-ethics) and not moral guidance (normative ethics). The philosophers who followed him disagreed with him on most things, except for his attacks on naturalism. So we should now turn to look at G. E. Moore, the man who nudged moral philosophy in the direction of linguistic analysis.

Intuitionism

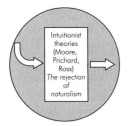

Intuitionist theories (Moore, Prichard, Ross)
The rejection of naturalism

Naturalism claimed that moral judgements rest on certain natural properties or facts about the world, and so we can make moral judgements simply by examining those natural facts. But if naturalism is wrong, and if we can't somehow *reduce* moral terms to natural ones, then how do we come to make moral judgements? Perhaps the answer is that we just do. Moral judgements express such basic truths that we don't need to justify or explain them in terms of anything else. This rejection of a reductive position leads to the claim that moral judgements are intuitive or self-evident, and so in no need of being justified by any kind of argument. The theory that moral judgements are known intuitively is called intuitionism. Like naturalism it takes a realist position, claiming that there are moral truths to be known, and that moral judgements are capable of being true or false. Unlike naturalism it thinks that moral values are irreducible to anything else; they are unique and we should recognise them as such.

Intuitionism had been around for a number of centuries before the twentieth century, one form of which was the popular 'moral sense' theory of David Hume's time. But in the early twentieth century two influential forms of intuitionism developed from the reaction against naturalism. These were what we might call 'consequentialist intuitionism', supported by G. E. Moore, and deontological intuitionism, held by H. A. Prichard and W. D. Ross. We have already touched on Prichard's and Ross's theory when we looked at some problems with Kant's deontological ethics (page 46 above) and we will return to them below. First, however, we shall look at Moore's consequentialist version of intuitionism.

Consequentialist intuitionism – G. E. Moore

Moore

> *Beg it may be noticed that I am not an 'Intuitionist' in the ordinary sense of the term ... [W]hen I call such propositions 'Intuitions' I mean merely to assert that they are incapable of proof; I imply nothing whatever as to the manner or origin of our cognition of them.*[143]

We noted above that intuitionism has had a long history, and the great debate amongst these moral philosophers was 'where do our intuitions come from?' Some, such as Francis Hutcheson (1694–1746), said our moral intuitions stemmed from an internal, god-given, moral sense (analogous to our other five senses) through which we could intuit what was right and wrong. Others, such as Samuel Clarke, said our intuitions stemmed from a rational faculty in our mind that had the power to grasp moral truths (analogous to our capacity to grasp mathematical truths). G. E. Moore had no interest in this debate about the origins of our moral intuitions, which is why he said he wasn't an intuitionist in the ordinary sense of the term. Moore's concerns lay elsewhere.

Moore was not a great systems builder, and his influence stems from his analysis of moral concepts and language in *Principia Ethica* (1903). Not that philosophers hadn't analysed ethical concepts before (they had been doing that since Socrates); it's just that no philosopher had done it in quite the same clear and careful way that Moore did. Moore changed the face of moral philosophy, at least in Britain and America, not so much in what he said, but in the questions he asked and the way he asked them. Moore thought it was possible that moral philosophers had been trying to answer questions that simply couldn't be answered. So he drew the attention of Anglo-American philosophers to 'being clear about the question'.

As a consequentialist, Moore believes the moral worth of an action is determined by the good effects it brings. So we need to decide what these effects are. In other words, the question we should be asking is, 'What is Good?'. The answer that Moore has reached by the end of *Principia Ethica* is that what is good cannot be defined, but is known intuitively. This is why his approach is known as intuitionism. Because 'good' is indefinable it cannot be reduced to 'the greatest happiness', or to 'what people desire', or any other such non-moral good. In order to clarify what he means by indefinable Moore likens the word 'good' to 'yellow'. If we try to say that 'yellow' means 'light travelling at a particular frequency' then we are simply wrong – yellow refers to what we see when we see yellow objects, not to 'light-vibrations'. So for Moore 'yellow' is clearly comprehensible to us, yet we are not able to define it in terms of anything else. The same goes for 'good', we know what it is when we see it, but we cannot define it in any other terms. But for Moore it is important to note that moral properties are unlike natural properties such as 'being yellow', as we do not observe them through our ordinary senses. Moral judgements are evaluative rather than factual and so cannot be justified by purely empirical observation. Moral terms are *self-evident* and can only be known by what Moore calls 'intuition'.

experimenting with ideas

Imagine that a series of philosophers from across history appeared on a TV quiz show, and were asked the question 'what is good?'. Write down the answers that you think the following philosophers (see over) would give to that question.

Moral philosopher	Their answer to the question 'What is good?'
1 Plato	
2 Aristotle	
3 Aquinas	
4 A divine command theorist	
5 Hume	
6 Bentham	
7 Mill	
8 An egoist	

■ The open question argument

The problem as Moore sees it is that most philosophers down the years have been wrong to try to define 'good' in other terms: they have failed to see that 'good' is indefinable. In order to support this view Moore presents us with a dilemma. When we ask the question 'What is good?' Moore says that we are faced with three possibilities:

Either 1) 'good' is indefinable
Or   2) 'good' is definable
Or   3) 'good' means nothing at all and 'there is no such subject as ethics'.[144]

The last option is given short shrift and rejected almost out of hand (although perhaps the NIHILISTS who we examine at the end of this chapter might disagree with Moore here). This leaves us with only two options: either good is definable or it is not. In order to show that good cannot be defined Moore offers an argument which has become known as the 'open question argument'. Consider the argument as follows.

Any theory which attempts to define 'good' (for example, naturalism) is saying something equivalent to:

'Good' means X (where X is some fact or set of facts).

But, says Moore, for any such definition it will always make sense to ask:

But is X really good?

So, for example, if a utilitarian says 'Good means maximising pleasure and minimising pain for the majority' it still makes sense to ask 'But is it really good to maximise pleasure and minimise pain for the majority?' In fact (as we saw with some of the examples against utilitarianism) not only does this question make sense, but it is a question we would want to ask when some innocent person is being punished on utilitarian grounds (for example, to placate an angry mob).

Moore goes on. If good can be defined as X, then it shouldn't make any sense to ask 'but is X really good?' We can see this by looking at another definition, such as 'a bachelor is an unmarried man'. It just doesn't make sense to then ask 'but is an unmarried man really a bachelor?' because we would then be asking 'but is a bachelor really a bachelor?', which is an absurd question.[145] However, asking a utilitarian 'but is maximising happiness really good?' *is not* the same as asking 'but is good really good?'. Yet if the naturalist were right then the first question would be trivial: it *would* be like asking whether good is good. So the proposed definition must be inadequate. It must mean that 'good' and 'maximising happiness' are not the same. For Moore, we can always meaningfully pose the question 'but is X really good?' for every definition of good, including all naturalistic ones. It remains an open question whether or not it really is good. Moore believes that this open question argument shows that good is not definable, ruling out option 2. This leaves only option 1, namely that good is indefinable.

▶ criticism ◀ It may be objected to Moore's open question argument that the question only appears to remain open because the meaning of words such as 'good' are unclear in ordinary usage. So when the naturalist provides a definition of 'good' it is not surprising that we don't immediately recognise its accuracy. In other words, the reason we may wonder whether the promotion of pleasure really is good is only because we are still unclear in our minds about the proper signification of the term 'good'. So the naturalist would then argue that strictly speaking it does *not* make sense to ask whether an action that (for example) leads to the general happiness is in fact good.

■ The naturalistic fallacy

Having established that good is indefinable, Moore goes on to bring out a fallacy (a logical error or mistake) that he believes occurs in many arguments given by moral philosophers. The basic form of the fallacy is easy to understand: a term that is indefinable cannot be defined, and any attempt to define the indefinable is clearly fallacious. Armed with this Moore has a field day in his attack on naturalism, as he sees this fallacy occurring all over the place in such theories. Remember that according to Moore the concept 'good' is indefinable, and so it is a non-natural concept (it can't be defined in terms of anything natural). But naturalists such as the utilitarian philosopher John Stuart Mill are not only attempting to define 'good' (a fallacy because 'good' is indefinable) but they are trying to do so in naturalistic terms (a fallacy because 'good' is non-natural). What fools, thinks Moore, how could they have failed to see this! So all forms of naturalism are rejected by Moore because they are all guilty of the naturalistic fallacy. It's worth remembering that for Moore the naturalistic fallacy is just a special case of the more general fallacy of defining the indefinable.

We saw above (page 72) that Moore accused Mill of committing the naturalistic fallacy. According to Moore's interpretation, Mill attempts to define 'good' as 'desired', and then he goes on to say that it is happiness that we desire. Moore says:

the fallacy in this step is so obvious, that it is quite wonderful how Mill failed to see it.[146]

Moore

It seems clear to Moore that Mill is trying to define, in naturalistic terms, the indefinable (i.e. 'good') – which is the naturalistic fallacy. This attack on Mill's theory is what Moore became most famous for, and many philosophers took this to spell the end for utilitarianism. But we have already seen that Mill was not doing what Moore thought he was doing – Mill was not defining 'good' at all, and had no interest in defining good. He was just pointing out that people already pursue happiness as a worthwhile goal, so they already believe it to be good (no further proof is necessary). In which case Mill is not committing the naturalistic fallacy, and Moore's most famous argument collapses.

Moore's argument against naturalism may remind you of Hume's law, because it is drawing a sharp distinction between the moral realm and the non-moral realm. But Hume's argument is about the logical connection between these realms (you cannot derive an ought from an is) whereas Moore's argument is about the linguistic or semantic connection between moral and non-moral terms. In a nutshell Moore is saying that any attempt to give a naturalistic account of what it is to do good still leaves open the question of whether behaving in accordance with that account would be the morally good thing to do.

■ Moore's ideals and intuitions

The negative part of Moore's argument is over. He believes that he has established that good cannot be defined, and that any attempt to define it will be fallacious. He also believes that we know what is good, not through analysing it in ordinary, naturalistic terms (such as weighing up pleasure and pain) but through our discriminating intuitive faculty. So what is the positive part of Moore's argument, what does Moore think we should be striving for? In other words what actually is good according to Moore?

Goods may all be said to consist in the love of beautiful things or of good persons.[147]

Moore

At the end of *Principia Ethica* Moore describes those things he believes to be good (although he obviously doesn't define them because to define them would be to commit the fallacy of defining the indefinable!). This final chapter, entitled 'The Ideal' is a fairly gushing account of the things that Moore believes are intrinsically valuable. Amongst these goods are, most importantly, the love of friendship and beauty. For Moore, we must strive to bring about these goods, and we must consider our actions in terms of their consequences: of whether they promote these goods or damage them. Alasdair MacIntyre points out that there was a large group of intellectuals, artists and writers (known as 'The Bloomsbury Group') who lapped up this final chapter, even calling it 'the beginning of a renaissance'.[148] Most of us would question, however, whether Moore was correct to say that love of friendship and beauty are 'by far the most valuable things which we know or can imagine' (section 113 of *Principia Ethica*). If this is as far our values extend then, as MacIntyre says, Moore has a highly impoverished view of what good is.

Moore identifies a) the love of beauty and b) the love of friendship as two goods that we should be striving for.

What other goods do you think need to be added to this list in order to make it more complete?

For MacIntyre, it was as if Moore had given some theoretical justification for the values that these intellectuals already held dear. But this raises the more important question of who is to judge whose intuitions of the 'good' are the correct intuitions? The hedonistic utilitarians could argue about which action promoted the most happiness, but because Moore believes the good is indefinable we can't really find common ground from which to resolve disagreements. At its most extreme end we find moral intuitions that are despicable. For example, Rudolf Höss, the commandant of Auschwitz (the Nazi extermination camp which murdered over a million Jews), wrote in his memoirs after the war that he felt what he had done was 'right'. Mill at least could give reasons against Höss' intuition by pointing to the enormous suffering of the victims of the Holocaust, but Moore could not give reasons against the Nazis beyond saying 'their intuitions clashed with most other people's intuitions'.

So how should we categorise Moore? Is he a moral philosopher, or a philosopher of language? Does he support a utilitarian approach, or is he against it? In the final chapter of *Principia Ethica* it becomes clear that Moore is not primarily a linguistic philosopher, although it was his attention to language that made him so influential. He had, after all, drawn the attention of moral philosophers to the precise nature of the questions they were trying to answer. But that wasn't all he was doing, as can be seen from the last chapter. Moore, like Bentham and Mill before him, is genuinely concerned with what things are good. Given that this search for what is good is so important to Moore, it is perhaps unfortunate that he is now mainly remembered as the man who accused Mill of the 'naturalistic fallacy'. Despite this rejection of naturalistic utilitarianism Moore has sympathies with a utilitarian approach. Firstly he is a realist, like Bentham and Mill, because he believes that 'good' refers to something out there in the world. Secondly Moore is a consequentialist, because he identifies moral value as lying in the outcome of actions. Thirdly some philosophers have even called Moore an 'ideal' utilitarian: ideal because he believes that goods we seek to bring about are 'ideal goods', things that are intrinsically good to a high degree. Perhaps most significantly though, Moore is an intuitionist because he believes these values were knowable by intuition. And it was Moore's intuitionism that brought about the attack from the group of philosophers known as the 'emotivists', as we shall see below.

Deontological intuitionism – Prichard and Ross

Before we turn to the emotivists, and other philosophers who took a hard anti-realist line towards moral concepts, we should briefly look at another form of intuitionism prevalent in the first part of the last century. Like Moore, these intuitionists believed that we grasp moral principles by intuition; like Moore, they believed that moral judgements refer to the world and can be true or false; and, like Moore, these intuitionists believed there are a number of different values that we have to recognise. However, unlike Moore, they believed that values lie in what is right, rather than what is good, and should be located in the actions themselves rather than in the consequences. So we can think of this type of theory as 'deontological intuitionism', in contrast to the consequentialist form proposed by Moore. There are two key figures in this movement, H. A. Prichard and W. D. Ross.

Prichard's most famous work was his article 'Does moral philosophy rest on a mistake?' published in 1912. In this paper Prichard presented himself as taking a whole new approach to moral philosophy, bringing to the subject a new clarity and focus. Prichard opens his article by saying that his increasing dissatisfaction with moral philosophy is due to its 'attempt to answer an improper question'. (This is almost exactly what Moore had claimed nine years earlier, but it seems that Prichard, who worked at Oxford University, was not wholly familiar with the philosophy of Moore, who was from Cambridge University, a full 60 miles away!) The mistake that Prichard is referring to is the incorrect belief that reasons can be given as to why something is our duty. Duty, Prichard thinks, is the ultimate moral value, but we cannot ever prove why something is our duty. This is in clear contrast to Kant who believed that reason could determine, through the categorical imperative, what we were obliged to do. However, Prichard believes that obligatoriness (the quality of some action being our duty) is only known through intuition, not through reason. He thinks that, as a matter of fact, when we feel obliged to do something this is *not* because we have worked out that it can be universalised, or that it brings about the greatest good. Rather, Prichard claims that our apprehension that something is our duty 'is immediate, in precisely the same sense in which a mathematical apprehension is immediate'.[149]

▶ criticism ◀ So, just as it is self-evident that 2 + 2 = 4, Prichard believes that it is also self-evident whether an act is our duty or not. But what happens if we disagree with someone about whether a course of action is a duty or not? For example, if we wish to persuade a Nazi officer that they had a duty to *disobey* an order which would increase the number of people being exterminated in Auschwitz?[150] Here the analogy with mathematics doesn't hold, as the alleged self-evidence of mathematical truths can be double-checked through calculations and through consultation with experts. But the self-evidence of our duties cannot be checked against anything to see if it is correct, and it seems that Prichard can say little more to the Nazi officer than 'your moral intuitions are defective'. We saw Moore have similar difficulties with this challenge above, and it is a serious problem for intuitionists.

▶ criticism ◀ W. D. Hudson believes that there is a further problem with Prichard's mathematical analogy. This is that with mathematics we never have to choose between two self-evident, but conflicting principles or axioms.[151] Yet when it comes to obligations there are moral dilemmas in which we do face such a conflict, where two duties seem to have equal weight and yet point in opposite directions (for example, in our on-going confrontation with the mad axe murderer: we have a duty to be honest, but also a duty to prevent harm to others). It was W. D. Ross, another deontological intuitionist, who proposed a procedure for dealing with such conflicting duties.

Ross, like the other intuitionists, was a realist in the sense that he believed moral terms (used when judging the right course of action) actually referred to some feature of the world. For Ross, we build up principles about what is right or wrong on the basis of experience, through the same process of induction as we gain most of our concepts about the world. (A child learns about the properties of food by repeatedly dropping food from her high chair and, on the basis of her observations, by the age of 3 she is able to make the generalisation that 'dropped food splats'. Unfortunately this realisation simply encourages her to carry on doing it!) So we might notice that whenever people lie then this is accompanied by the intuition that it is wrong. Using induction we can then generalise from these individual instances of lying being wrong to the moral principle that 'lying is wrong'. So whilst our intuition guides us to the moral qualities of a course of action, we use 'intuitive induction' to arrive at a list of moral principles (of what we ought to do). Ross lists many such principles, but is careful to say that the list is not exhaustive (more might always be discovered in the future). Ross calls these principles PRIMA FACIE DUTIES and they include all the usual suspects: beneficence (the obligation to promote the welfare of others), non-malevolence (the obligation not to harm others), justice, promise-keeping, honesty, etc.

What is important is that these duties cannot be drawn from one single principle and Ross, like Moore and Prichard before him, recognises all these *prima facie* duties as basic and irreducible. Ross rejects Kant's claim that 'only acts done from the motive of duty are right', partly because Ross believed that we had no control over our motives. But Ross also rejects Mill's claim that 'only acts that maximise happiness are good' because he argues that a consequentialist approach frequently clashes with other values that we intuit (such as preserving civil liberties, or a duty to keep our promises, or a right not to be killed). We have already recognised this as a failure of consequentialism on page 65 above.

Now for Ross it is crucial that *prima facie* duties are not absolute, this is why he calls them *prima facie* (which means roughly 'at first sight'). *Prima facie* duties are the ragbag of obligations that we know from experience have a *tendency* to be right. When it comes to real-life situations we may find that these *prima facie* duties clash, but since these duties are not absolute we don't have the problems that Kant faced. For Ross, where there is a conflict of *prima facie* duties, we can determine by intuition which our actual duty is here, in this situation. So, in the case of the mad axe murderer, our actual duty will probably be our duty not to harm others, and so it would be justifiable to lie to him. Treating our moral principles in this way (as rough and ready, but which can be prioritised according to the individual situation) resolves the problem of conflicting duties that Kant faced.

The mad axe murderer is back again, and this time he's really mad. He has brought video evidence that he lent you his axe and on the same tape you can clearly hear you promising to give him the axe back again. However, you know that he hasn't been taking his medication recently and that his old desire to 'kill them all' is resurfacing.

What would be the relevant *prima facie* duties in this situation? Well, we know that we ought to 1) keep our promises and 2) tell the truth, but we also know that 3) we have a duty not to harm others. So there are three *prima facie* duties involved. According to Ross, intuition tells us that our actual duty in this case would be 'not to harm others', so we would break our promise to the axe murderer (we wouldn't give him his axe back) and we'd also probably lie to him about where the axe was.

Now refer back to the activity on page 44 above. (You promise to take your nephew to the park etc.) Read through the situations. Then, for each situation:

a) Write down the relevant *prima facie* duties (these may well be the two duties that apparently conflict, but you might think of others too).

b) Which of these *prima facie* duties does your moral intuition tell you is your actual duty in this situation? In other words, which moral principle would be the right one to follow in this situation?

Further criticisms of intuitionism

Intuitionism raises puzzling questions to do with what kinds of things exist in the world (ontological questions); and questions to do with knowledge, or how we come to know things (epistemological questions). For what the intuitionist does is to introduce some odd things into the world, namely moral facts. Intuitionists like Moore and Ross must believe in the existence of simple indefinable properties – properties of a peculiar 'non-natural' or 'normative' sort. And this commits them to an unusual ontology, namely the existence of non-natural properties of the world. At the same time they believe in a special faculty of moral intuition, which enables us to have knowledge of morals. So they are committed to quite an elaborate epistemology. J. L. Mackie says that *all* realists are committed to the existence of these very queer moral entities or properties, it's just that only the intuitionists are honest about them![152] For Mackie the very queerness, or oddness, of moral objects and properties should make us suspicious – they are unlike any other object or property *because they don't exist*!

It is often objected that these mysterious or queer entities (i.e. moral properties) have been introduced into the analysis in a way which avoids really addressing the questions meta-ethics was concerned with, that is: how ethical judgements are justified, what precisely they are, in what way they relate to other kinds of judgements and so forth. Isn't an appeal to intuition a simple expression of bewilderment – a failure to find an answer to the question of how we are able to apply the property of 'goodness' to things? It introduces properties and objects in an *ad hoc* manner but fails to explain anything. This is a criticism similar to Mackie's 'argument from queerness', and it is made by G. J. Warnock who finds it astonishing that people like Moore and Ross believe that 'there is a vast corpus of moral facts about the world – known, but we cannot say how; related to other features of the world, but we cannot explain in what way; overwhelmingly important for our conduct, but we cannot say why'.[153]

The very indefinability of moral concepts on which the intuitionist insists seems rather to avoid discussing what is at issue. For, while they admit that moral properties are different from other sorts of properties, they refuse to discuss what this difference is. And if we ask what, for example, 'goodness' is we are simply told that it is indefinable. But surely the property of being good is not independent of any other kinds of facts about it. There is, in other words, some reason that can be given as to why certain acts are good. When the utilitarian argues that an act is good because it reduces suffering this makes a lot of sense. And this suggests that there is some connection between the ascription of a moral property and other sorts of properties. But the intuitionist fails to explain this connection.

If moral properties were intuited it would seem that we could not be in doubt about them, and yet often we are. Further it would be meaningless to disagree about them, and yet we often do. How does intuitionism account for the apparent fact that our obligations are not always self-evident, and that in cases of conflict of duties it is not at all clear what we ought to do. No explanation is given by intuitionism as to how there is room for disagreement and dispute in matters of morality, and it is difficult to square with the apparent diversity of systems of moral belief.

Hume insists that ethical judgements are in themselves motivating or 'practical' in the sense that, if we accept such a judgement, we must have some motivation for acting according to it. But according to an intuitionist an ethical judgement merely ascribes a property to something. Now on this view it is entirely possible for us to accept the moral judgement and still have no motivation to act one way rather than another. In other words, if moral properties are simply ascribed to actions much as other properties are, but these moral properties are different from other sorts of properties (in virtue of being 'non-natural'), then why does this unexplained difference constitute any reason for being obligated by the property in question? Why is *some* information about the properties of things and of actions irrelevant to questions about what is to be done, while some other information apparently is not? In other words intuitionism seems implausible because ethical judgements do not seem to be simply about ascribing properties of whatever kind, but rather about expressing feelings or approval or disapproval, or about recommending or prescribing behaviour. This is what the emotivists and prescriptivists claim, as we shall see below.

■ **Figure 3.6 A reminder of some of the main features of the different realist theories**

Before we move on to look at those theories that reject moral realism, here is a table that sums up a few of the key features of the moral realist theories we have just examined.

	Do moral terms refer to something independent of humans?	Can moral terms be understood in non-naturalistic terms?	Do moral values lie in the consequences of a course of action?	Is there more than one thing that has moral value?	Can moral principles and values be grasped by intuition?
Rationalism	Yes – to the moral law	Yes – in terms of the moral law	No	The ultimate moral value lies in the moral law	No
Naturalism	Yes – to natural goods	No	Yes – for hedonistic utilitarians	No – for utilitarians Yes – for Aristotelians	No
Consequentialist intuitionism	Yes – to non-natural goods	Yes – in terms of intuitions	Yes – for ideal utilitarians	Yes – there are several ideals	Yes
Deontological intuitionism	Yes – to non-natural obligations	Yes – in terms of intuitions	No	Yes – there are many obligations	Yes

Non-cognitivism/moral anti-realism

> *Ralph leapt to his feet. 'Jack! You haven't got the conch!*
> *Let him speak.'*
> *Jack's face swam near him. 'And you shut up! Who are*
> *you anyway? Sitting there – telling people what to do.' …*
> *'The rules!' shouted Ralph. 'You're breaking the rules!'*
> *'Who cares?' …*
> *Ralph summoned all his wits. 'Because the rules are the*
> *only thing we've got!'*[154]

William Golding, Lord of the Flies

Ralph and Jack are in trouble – they are twelve years old, they are rivals who hate one another, they are on a desert island and there is nothing and no one to stop them slashing each other's throat or worse (and on this island there is much, much worse). Ralph is right, the rules are all they've got, or at least all they have to prevent their fragile little society from shattering. The question is, where do the rules come from? Ralph's rule, that you can only speak at an assembly if you're holding a conch shell, is something transported from another culture, another country, far, far away. In this new context the rule is as fragile as the shell he holds. Jack's rule, the rule of physical power, is one that he develops as a hunter and exploits to terrifying effect as the new chief. In the end the culture that turns the boys into a unit is a culture based on fear, on hatred of outsiders, on superstition and violent ritual. These boys are making up their moral principles as they go along, and it's not pretty.

The question we asked at the beginning of this chapter was: do we discover or invent the moral rules and principles that we feel bound by? Are Ralph, Jack and the rest simply discovering principles that other cultures have discovered, or are they inventing them? The realists of the last chapter believed that moral values are discovered or intuited. These realists had the corresponding (cognitivist) belief that moral judgements could be true or false, because the key terms such as 'good' and 'right' referred to certain properties or facts in the world, whether natural (in the case of utilitarians) or non-natural (in the case of intuitionists).

But in this chapter we are going to look at a number of theories that reject realism. Indeed they have little in common except that they reject realism. These 'anti-realist' theories believe that moral values are *not* discovered or intuited: they aren't 'out there' in the world at all. Anti-realists have a corresponding non-cognitivist approach to the status of moral judgements: moral judgements are not propositions about the world, and as such they are neither true nor false. According to anti-realists, moral judgements have some other meaning or purpose, or, for some cynics, they are simply nonsense.

The influence of Hume on anti-realism

Although Hume is not an anti-realist (and he is considered to be a naturalist, and hence a realist, by many commentators[155]) certain comments he made proved to be influential on anti-realism. We have already seen him claim in his *Treatise of Human Nature*:

Hume

> *Where a passion is neither founded on false suppositions, nor chooses means insufficient for the end, the understanding can neither justify nor condemn it. It is not contrary to reason to prefer the destruction of the whole world to the scratching of my little finger.*[156]

Reason cannot provide us with a motive for action. However, this approach need not imply that moral judgements are made on the basis of a simple examination of the facts revealed to us through experience. For Hume agrees with the rationalist, in the claim that value judgements cannot depend on sense perception. We cannot see, hear, smell, etc. good or evil. In his *Treatise* Hume argues that an empirical examination of a vicious act, of murder for instance, can never reveal to us any thing we can term 'vice'. That is, there is nothing about the event itself, no fact which we can observe, which constitutes its being wrong. So where then do ethical judgements come from? Hume argues that all our preferences including our moral ones must be based upon passions, i.e. our basic feelings and desires.

Hume

> *So that when you pronounce any action or character to be vicious, you mean nothing, but that from the constitution of your nature you have a feeling or sentiment of blame from the contemplation of it. Vice and virtue, therefore, may be compared to sounds, colours, heat and cold, which, according to modern philosophy, are not qualities in objects, but perceptions in the mind.*[157]

Thus ethical judgements are grounded in experience not reason, that is, they are a matter of our own 'feelings' or 'desires'. While in this sense they are subjective or mind-dependent, Hume nonetheless tries to argue that they are objective insofar as they are rooted in facts about human nature. We do not choose these desires; they are simply given to us by our biological heritage. We are just the kind of creature that has the feelings that we do, and it is these shared feelings which constitute morality. On Hume's account, our ethical nature is characterised by the capacity for *sympathy*, or the ability to feel with (empathise with) others. On such an account any variations in moral codes must be a consequence of differing social conditions, while ultimately all such codes must express some fundamentals which humanity shares. This appeal to the innate sympathy in human nature makes Hume's theory a broadly naturalistic one (with a touch of moral sense theory thrown in). But philosophers in the twentieth century who rediscovered Hume found that his comments about feelings and passions led them to a different, *anti-realist*, conclusion.

Just as there is no single cognitivist/realist theory, so there is no single non-cognitivist or anti-realist theory. Anti-realism comes in various forms, and here we will be looking at four types namely: emotivism, prescriptivism, relativism and moral nihilism. The first two of these follow on, in historical terms, from intuitionism; the last two theories have been entertained by philosophers since at least Plato's time but have only hit the cultural mainstream with the demise of religion in the last two hundred years.

Emotivism

Ayer

> In every case in which one would commonly be said to be making an ethical judgement, the function of the ethical term is purely emotive. It is used to express feelings about certain objects, but not to make any assertion about them.[158]

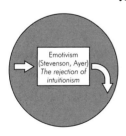

Emotivism
(Stevenson, Ayer)
The rejection of
intuitionism

Emotivism can be seen as a reaction against intuitionism. Alasdair MacIntyre thinks it is no coincidence that most of the emotivists studied under intuitionists.[159] Remember that Moore thought that we knew what was 'good' through intuition, for example the love of friendship and beauty. Now, among a certain intellectual elite, Moore's examples of 'goods' seemed obviously correct. But to everyone else, including many of Moore's pupils (such as C. L. Stevenson), what seemed obvious was that what Moore thought of as 'goods' were simply an expression of his own feelings and attitudes, to which he had given an objective spin that simply wasn't justified. So the theory of emotivism can be seen in part as a reaction against Moore's confident pronouncements as to what was and wasn't good.

The strongest statement of emotivism as a moral theory came from A. J. Ayer (1910–1989). He was a British philosopher who was very much under the influence of a group of Austrian philosophers known as logical positivists. These philosophers were angered by the gibberish that they thought many philosophers, particularly in the nineteenth century, had a tendency to spout. Language, they said, was only meaningful when it referred to the world; if we go beyond this then we venture into nonsense. Ayer was greatly affected by this idea and in 1936 he wrote a book called *Language, Truth and Logic* that popularised logical positivism in Britain and America. The theory of meaning that is now associated with Ayer is the verification principle and it is a kind of test that sentences must pass if they are genuinely meaningful. The verification principle states that:

A sentence is meaningful if and only if
either   (a) it is a tautology (i.e. true by definition)
    or   (b) it is verifiable through sense experience.

What the principle is saying is that in order to say something meaningful we must know what makes our statement true. Ayer believed that if a statement wasn't a tautology (i.e. true by definition), and if there was no empirical way of discovering its truth, then it was meaningless. Like all positivists Ayer put a lot of faith in science and in our observations of the world. He used the verification principle as a tool to sort out the good from the bad, the philosophical sheep from the metaphysical goats.

Read through the following sentences and decide for each whether or not it meets A. J. Ayer's verification principle (i.e. whether it is capable of being true or false).

1 Stealing money is wrong.
2 There is life after death.
3 A bachelor is an unmarried man.
4 It is good to give money to charity.
5 It is your duty to tell the truth.
6 There are tiny pixies that live in my fridge who disappear without trace as soon as I open the door.
7 The universe is expanding.
8 Bondi Beach contains more than 1 billion particles of sand.
9 It is wrong to abort a 20-week-old foetus.
10 The sunset over Victoria Falls is the most beautiful sight on Earth.

So what did Ayer have to say about judgements of value, which include such terms as 'right' and 'good'? He agreed with those who claimed that these terms were unanalysable, but that is because he said there is nothing to analyse. 'Good' and 'right' are what Ayer calls 'pseudo-concepts': they don't

experimenting with ideas

Non-cognitivism/moral anti-realism

refer to anything at all. So if they do not refer to any property of the world, then moral judgements are not propositions and are not capable of being true or false. According to Ayer's verification principle, moral judgements are therefore meaningless. Given the frequency of moral judgements in our everyday lives, and their importance to us, what then does Ayer think is behind moral language? He concludes that moral terms are simply expressions of emotions or feelings, like going 'boo!' or 'hooray!'. So when I say:

Ayer

> *'Stealing money is wrong' I produce a sentence with no factual meaning … It is as if I had written 'Stealing money ! !' – where the shape and thickness of the exclamation marks show … that a special sort of moral disapproval is the feeling which is being expressed.*[160]

Now this 'emotive' account of moral terms was not new. Ogden and Richards had said almost the same thing thirteen years previously in their book *The Meaning of Meaning* (1923), writing that ' "good" … serves only as an emotive sign expressing our attitude'.[161] So emotivism claims that moral assertions express attitudes or feelings. By arguing that all ethical statements are simply expressions of emotion, a bit like expletives, Ayer is taking a non-cognitivist stance towards moral terms. 'Good' doesn't refer to anything in the world, but is only an expression reflecting something in me. It is important to emphasise that, unlike Hume's position outlined above, emotivism denies that moral expressions *describe* feelings or emotions any more than they describe other empirical facts. This what leads Hume back into a naturalist view of ethics. But on an emotivist account moral terms *express* a feeling, much as does a frown or an angry tone of voice.

The American philosopher C. L. Stevenson went a step further than Ayer in analysing the emotive meaning of moral judgements. He argued that moral judgements which employed terms like 'good' and 'right' were not simply expressions of a feeling, as Ayer had maintained. More importantly, thought Stevenson, they were also attempts to influence other people, to persuade them to feel as we feel and to have the same attitude that we have. So Stevenson might say that when we claim 'that's a good album' we mean 'I like this album; you should do so as well.' Similarly if we say 'abortion is wrong' we mean 'I disapprove of abortion and so should you'. So Stevenson is able to give an account of how moral terms motivate or guide action – they do so like someone shouting or urging us to do something, they motivate through the power of the emotion behind the words.

ACTIVITY Revisit sentences 1, 4, 5 and 9 on page 159 and write down the emotive meaning that Stevenson would find in them.

So emotivism opposes intuitionism by not regarding moral propositions as descriptive. They do not ascribe a special property to events. This means that they are not informative. They are not intended simply to indicate facts, but are rather designed to influence other people's behaviour by conveying approval or disapproval. So emotivism has the advantage of doing away with the mysterious 'non-natural' properties of intuitionism. It also connects moral judgement with conduct in an intelligible way, which, as we have seen, intuitionism cannot (above on page 155).

The disagreement between emotivists and intuitionists turns on their analysis of simple ethical propositions. Consider the following propositions (illustrated in Figure 3.7): Boris is big, and Boris is bad.

■ **Figure 3.7**
According to the emotivist, the intuitionist's mistake is to think there must be something in the world corresponding to the expression 'is bad', and so to imagine that there must be a non-natural property – badness – that Boris possesses

Both these propositions have the same basic grammatical form. They both have a subject term ('Boris') which picks out an individual in the world (Boris himself). And both statements have a predicate term ('is bad' and 'is big') saying something about Boris. Now, the intuitionist claims that what is ascribed to Boris in both these statements is a property which we can discover in the world. Both bigness and badness are real properties of people, albeit natural and non-natural ones respectively. And it is here that the emotivist takes issue with intuitionism. The emotivist claims that, although these two propositions are superficially similar, in reality they are very different. While the first does indeed ascribe a real property to Boris, the second does not. Badness is not really a property of people or actions at all. This means that the second proposition is deceptive as it leads us to look in the world for something corresponding to the word 'bad'. And this is the error of the intuitionist who, having searched around for something corresponding to the word 'bad' and having failed to detect anything in the normal way (being unable to see, or hear, or smell Boris's badness), concludes that badness is a very peculiar or 'non-natural' property. But in reality, says the emotivist, there is no such thing. For the real meaning of 'Boris is bad' is closer to 'Avoid Boris!' or 'Boris, yuk!'; that is to say, it expresses disapproval and does not ascribe any objective property to him at all.

Some criticisms of emotivism

One conclusion that can be drawn from emotivism is that value judgements are not rational and so no rational agreement is possible on ethical matters and no knowledge can be had of them. Different people feel differently about different things and each has equal right to their opinion: I like strawberry ice-cream, you like chocolate ice-cream; I feel 'ugh!' when I think about capital punishment, but you feel 'hurray!'. If emotivism is correct then there is no point in having a moral discussion, since two people cannot really contradict each other when they appear to be expressing a disagreement over some moral issue.

The immediate difficulty with this conclusion is that it appears to misunderstand the true character of moral judgements. When I claim that 'abortion of a 20-week-old foetus is wrong' I intend to contradict your claim that 'abortion of a 20-week-old foetus is permissible'. For when we disagree on a moral issue we argue with reasons and it seems as if we are literally contradicting each other; we are not just expressing conflicting ethical attitudes or feelings. Emotivism appears to make such rational moral argumentation impossible. If moral judgements were purely subjective it would be senseless for me to condemn someone who professed a different moral attitude.

This objection, however, need not be fatal, and an important lesson needs to be drawn from the emotivist's defence. For emotivism can allow for rational dispute over matters of fact (for example, whether or not a 20-week-old foetus can feel pain, or can survive outside of the womb), and over the definition of terms (for example, whether a foetus is a person, or a potential person). So if we are in disagreement over some issue, it may not be irrational to argue so long as our disagreement concerns something objective, such as a factual belief about the world, or concerns the meaning of the terms we are using. The rational approach, according to the emotivist, is to seek out any shared values that we have and use these as leverage in the argument. In the case of the argument over the abortion of a 20-week-old foetus, we may both share the view that harming innocent human beings is wrong. If I can demonstrate that the foetus is a human being (for example, by showing that a foetus has complex responses, can survive outside of the womb with special care, has all the necessary body parts in place, etc.) and that it can be harmed (because it feels pain), then the other person may come to agree with me on this argument. What has happened here is that the pro-abortionist did not initially realise that their moral position was actually inconsistent, because they were unaware of certain facts.

Despite this defence of emotivism, while particular value judgements may be a matter for rational debate, ultimately, on an emotivist account, the criteria on which we base such judgements boil down to the expression of feelings. And in the final analysis any reasons I may offer for why something is wrong can only reduce to some gut feeling for which no justification can be offered. Thus any sense that there is a rational basis for moral dispute is illusory.

We said above that emotivism explains how moral judgements motivate action. So ethical statements may be instruments for the control and influence of social behaviour etc. But so are advertisements, political speeches, bribes, blackmail, orders and so forth. In order to influence someone's behaviour, in other words, I may engage in moral exhortation, but I may also threaten, plead with or bribe them. This observation raises the question of what, if anything, is distinctive about purely *moral* discourse, for according to emotivism it would seem that it is 'ethical' to deploy any effective means to persuade someone to adopt a certain kind of behaviour. The consequence is that there can be no way of saying whether a moral argument is good or bad, but only whether or not it has the desired effect (i.e. to motivate a change in other people's behaviour), and thus ethics appears to be on a par with propaganda and rhetoric.

Emotivism is also mistaken in claiming that moral discourse always involves itself in trying to change attitudes or influence action. For it is possible to condemn someone's behaviour, without holding out any hope of influencing it. Moreover moral discourse can be meaningful without its being any expression of an emotional state. I can express a moral opinion without being emotionally excited, for example when giving someone moral advice. Indeed often it is regarded as important to be dispassionate in evaluating a moral dilemma, since our emotions can cloud our ability to make moral decisions (see page 227).

Kantian theorists may turn to the principle of universalisability to resist the claims of emotivism. For, following Kant, they may insist on the need for the element of *reason* in moral conduct. In other words there is a crucial difference between saying that something is right or wrong, and expressing a liking or dislike for it. If I do something because I ought to do it I will be prepared to act the same way if the same circumstances arise. But this is not true of feelings. If I do something because I feel like it, not because I ought to, there is no commitment to acting in a similar way in similar circumstances. Moral judgements, in other words, refer beyond the particular case in a way that feelings or emotions do not. Further they involve not just how I ought to behave in certain circumstances, but how *anyone* ought to behave in such circumstances. What this means is that to make a moral judgement implies having principles; and while non-rational beings can have feelings and express them, only a rational being can hold universal principles of this kind.

Finally we should return to the historical point that Alasdair MacIntyre drew our attention to at the beginning of this section. MacIntyre isn't surprised that emotivism arose when it did as a successor to the intuitionist theories that came before. (For example, A. J. Ayer studied at Oxford, where the views of Prichard and Ross prevailed, while C. L. Stevenson studied under Moore at Cambridge.) This is because the intuitionists confidently proclaimed that they could intuit what was 'right' or 'good'. The emotivists then pointed out that all the intuitionists were doing was expressing their own preferences and attitudes; except the emotivists ambitiously went beyond this and claimed that all moral judgements, not just 'moral judgements made by intuitionist philosophers circa 1930', were expressions of feelings (which is a dramatic oversimplification of the uses of moral terms). MacIntyre maintains that the emotivists 'confused moral utterance at Cambridge after 1903 ... with moral utterance as such'.[162] If MacIntyre is right then this undermines the emotivists' claim that their analysis applies to moral judgements everywhere and at all times.

Prescriptivism

All the words discussed [i.e. 'right', 'good' and 'ought'] have it as their distinctive function either to commend or in some other way to guide choices or actions.[163]

Hare

Prescriptivism
(Hare)
The rejection of emotivism

Prescriptivism can be seen as a development of emotivism, insofar as it further explores the uses and purposes that moral judgements have in our dialogue with other people. But it views emotivism as too simplistic: moral terms are not just expressions of feelings, they have other much more important uses, which are to prescribe and commend, to tell other people how they ought to behave.[164]

Like emotivism (and unlike intuitionism), prescriptivism denies that values are kinds of facts. In other words it denies that moral discourse is informative and that moral judgements state moral facts. The prescriptivist reasons that no proposition asserting what we *ought* to do can follow from a proposition simply stating what *is* the case. While we may learn from experience that pain is unpleasant (a matter of fact), we cannot infer that it ought to be alleviated (a matter of value). In the latter instance we are not talking about what is the case, or what is a fact now, but precisely about what is *not* the case, but ought to be made the case. A call to action cannot be a simple logical consequence of statements of fact.

By this familiar line of thought the prescriptivist is led to concentrate on the practical character of the language of values. In other words, prescriptivism tells us what kind of thing moral language is. To make moral judgements like 'stealing is wrong' comes close to issuing a command, or giving advice, or offering a recommendation. So according to prescriptivism when John Stuart Mill claimed that 'happiness was desirable', what he really meant was not that 'happiness is something we are able to desire' but that 'happiness *ought* to be desired'. In other words by using the moral language of desirability Mill was commending happiness as something we should strive to reach. Thus, against the emotivist, the prescriptivist argues that ethical propositions are not expressions of the way the speaker feels, but exhortations to action. Moral prescriptions are not about influencing behaviour through an expression of approval, but consist in my telling you what to do. So to see the distinction between emotivism and prescriptivism it is important to distinguish (a) my telling you what to do from (b) any effects or consequences of my so telling you. The prescriptivist focuses on what I am doing *in* saying 'you ought to repay the money', that is, recommending a certain course of action; whereas the emotivist highlights what I may hope to achieve *by* saying it (namely for my emotive exclamations to prompt you to give me my money back). If rationalist and naturalist theories compared value judgements to statements of fact, and emotivist theories compared them to exclamations, then the prescriptivist compares them to commands.

Kant also regarded moral judgements as akin to commands or, as he had it, 'imperatives', as did the natural law theory and, most obviously, the divine command theory, which compared moral principles to generalised commands, such as the Ten Commandments of the Old Testament. However, according to the principal exponent of prescriptivism, R. M. Hare (1919–), moral prescriptions differ from commands in that they do not simply speak of the obligations of a particular person in a particular situation, but imply that anyone and everyone, in a relevantly similar situation, would be likewise obliged. For the moral judgement that I make in a certain situation must be founded on certain features of that situation; and accordingly I must, in consistency, be prepared to make the same judgement in any situation which shares those features and does not differ in any other relevant respect. Hare, in other words, follows Kant in regarding *universalisability* as essential to the logic of ethical judgements. In this respect they differ from aesthetic and other judgements of value.

ACTIVITY Revisit sentences 1, 4, 5 and 9 (from the activity on page 159 above) and write down the prescriptive meaning that Hare would find in them.

The immediate advantage of such an approach over that of emotivism is that it enables us to avoid the conclusion that moral discourse is fundamentally non-rational. The problem of getting somebody to do something, or of influencing her feelings with that end in view, is simply the problem of employing effective means to that end; and those means need not involve my putting forward reasons. For, as we saw, for a judgement to be 'emotively' effective it is required only that it works to influence behaviour. Yet it seems to be essential to our concept of morality that we can ask for a rational response to practical questions. Prescriptive discourse is therefore concerned to answer questions about conduct, as contrasted to informative discourse which seeks information about matters of fact. In giving moral advice, or arguing a moral point, what we are engaged in is a rational attempt to show that our position is *consistent* with the logical character of ethical discourse, namely its being prescriptive and universalisable. Thus it is solely in virtue of the universalisability of moral propositions that rational argument is possible.

According to such an account we are able to have moral disputes because we can advocate different moral principles. So long as there is consistency in what we prescribe we are speaking the language of morals. In other words, the prescriptivist affirms that any imperative to action which can be universalised and consistently adhered to must count as an ethical principle.

Criticisms of prescriptivism

Is it really plausible to suppose that all moral discourse is primarily and essentially concerned with telling people what to do? Surely as well as prescribing we may deploy moral terms in order to advise, implore, command, confess and so forth. In other words, Hare restricts his analysis to those contexts in which one speaker addresses to another a moral judgement upon some course of action.

This objection, however, is perhaps based on a misunderstanding. For what the prescriptivist surely intends is to stress the interconnection between moral discourse and action. Thus while moral utterances clearly do not always tell someone what to do, it is plausible to hold that the acceptance of a moral proposition consists in acting in a certain way if the appropriate circumstances arise. Nonetheless, while it is clear that there is an interdependence between ethical pronouncements and behaviour, we can raise questions about the prescriptivist explanation of it.

◼ Is value given by the form or the content of moral judgements?

We saw in the discussion of Kant (page 45) that it is possible to have universalisable principles which are consistent and yet which we would be disinclined to call 'moral' (such as that you should always look after yourself). The prescriptivist (following Kant) presumably thinks that this is not possible. For what is morally objectionable, they suppose, is to make moral judgements which do not give proper weight to the well-being, wants or needs etc. of those concerned. Thus any rational agent would be required in her practical judgements to pay regard to the interests of others. But this defence of the universalisability principle is surely based on an equivocation. For what the agent may like or want is not the point at issue. If I commend, or adopt as right, some course of action which grossly damages the interests of another, you may point out to me that I would not like it if my own interests were damaged in that way. There is, however, no reason why I should not admit this, and yet still maintain that, if our positions were reversed, that other person would be *right* to damage my interests as I now propose to damage theirs. All that I am required to do is to concede that neglect of my own interests by others would be morally unobjectionable. If this is right then there appears to be no limit on what practical judgements **167** we can consistently make. And so we can simply decide what our principles are. It would seem that we are left with the view (not unlike Jean-Paul Sartre's view[165]) that morality is constrained only by good faith and consistency, and that nothing can *determine* us to adopt any particular principles.

Such a position, because of its implication that each individual simply chooses what they value without appeal to reasons, threatens to degenerate into relativism, which we return to below. The question is whether the reversibility test (i.e. treating oneself both as the subject and object of an act) could operate as a sufficient constraint on moral choices to generate a substantive normative ethics. Does prescriptivism imply that any prescription could be moral, for example 'thou shalt not step on the cracks on the pavement'? It may be that Hare can reasonably answer in the affirmative but point out that we can still dismiss such a person since they are crazy according to the majority, just as we do when people believe anything crazy.

The issue that this discussion raises is whether it is the content of what we judge which makes a judgement moral, or whether it is the form of the judgement. Kant, Hare and Sartre appear to argue that it is the form which matters. The judgement must be a universal one, or must be authentic and consistently lived by. But such accounts appear to leave out something crucial: such formal features appear to leave the content of what we judge untouched. And yet, it seems that a judgement, in order to be properly moral, has to have something to do with the concern for the welfare of others (we saw this brought out on page 17 above, when our intuitions suggested that a moral action had a significant effect on others).

What we have been seeing is that non-cognitivism can readily lead into *relativism*. If values depend exclusively on the way we feel – if moral judgements are mere expressions of sentiment and not descriptions of facts, then unless we can establish (as Hume hoped to) that human beings share a common moral 'nature' we may conclude that there is nothing in the nature of things or of mankind to determine them to be one way rather than the other.

Ethical relativism

As I walked between New Guinea valleys, people who themselves practised cannibalism and who were scarcely out of the stone age routinely warned me about the unspeakably primitive, vile, and cannibalistic habits of the people I would encounter in the next valley.[166]

Jared Diamond

Ethical relativism

According to relativism, moral judgements are relative to the standards that each society has. Lots of different societies means lots of different standards. So, while our culture might judge all forms of cannibalism to be vile, in the Grand Valley of Papua New Guinea there is clearly a finer distinction to be drawn. Because of the geography of the Grand Valley, no culture has come to dominate. There are five thousand languages spoken in the world today, and one thousand of them are spoken in New Guinea, each of them mutually unintelligible to their neighbouring language, and dozens bearing no relation to any other language on Earth. Unlike the rest of the world, where a few cultures came to dominate and subsume other cultures[167], there was no such colonisation or conquering of Papua New Guinea's Grand Valley. No single language, no single culture and no single moral code. It is a relativist's dream, for here we can see, within an area the size of Texas, just how radically different moral codes can be. And which of these moral codes, which form of cannibalism or vegetarianism, are we to say is the absolute one, the right one?

Early examples of moral relativism can be found in Ancient Greece. We saw (page 10 above) that Protagoras claimed that 'man is the measure of all things', and in Plato's *Republic* the character Thrasymachus also takes a relativist line. He argues that justice is the interest of the stronger, meaning that doing what is right means doing what you are told by those in power. It follows that moral judgements are relative to the principles of conduct laid down by certain authorities. Ethical relativism then is the view that moral values vary from time to time, place to place, or culture to culture. The ethical relativist claims that there are no universal moral truths and that any rational justification for a moral position is in vain. The ultimate consequence of rejecting moral cognitivism or realism is that two conflicting basic moral judgements appear to be equally valid (as we saw in the discussion of emotivism). Thus the relativist argues that what is right or good according to the moral code of one individual, or of one society, need not be right or good for another, even if the situations involved are similar.

Ethical relativism is argued for from the (allegedly) empirically observed fact that peoples from different societies adhere to different basic ethical beliefs. Cannibalism and human sacrifice are acceptable forms of conduct in some societies, while not in ours. (Among the Aztecs, the two went hand-in-hand, with sacrificed victims taken from temples and distributed throughout the capital city for use in stews.[168]) The relativist points out that the ethical beliefs of different peoples and cultures conflict, and concludes that no values are **169** universal to all mankind. This, as we saw in Chapter 1, was probably the impetus behind the Sophists' relativism in Ancient Greece. More recently, ethical relativism has derived support from the explanations of people's moral beliefs offered by the social sciences.

In the past one hundred years or so there has been an increasing momentum of ethical and cultural relativism, driven by key figures in the social sciences. Sigmund Freud's concept of the superego, for example, appears to lead to relativism since (he claims) our moral sense is inculcated in us by the representatives of society (i.e. our parents). A relativist perspective can also be drawn from the Marxist argument that it is the ideology of the ruling class which determines the morality of a society. This implies that the morality of bourgeois philosophers like Mill or Kant can have no claim to objectivity. (Although Karl Marx does appear to believe that some things can be universally condemned, such as the oppression and false consciousness of the proletariat.) According to relativism, Moore's question 'What is good?' can only be equated with what a particular culture *believes* is good. And what a culture believes to be good is, roughly, what members of that culture (philosophers and non-philosophers alike) end up believing to be good. This kind of account suggests that we are not free to choose our beliefs and principles. And if social conditioning defines values, then the appeal to social authority is the only legitimate means to justify our ethical beliefs. A value judgement, therefore, is to be justified exclusively by appeal to certain social norms and conventions: the *mores* of a particular culture.

ACTIVITY   Revisit Primo Levi's account of how theft was judged in Auschwitz on page 122 above. According to Levi, thieving is judged differently at different levels within the extermination camp.

1 At the level of civil law how is theft judged?
2 Within Buna, the factory, how is theft judged by the SS?
3 Within the camp itself
   a) how is theft judged by the SS,
   b) how is it judged by the civilians,
   c) how is it judged by the prisoners?
Do you think Levi's description supports a relativist account of morality? How do you think a realist might go about judging 'theft in Auschwitz'?

Criticisms of ethical relativism

There is a tendency to suppose that if you have explained someone's values or beliefs, by showing what caused them, you have somehow invalidated them. If I only hold the values

I do because they have been handed down to me by my society (Marx), or my parents (Freud), then they would seem to have no genuine worth and so relativism seems to degenerate into moral scepticism. However, this objection, as it stands, can be resisted. For to show that a moral belief has a cause is no more to undermine it than it would be in the case of a factual belief. The cause of a belief does not determine whether or not the belief is true. And similarly, the fact that I believe that it is wrong to pull the legs off spiders because my mother told me it was wrong, doesn't show that I am mistaken. Consequently we need to be wary of rejecting relativism out of hand.

However, the *descriptive* statement that cultural practices differ does not entail the *prescriptive* statement that ethical statements are relative. So the fact of cultural diversity cannot establish that there are no objective moral truths or values. To think it would be to violate Hume's law. In other words, it could be the case that people from different cultures hold to different moral codes, but this by itself doesn't show that each is equally valid. It could be that some (for example, cultures which condemn cannibalism) are better, in moral terms, than others (for example, cultures that condone cannibalism). And so, using only anthropological evidence, ethical relativism must remain unproven as a hypothesis.

We may not be able to *prove* ethical relativism by pointing to the diversity of cultural values, but relativism may still be the best explanation of this diversity. For if moral values were universal we would expect each culture to agree. However, the ethical realist has a response to this. For it may be argued that all apparent differences of moral beliefs are in reality the consequence of disagreements about the *facts*, while fundamental values remain absolute and are shared by everyone.[169] Thus even if cultural relativism is true (i.e. even if people in different cultures have different values) this does not establish the truth of meta-ethical relativism, for if their values differ this could be due to incompleteness or errors in the *factual* beliefs, be they empirical, metaphysical, religious or whatever. (This argument is also familiar from our discussion of emotivism above.) To establish that different people agree about all the facts is no easy matter, since different cultures tend to have divergent conceptual understandings. What this means is that the claim of cultural relativism, which is essentially made in the field of normative ethics, cannot establish any meta-ethical relativism. The ethical realist, in other words, can happily accommodate the divergencies between the moral beliefs of different cultures (and individuals), by arguing that they are the consequence of divergent factual beliefs. Ethical relativism, therefore, remains unproven.

Relativists sometimes argue that the fact that people with different values are equally justified in holding them implies that we cannot meaningfully condemn them and therefore that we ought to be tolerant of them. Tolerance is a difficult ideal to maintain, and it tends to crack when it is tested to its limits. In the film *The Long Goodbye* Philip Marlowe, the ultimate cool, laid-back private detective, goes through life telling everyone that 'It's okay by me'.[170] But it turns out that it's not really okay by him that his best friend lied to him about murdering his wife. So Marlowe kills his best friend – his friend had pushed his tolerance to the limit, and it cracked.

But to some philosophers it is a mistake to infer from relativism that we should be tolerant and avoid condemning others. It may be true that we have no *rational* justification for condemning other people. But this is the whole point that the relativist wants to make: moral judgements are never rational. But this doesn't mean we have no moral right to make them. And it doesn't of course mean that we shouldn't be tolerant of others. We will be tolerant of other cultures, if that is something that our culture values. Note, though, that such tolerance quickly leads into an important paradox for liberal morality. For if you are committed to being tolerant of other cultures, then what do you do when the people in the other culture are not tolerant? Do you tolerate their intolerance, or not? If you do, then you are countenancing intolerance, and if you don't you are being intolerant.

Here it is worth returning to our first point, where we were worried that explaining our values as originating from social conditioning undermined them. Now, while it is true that showing that the origin of someone's beliefs comes from indoctrination doesn't show that they are false, it doesn't show that they are true either. And many would claim that the values need to be chosen for good reasons in order to have value. Kant, for example, would argue that it is the autonomous or free decision of an individual which contains the foundation of the values they hold.

Similarly, recall the lesson we learned from our discussion of the divine command theory in Chapter 2, namely that God could not determine what is valuable, simply by commanding it. For it is often thought that if something is wrong then it is wrong, and no god could change this fact. Now, if this is correct, then it seems to follow that no being can make something right or wrong just by commanding it. And yet this is effectively what the ethical relativist is saying. She is saying that a society makes an activity wrong by disapproving of it.

Another way of seeing this point is to recognise that if you are caught within a moral dilemma it helps little to be told what the beliefs and customs of your society are. And people can, after all, decide to go against the prevailing attitudes. It is difficult for the cultural relativist to account for a moral non-conformist. In other words, relativism appears to have the absurd consequence that an opinion poll could prove the non-conformist wrong since, as a matter of fact, his society approves of something else. This would suggest, for example, that everyone who didn't vote for the winning party at the last election was *wrong*, and that those who believe it is wrong to eat meat, because they are in the minority in this culture, must for that reason alone be mistaken.

■ Can there be moral 'progress'?

Another important argument often used by realists against relativism is that we often judge that one moral code is better than another; but if there is no absolute moral standard, we have no right to make such a judgement, because there is nothing in respect of which we can compare the two codes. Similarly relativism appears to rule out of court the possibility of condemning the actions of other societies. Thus the relativist seems committed to claiming that, while slavery is bad in our society, it may very well be good in other societies. We may find it difficult to accept that condemnation of the customs of other societies is misguided, and that disagreement or argument is senseless between different cultures. In a similar vein, note that we may want to claim that the abolition of slavery, or the enfranchisement of women, represents a moral improvement to our society. So society today (at least in these respects) is better than it was – there has been moral progress. However, for a relativist, it is difficult to concur with this intuition. For if values are relative to the culture you are in then, as your culture develops, its values can *change* but cannot be meaningfully said to improve. Again, to say that they have improved would appear to suppose that there is an absolute standard, a moral yardstick, against which today's values and yesterday's can be compared.

However, do we really need an absolute standard against which to compare two moral codes in order to claim that one has made greater moral progress than another? Perhaps we can compare two codes without having a standard, just as we can compare the length of two sticks without having a standard third stick. Thus to compare two codes all that is required is that I take one code as a standard and stick to it in judging others. Certainly from our perspective it may not be problematic to claim ourselves superior, precisely because from our perspective we must be, since it is us who define what is good.

But this still seems to leave the question as to how we judge which code to use. What justification have we for regarding our values as the standard, and then going around judging others by them? If there is no independent rational basis for preferring our own code to others, doesn't this imply that we have no right to use it in condemning others? Certainly it implies that there cannot be any *moral* justification of what moral code to use. But a relativist may accept this conclusion and argue that to expect one is nonsensical. Perhaps this is just what we do. We adopt the values of our society and act according to them, and this is what it is to act morally. And if we have decided to act morally there cannot be any further moral question to be asked as to why.

If the prevailing customs define what is right, then it would be impossible to make a moral case against them. Thus relativism does imply, according to the realist, that we cannot speak meaningfully of moral progress or decline. Of course the relativist can account for progress in the sense that the actions of society conform more and more closely to our standards, but not that the standards themselves are somehow getting better. The difficulty for the relativist would be to make sense of the notion that moral standards might themselves progress. To do so she would need further standards by which to judge moral changes. For we can only get progress if we have some normative criteria or standards by which to judge change.

Note that the realist has less difficulty here, since he claims that there is indeed some objective set of moral standards which are the same for all people and all times and that it is through approximation to these standards that we achieve moral progress. One obvious problem for the realist, however, is that if we do not know what the objective standard is, how do we know that we are progressing towards it or declining from it? Nonetheless the relativist seems to be in the more unhappy position of having to say that past standards are wrong (because different from his present ones) and also that any future changes in standards are wrong for the same reason. Thus moral change between past and present is necessarily progressive, and moral change between present and future is necessarily retrogressive!

Let us know turn our attention to one last form of moral anti-realism. It is the most extreme of them all, because it rejects any justification of morality at all. Where the emotivists and prescriptivists sought to uncover the real purpose and meaning of moral judgements, and where relativists saw moral judgements as the glue holding together particular societies (albeit different glue for different societies), nihilists reject morality outright. In its most radical form, NIHILISM claims that moral judgements refer to nothing and they have no value. That's it, end of story.

Moral nihilism

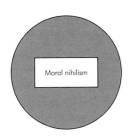

*He's lying against a back wall, propped up. The face is
bloated and pale and the eyes are shut, mouth open and the
face belongs to some young, eighteen-, nineteen-year-old boy,
dried blood, crusted, above the upper lip. 'Jesus,' Rip says.
Spin's eyes are wide.*

*Trent just stands there and says something like 'Wild.'
Rip jabs the boy in the stomach with his foot. 'Sure he's
dead?' 'See him moving?' Ross giggles ...* [171]

Bret Easton Ellis, *Less Than Zero*

Bret Easton Ellis' characters clearly have issues. We might, in
today's politically correct language, call them 'ethically
challenged'. They just don't have a sense of morality. It's not
that they're particularly immoral, it's more as if ordinary
moral feelings or a moral sense or sympathy (the kind that
Hume was talking about) are simply absent from them. This
makes their behaviour all the more chilling as there is no scale
of 'right' and 'wrong' against which Ellis' characters can
measure their conduct. Without articulating it, these
characters are what we might call nihilists.

The term 'nihilism' was coined by the Russian novelist Ivan
Turgenev (1818–1883), in his novel *Father and Sons*. He used
it to describe a young rebel, Basarov, who rejected all moral
values (*nihil* in Latin means 'nothing'). Later it became
associated with the anti-Tsarist movement who rejected the
feudal system and the moral orthodoxy of Russia in the
nineteenth century. In philosophical terms, nihilism is a radical
scepticism about the possibility of justification of ethical
principles and judgements. It is the view that there are no
moral facts, no moral truths and so no possibility of moral
knowledge. In its moderate forms it may not recommend
abandoning morality, since morality may express something
other than facts, such as feelings or attitudes (compare this
with emotivism). But radical nihilism claims that ethical
discourse is fundamentally confused and should be abandoned.

Nihilism is a much more worrying, and more exhilarating,
theory than the anti-realist positions that we have looked at
so far. While Anglo-American philosophers such as Ayer and
Hare were buried in the meta-ethical analysis of meaning, on
the Continent the existentialists were engaged in a much
more exciting project, and one with troubling nihilistic
leanings. Just after the Second World War the philosophy of
existentialism swept through France and post-war Europe. In
some forms existentialism smacked of nihilism, at least as
represented in the early works of Albert Camus (1913–1960)
and Jean-Paul Sartre (1905–1980).

At one point I heard him say, 'Has he even expressed any regrets? Never, gentlemen. Not once in front of the examining magistrate did he show any emotion with regard to his abominable crime.'... Of course, I couldn't help admitting that [the prosecutor] was right. I didn't much regret what I'd done ... I'd have liked to have explained to him in a friendly way ... that I'd never really been able to regret anything. I was always preoccupied by what was about to happen, today or tomorrow.[172]

Albert Camus, *The Outsider*

Camus' novel *The Outsider* is probably the best-known existentialist novel. In it the protagonist, Meursault, murders an Algerian man on a beach for some very hazy reasons: the man was part of a gang intimidating an acquaintance of his, Meursault felt threatened, the sun was in his eyes, he was hot and uncomfortable ... None of these things really explains why Meursault had to then go and shoot the man five times. At the trial Meursault is condemned to death because of his attitude: he confesses that he is more annoyed than regretful at what he's done. He is an outsider and, as Camus says, he is punished because he is too honest about his feelings, he 'doesn't play the game ... he is driven by a passion for truth'.[173] For Camus and Sartre, conventional morality appears to get in the way of the much more important business of living an *authentic* life.

Jean-Paul Sartre proposed a philosophy of radical freedom, in which humans are not bound by any moral obligations. For Sartre, human existence is essentially one of freedom: we are not determined to act in certain ways, as the Marxists, Freudians and Darwinists seemed to say. Moreover, we do not have a human nature, as practically every philosopher since Socrates has claimed (although these philosophers disagreed as to what our nature was – for Sartre they were all wrong). There is no purpose to our lives, as the Aristotelians and religious philosophers have maintained. And most importantly there are no moral laws or principles that bind us or oblige us to behave in certain ways. In one of his lectures Sartre misquotes the Russian novelist Dostoyevsky, but this sums up his position quite nicely:

If God did not exist, everything would be permitted.[174]

For Sartre, the absence of God (the only possible creator of human nature, essence, function and moral laws) means that we are absolutely, terrifyingly free. Of course Sartre admits that we do not feel free and we very often do not act as if we were free, but this is because we live inauthentic lives; we live in 'bad faith' believing we are bound by objective moral laws.

For Sartre, we must strive to be authentic, to embrace our freedom and to recognise that we invent morality as we go along. In this respect the act of moral creation 'is comparable to the construction of a work of art'.[175] Just as the artist does not have to follow any rules, or adhere to any values, or meet any predetermined purpose, nor do moral agents like us. So we must invent and create morality as we go along.

We can see now why both Camus and Sartre seemed to be promoting moral nihilism, because for them being authentic meant challenging the obligations that society binds us with. These moral rules have no objective basis and must be cast aside. But at the same time both Sartre and Camus wished to condemn the practices of oppressive political regimes (the Nazis across Europe, the French in Algeria). Sartre spent much of his life trying to find an existential ethic that was authentic (insofar as our freedom was preserved) but which gave us the foundations from which to show others how to act. Not surprisingly it is widely held that he failed in this mission.[176]

Before the existentialists, the German philosopher Friedrich Nietzsche (1844–1900) dramatically proclaimed the death of God in *Thus Spake Zarathustra* (1885). This proclamation was intended to signal Western man's realisation in the nineteenth century that there is no objective basis for moral action. This recognition is, for Nietzsche, and for existentialist thinkers as such, the starting point rather than the end point for any moral philosophy. In other words, existentialism is perhaps best regarded as an attempt to produce some positive reaction to radical moral scepticism. Since values are not *given* to us by the nature of things, the existentialist demands that we take responsibility to forge our own. Søren Kierkegaard (1813–1855), for example, argued that any attempt to justify one's moral position seems to involve appeal to premises which in turn must be vindicated, and that the only way to avoid an infinite regress of reasons is to simply *choose* to stand by certain premises.

According to Nietzsche the supposed universalisable character of moral judgements that we make is not an expression of reason, as Kant argued, but represents an attempt to bind and control the exceptional individual of whom the majority is resentful. Christianity is a 'slave morality', a morality of the weak, intended to exert power over the strong. The slave morality inverts the master values of pride, courage and personal merit, replacing them with humility, meekness and equality. Nietzsche argues further that the notions of objectivity and truth generally are simply expressions of the 'will to power', the striving for freedom and strength. What we take to be facts, therefore, are as much expressions of our values as any ethical pronouncement. Because there is no absolute truth in morality or anything else, but merely a power struggle between competing value systems, what is required is a 'revaluation of all values' which will affirm life and power.

A nihilist who sticks to her position, and refuses to admit the validity of any moral pronouncements, would appear to be unassailable. How then might we dissuade the committed ethical sceptic of the importance of moral beliefs? Taking our cue from certain treatments of the radical sceptic about the possibility of knowledge generally, we might ask what kind of a justification of a moral belief is the nihilist after? Clearly she is impressed by the logical impossibility of deriving an *ought* from an *is* but, despite this, can we really think of value terms as having no connection at all with facts? Surely some facts are so closely bound to evaluative pronouncements that to divorce them is no longer to be intelligible. For the nihilist is committed to saying that happiness is no more good than bad, even that pain could be regarded as a good thing. In other words, the nihilist can be accused of denying something so fundamental to what it is to speak meaningfully about practical decision-making and human existence that ultimately we cannot understand her. If, as the nihilist claims, anything goes in value judgements, we cease to think of the person as communicating at all. While there is no way the nihilist can be proved wrong, her position is, it may be claimed, futile.

■ **Figure 3.8 A reminder of some of the main features of the different anti-realist theories**

	Do moral terms refer to something independent of humans?	Do moral terms have a non-descriptive meaning?	Do moral terms influence action?	Are moral values invented?	Should we completely reject ordinary moral values?
Emotivism	No	Yes – an emotive meaning	Yes – through emotional impact	No	No
Prescriptivism	No	Yes – a prescriptive meaning	Yes – through commendations	No	No
Relativism	No	No	Yes – for people in a particular society	Yes – by society	No
Nihilism	No	No	Yes – they oppress people!	Yes – by us	Yes

In our analysis of meta-ethics it seems that we have strayed too far from our original interest in moral philosophy. After all, we came to ethics because we were concerned about how we should live, what we should do with our lives, what sort of people we should be. In Chapter 2 we saw how normative ethics helped us with this project, by seeking a coherent framework that could underpin our reason for action. However, normative ethics threw up many questions that needed to be addressed: most importantly whether we *decide* what is the right thing to do (as anti-realists might say) or whether we *discover* what is the right thing to do (as realists might say). So meta-ethics can help us clarify what it is that we're doing but, in Anglo-American philosophy at least, it seemed to become bogged down in the analysis of moral judgements and terms.

It is time now to return to our original concern – how we should live. So in the next chapter we shall look at three issues that test our moral beliefs and theories: first, the status and value of life before birth; secondly the status and value of life before death; and thirdly the status and value of non-human lives.

Key points: Chapter 3

What you need to know about **meta-ethics**:

1 Meta-ethics analyses what is going on in normative ethics. Moral philosophy took a distinct turn away from normative ethics and towards meta-ethics in the first half of the twentieth century – as part of the 'linguistic turn'. In particular, meta-ethics raises questions about the meaning and nature of moral judgements and of the evaluative terms (good, bad, right, wrong) employed in these judgements.

2 Some philosophers make an ontological commitment to moral properties and objects – they believe that there are things that exist 'out there' in the world to which terms like 'good' and 'right' refer. These philosophers are known as moral realists. Other philosophers don't make such an ontological commitment: they don't believe that 'good' or 'right' refer to anything out there in the world at all. These philosophers are moral anti-realists. Mirroring the realist/anti-realist debate about the ontological status of moral terms (about whether they refer to anything that exists or not) is a semantic debate about the meaning of moral judgements. On the one hand, cognitivists believe that moral judgements refer to the world; they are propositions that correctly or incorrectly reflect the world: in other words, moral judgements can be true or false. On

the other hand, non-cognitivists do not believe moral judgements refer to the world, and so they also don't believe that they are capable of being true or false.

3 There are three common forms of moral realism – rationalism, naturalism and intuitionism.

a) Moral rationalists believe that reason alone can help us to determine what is right. For Aquinas, reason enabled us to understand the natural law that governed the universe, a law which governed the proper purpose of everything as God intended. For Kant, reason helped us to determine the moral law through the categorical imperative: these revealed moral duties which were universal.

b) Moral naturalists believe that what is good can be analysed in naturalistic terms. For Aristotle, 'good' could be understood in terms of the successful fulfilment of our function. For the utilitarians, 'good' is understood in terms of the impact an action has on the pleasure, pain or happiness of the population as a whole. For egoists, 'good' is understood in terms of the benefits an action brings about for me as an individual.

c) Moral intuitionists believe that we can determine what is right or wrong through our moral intuition. For Moore our intuitions reveal what things are good (and there are a number of goods) and he thought we should strive to bring about these good states of affairs through our actions – he was a 'consequentialist' intuitionist in that respect. For Prichard and Ross our intuitions reveal what is right. These 'deontological' intuitionists believe we have certain obligations (and there are a number of obligations) that we must adhere to.

4 Some philosophers believe that ethics is 'autonomous' and this leads them to reject naturalism. They believe that ethics forms a unique and distinct realm which cannot be reduced to or analysed in terms of other things. Hume believed in the *logical autonomy* of ethics, claiming that it was a logical error to derive an 'ought' from an 'is' (i.e. to use factual premises to support an evaluative conclusion). Some philosophers believed that naturalism makes this kind of error, but that is a highly problematic claim (especially since Hume himself was a naturalist). Moore believed in the *semantic autonomy* of ethics, claiming that you could not define moral terms in non-moral terms. Specifically, Moore thought that moral terms were indefinable *and* non-natural and that it was a double fallacy a) to try to define them and b) to do so in naturalistic terms. So Moore accused naturalists and in particular the utilitarians, of committing this naturalistic fallacy. However, many

philosophers doubt whether in fact the utilitarians are guilty of this fallacy.

5 There are four common forms of moral anti-realism: emotivism; prescriptivism; relativism; and nihilism.

a) Emotivism can be seen as a reaction against the objective pronouncements of the intuitionists about what was right or good. It seemed to A. J. Ayer that these pronouncements were really just expressions of personal approval or disapproval. So moral judgements had an emotive meaning, but no factual content at all (they were neither true nor false). C. L. Stevenson found a further emotive element in moral judgements, namely that they were attempts to persuade other people to feel the same way.

b) Prescriptivism can be seen as a reaction against emotivism. Prescriptivists such as R. M. Hare agreed with the emotivists that moral judgements weren't being used to describe the world, and that they had a non-descriptive meaning. But Hare felt that emotivism hadn't captured the real use of moral judgements, which was to issue recommendations about how other people should act. So moral judgements are meant to guide action, and to urge everyone in a similar situation to behave in the same way.

c) Ethical relativism as a moral position has been around since at least the Ancient Greeks. It says that what's good for you might not be good for me, and vice versa – there is no possible objective position from which to judge whose moral principles are correct. What counts as 'good' or 'right' is relative to the culture or individual making the judgement. The popularity of relativism spread in the twentieth century as various social sciences claimed to have shown a) that societies from around the world and across history had radically different moral rules; and b) that how society arrived at moral rules could be explained in deterministic terms. (Freud: we are socialised into moral values by our parents; Marx: we are indoctrinated into moral values by the ruling classes.)

d) Moral nihilism goes further than all other anti-realist theories. It advocates a rejection of all moral principles and values – they refer to nothing. At best they are illusions that society creates; at worst they are shackles that prevent us from living a truly authentic existence. Sartre's existentialism leans towards nihilism as he thinks the only possible foundation for objective moral values is God, but since there is no God there are no objective moral values.

Practical ethics

Introduction

In many a story there is a moment where the hero or heroine has to make a decision. Should Hansel and Gretel's father give in to his wife and take the children to the forest and leave them to die; or insist they stay and so risk the whole family dying of starvation? Should Judas stay loyal to his friend or accept the 30 pieces of silver and betray Jesus to the Romans? Should Frodo volunteer to take the Ring of Power to Mount Doom and destroy it, or should he go back to the safety of the Shire?[177] In some people's lives the issues they face may be less momentous, but can still feel equally pressing:

> *Often in department stores I would get stuck behind two motionless passengers [on the escalator] and want to seize their shoulders and urge them on like an instructor on an Outward Bound program, saying, 'Annette, Bruce – this isn't the Land of the Lotus Eaters. Don't you see you're on a moving stairway ... Don't you see that when you two stop, two abreast, you are not only blocking me? Don't you see that you indicate to all those who are right now stepping onto the escalator at the bottom and looking timidly up for inspiration ... They were wavering whether to stand or to climb, and you just sapped their wills!* You made them choose to waste their time! *Thus you perpetuate a pattern of sloth and congestion that may persist for hours. Can't you see that?'*[178]

Nicholson Baker, *The Mezzanine*

Somewhere in between the microscopic dilemmas of Baker's over-anxious protagonist and the life-changing choices made by the characters in the stories above, there are the dilemmas that we each must face in our own lives. The question is: can moral philosophy equip us with skills or strategies to help us make these decisions? What use are the normative theories we have studied when it comes to the real world? At the end of this chapter we will look at how moral philosophy can contribute to better moral decision-making. First, though, we will turn to three practical moral problems and examine how the different normative theories we have examined can be deployed to help us to try to resolve them.

Whether you believe that morality should be concerned with outcomes, with staying true to certain principles, with following the word of God or with becoming a virtuous person, it is perhaps inevitable that you will be confronted, at some points in your life, with genuine ethical dilemmas. The great sacred and philosophical texts may offer pronouncements on specific issues, such as whether it is right to commit adultery, to eat pork or to steal, but there will always be other issues on which no direct advice is given and then you will still be left with the problem of how to apply your ethical theories to actual situations in the world. In modern times, scientific developments throw up new dilemmas that these texts could not have addressed, such as whether human cloning is morally acceptable, or whether genetically modified soya beans should be grown. So the range of new dilemmas we have to face changes as society changes. Questions of how to approach such dilemmas and how to apply normative ethical theories to them fall into the domain of practical ethics.

So practical ethics (sometimes known as applied ethics) examines how an ethical theory such as utilitarianism can be applied to situations in the real world. It is this type of problem that is often the most absorbing, as it requires getting involved in the nuts and bolts of contemporary moral dilemmas. We find ourselves having to question and defend our own beliefs about controversial issues. We also discover the conflicts and tensions that may exist within our own moral intuitions. For example, you may come to question why you believe abortion is morally permissible and yet infanticide not. At the same time, practical ethics can uncover problems within ethical theories, for instance if the theory turns out to have unpalatable consequences. In sum, reflecting on the application of theory to practice can:

- bring out many of the problems within the moral theory itself
- lead to criticisms of and alteration to that theory
- reveal inconsistencies in our own moral opinions
- lead us to reflect on our own moral beliefs. Do they adhere to one moral theory or several, each having priority in different situations?

During our study of practical ethics the issue of death comes up frequently. Abortion, euthanasia and animal rights all revolve around the value we place on life and death. If we are to address these issues properly we need first to think about the value of life and where this value derives from. In other words we need to address some meta-ethical questions first before turning to practical issues.

The ethics of killing

Most of us believe that killing is wrong; but the question moral philosophers inevitably pose is *why* is it wrong? What is being demanded here is some kind of explanation of, or justification for, this belief. But there is an additional issue that philosophers are interested in. We tend to suppose that killing human beings is in some way worse than killing animals, but why is this? Why, if killing is in itself wrong, should it not be equally bad to kill a rat in your kitchen? Traditionally, in the West at least, the judgement that killing humans is morally worse has gained support from religious circles. The Old Testament, for example, suggests that God commanded us not to kill humans but gave us dominion over animals to use as we wish.[179] However, certain contemporary philosophers have argued that this is a form of irrational prejudice, akin to racism or sexism. Singer calls the tendency to treat our own species as morally privileged *speciesism*. So in order to determine whether this attitude is anything other than another form of chauvinism we shall need to consider whether there are any cogent reasons to support the view that it is more wrong to kill a human than an animal.

These are the two questions we need to address:

(i) Why should it be wrong to kill *any* living creature, human or otherwise?
(ii) Why should it be morally *worse* to kill a human than a non-human animal?

In this section we shall briefly examine four positions on why killing is wrong: classic utilitarianism, preference utilitarianism, a rights theory and Kantian theory. We shall examine how virtue theorists cope with practical ethics in general below, on page 188.

Classic utilitarianism

Utilitarianism in its traditional form has difficulties with answering both questions. The problem with (i) is that according to the utility principle an action is valuable according to its tendency to produce pleasure and minimise pain. But if a creature cannot feel pleasure or pain because it is dead, then surely it is taken out of the equation and no longer contributes to the 'utility calculus'. So there would seem to be nothing really wrong with killing, so long as we do it painlessly. An obvious response to this is that the killing of sentient creatures is wrong to the extent that it prevents them from enjoying any future pleasure and happiness. Nonetheless, it is not obvious that we can make meaningful comparisons between the amount of pleasure possessed by a non-existent creature which can experience nothing, and the sum of pleasure it would amass if it had lived.

The problem with (ii) is that if a human is killed then this is surely no worse than if a non-human, such as a rat, were killed, since utilitarianism says nothing about humans being more valuable than rats. All that matters to the value of a life is the pleasure or pain it is capable of experiencing, and in this respect it is not obvious that humans differ significantly from other animals.

A utilitarian can give three different responses to this:

a) When a human being is killed then there is pain caused to the people left behind – their relatives and loved ones. Therefore killing a human is wrong and is also worse than killing a rat because the suffering (although only indirect) that is produced as a consequence is greater.

b) Secondly, a human is capable of understanding that they are going to die. They have an idea of their future self, and so can recognise that if they die they are to be deprived of the future happiness they might have. This recognition serves to diminish the happiness they have now in a way that couldn't concern a rat. As with the first response, however, this is only an indirect ground for saying that killing a human is worse than killing other animals, since it is not about the actual happiness of which they are to be deprived, but only about the pain caused by dwelling on the fact of their imminent death. This means that this response doesn't really affect the killing of people painlessly and by surprise. So long as they don't know it is coming and it is quick, it seems it can't really be worse to kill a human than a rat.

c) The third option is for the classic utilitarian to accept that the killing of humans is no worse than killing other animals. What is wrong is killing sentient creatures who have the capacity to feel pleasure and pain, simply because it causes pain and deprives them of future happiness. Bentham said to ask not whether it can think, but whether it can suffer, meaning that humans are on an equal footing with animals in terms of the value of their lives.

Preference utilitarianism

Preference utilitarianism is the view that an action should be judged by *the extent to which it conforms to the preferences of any being affected by the action and its consequences.* Now, a preference utilitarian such as Peter Singer has little difficulty in giving an answer to (ii) but finds (i) much harder. To see how they can deal with (ii) we need to suppose that humans differ from other animals in that they have a developed consciousness of self and a conception of their future selves. Whereas other animals are able to experience pain and pleasure, humans, on this view, are distinctive in that they are aware of themselves as agents persisting through time. Because of this awareness, a human being is capable of possessing a greater array of preferences than an animal. In particular, a human being is capable of having the explicit preference not to be killed. Indeed, the preference not to be killed is the most important preference, because any other preferences we may hold, such as going to the pub, depends on this one being fulfilled. After all, I could not want to go to the pub if I were dead, and in this sense all my other preferences rely on my fundamental preference to stay alive. However, if non-human animals, as it is argued, cannot form the concept of a future self and therefore are incapable of holding any preferences about that self, then they cannot prefer the prospect of being alive tomorrow, rather than dead. It follows that a non-human animal's life is less valuable than a human being's.

Now, it might be objected that all animals fear death as is evidenced from their behaviour when faced with mortal danger and therefore that they do have the preference to stay alive. A fish, for example, will struggle when caught, in an effort to avoid suffocation and return to the water. However, defending the preference utilitarian here, Singer suggests this is only an appearance. The fish is really struggling to escape the pain it is experiencing. It doesn't realise that it is facing its own imminent demise because it has no concept of death, and without the explicit recognition of this, it cannot be said to know that it is about to die.

So if we accept that animals have fewer preferences than humans we have a reasonable way of dealing with (ii), but what of (i), namely why it is wrong to kill living creatures in general. If most, if not all, non-human animals have no conception of self and so no preference to stay alive, it seems there can be nothing wrong with killing them. It seems, therefore, that the preference utilitarian is committed to the view that it isn't wrong to kill animals so long as it is done painlessly. However, it has to be said that most people's moral intuitions incline to the view that an animal's life has some value, even if not a value equal to a human being's and so this consequence of the theory will be unpalatable to many. This might suggest that we should turn to a rights-based approach, in other words a theory which allows for some intrinsic value for a creature life.

Theories based on rights

Do foetuses have a right to be born? Does a woman have a right to abort a foetus? Do animals have a right to life? Or do humans have a right to kill animals for food? A rights-based theorist such as Michael Tooley claims that only beings which can 'conceive of themselves as distinct entities existing over time' have a right to life,[180] and this brings his theory closer to the preference utilitarianism of Singer. Tooley is claiming that to have a right to X presupposes having a desire for X, and therefore only creatures with a desire to stay alive have a right to life. Any creature with no concept of their future self and thus no concept of life or death has no right to life. This gives Tooley an answer to question (ii): it is worse to kill a human than a rat because we have a right to life. Other animals have no such right; they only have the right not to suffer. A being with the elevated moral status that comes with being able to consider its future self is often termed a PERSON. A person is not the same as a human being since not all humans have the capacity to consider their own futures, for example those in a permanent vegetative state, or still in the womb. Tooley's approach also suggests that abortion is justified, since a foetus has no conception of its future life, is not yet a person, and so is not capable of wanting to stay alive. By contrast, the mother is able to reflect on her future life with or without a child to bring up, and so has a right to choose either option.

Kantian theory

Kant's second formulation of the categorical imperative tells us that we should never treat another person merely as a *means*, but always as an *end*. What this tells us is that it is morally wrong for us to *use* someone in order to gain something that we want; in other words, to use them as a means to our own ends. Rather we must respect their AUTONOMY. Other people are free agents, and their freedom to choose their own ends must be uppermost in our minds in all our dealings with them.

This idea of respect for others' autonomy gives us a fairly straightforward way of answering question (ii). Any kind of violation of someone's autonomy, such as when I lie to you or harm you, is to be avoided, but killing a person is the *worst* violation of someone's autonomy, because choosing life is the fundamental choice of an autonomous agent. It is fundamental because it underlies all other choices, and by choosing life I choose to have choices. If someone kills me then they are not just denying me of one choice, but of all choices and of my capacity to choose. Therefore killing an autonomous person is an appalling act, but killing a non-autonomous creature, perhaps a rat, is not so appalling because they have not chosen to remain living. So Kantian theory gives us a similar solution to the problem of why humans' lives should be considered more valuable than animals' lives to the solution given by preference utilitarianism and the rights-based approach considered above. However, Kant's response to question (i) must be that it is not in fact morally wrong to kill any non-autonomous, non-rational creature. If, as seems likely, rats are incapable of reflecting rationally upon a situation they find themselves in, and freely coming to a decision about which course of action to take, if, in other words, rats simply act according to their instincts, then they are not members of the moral community and so can be disposed of as we see fit. And Kant himself does explicitly affirm this consequence of his theory. Animals, he claims, exist merely as a means to man's ends. (We discuss a Kantian approach to animal rights in more detail below.) Their lives have no intrinsic value. Moreover, suffering is not, on this account, a relevant moral consideration in our treatment of animals, meaning there is no intrinsic reason why we should avoid causing them pain, a consequence which may have seemed acceptable in Kant's day but which sits uncomfortably with contemporary moral attitudes.

We have now a broad picture of how consequentialists and deontologists might make a judgement about the morality of killing. The bulk of this chapter examines in some detail the morality of killing as it arises in three concrete ethical issues, namely abortion, euthanasia and animal rights. But before we look at these issues it would be worth revisiting virtue ethics to see what it has to say about practical ethics.

A virtue approach to practical ethics

We saw in Chapter 2 that both deontological and consequentialist approaches were able to provide formulae, i.e. over-arching principles, to guide our actions and tell us what we ought to do. However, we also saw that virtue ethicists shunned this calculative approach to ethics, partly because this isn't the way we experience moral dilemmas (they are messy, confusing, contain a bundle of values none of which can be ignored) and partly because the calculations very often yield recommendations which clash with our moral intuitions (this is true for both Kantians and utilitarians). In contrast, virtue ethicists urge us to take a more holistic approach, so that we are harnessing all the skills available to us in order to make a correct judgement; this also means balancing a number of different values that pull in different directions. For the virtue ethicist each situation presents itself to us differently, but over time someone who is virtuous will tend to conform to the sorts of values that deontologists and consequentialists espouse (trying to do good, trying to do what's right and fair, etc.) – which also means, in general, that virtuous people don't kill and don't encourage killing.

From the perspective of virtue ethics what do we actually judge? Well, we are judging character traits – our own and those of everyone else who holds a stake in the dilemma. But we are not judging solely on the basis of this particular action – rather we are seeing how our actions in this case fit within our overall character, viewed as existing over time. Aristotle wrote in the *Ethics* that 'a man will only be literate, then, only when he has both said something grammatical, and said it grammatically'.[181] What he is drawing out here is that the fact that you can mechanically follow a grammatical rule in, say, French, doesn't mean you are a French speaker. Similarly mere conformity to a moral principle (as some deontologists suggest) isn't what morality consists of. A virtuous person is someone who chooses an act and a) she knows what she's doing; b) she chooses it for its own sake; c) she chooses it from within, as it is embedded in her character. When we make a judgement about an action we are looking to see whether morality is ingrained in the person performing the act – do they have a virtuous character? Are they compassionate, sympathetic, just, generous, caring, etc. and if so then we must consider all their actions in this more rounded light.

experimenting with ideas

Gillo Pontecorvo's film *Battle of Algiers* (1965) explores the response of Algerian women to the continued colonial occupation of their country by the French in the mid-1950s. Their husbands and brothers, suspected guerrilla fighters, are tortured and executed, their families are bombed, they live under martial law. In the film we see in detail how two mothers – kind, gentle, loving, thoughtful – prepare and carry out attacks on the French: they plant explosives in restaurants and bars, knowing that civilians will be torn to pieces by these bombs.

1 What virtues do the women display, or fail to display, in carrying out the attacks?

2 What judgement might a virtue ethicist make here about their actions?

3 How would a utilitarian and a Kantian judge their actions?

4 What parallels are there between this situation and the response of some Iraqis to the occupation of their country by American and British forces in 2003?

5 What would you describe these women as: freedom fighters or terrorists? Why?

Virtue ethics also offers us action guides: it tells us that we ought to be virtuous, that we ought to do just what a virtuous person would do. This means paying attention to those we think are 'morally wise' – people who seem to know what to do in tricky situations, people who have the necessary skills to do the right thing. Virtue ethics also says that our actions needed to come 'from the inside', from the feeling that this is the right thing to do – this may be a motive of compassion or sympathy or justice etc. This is in stark contrast to Kant's approach where we were motivated by the moral law itself – by rules and principles, rather than our concern for others. So virtue ethics requires us to work harder over our whole life, in becoming ethically 'discerning'. In biomedical ethics, for example, some practitioners may be happy to have a set of procedures, or a checklist, which they can run through when faced with a moral dilemma. But the virtue ethicist maintains that this will not result in better decisions – merely more mechanical and inflexible ones. What is needed is for practitioners to become more discerning: to pay close attention to the wide range of factors that impinge on the moral dilemma, and through experience, practice, observing mentors and role models, become able to discern what the right thing to do is.

Such an approach may sound attractive, but what does virtue ethics actually mean at the sharp end? In other words what use is a virtue ethics approach when we have to make a tricky moral judgement? Ultimately, it would appear that the values espoused in virtue ethics are roughly the same as those of the other main normative theories we have examined. So, according to virtue ethics, we should help others, be fair, consider and respect other people, avoid causing harm, keep promises, tell the truth, be honest and so on. The only difference is that for a virtue ethicist these qualities need to become ingrained in us, so that acting on them is second nature. But the moral judgements and decisions we make will involve skilfully weighing up the situation and the values at stake, and using our wisdom to make the right decision. At the end of the book we look at some of the skills that we might need to develop in order to attain the virtue of practical wisdom (what the ancient Greeks called *phronesis* and what current theorists might call 'discernment'[182]). But for the rest of this chapter we will leave aside virtue ethics, returning to it in the final section.

experimenting with ideas

'He pulled the axe out, swung it up with both hands ... and almost mechanically, without putting any force behind it, let the butt-end fall on her head.'[183]

Have we at last come face-to-face with the moral philosopher's nemesis, the mad axe murderer? Rodya Raskolnikov is a typical ex-student: he is young, bright, introspective, jobless and lives in squalor. He cares about his family and he helps out the destitute people who live in his community when he can. His biggest problem is his landlady: he owes her a lot of money for rent, more than he could ever pay back, and there's talk of the police being called. He remembers discussions with fellow students where they talked about killing the landlady, and using her money to help people – reasoning that a thousand good deeds outweigh one crime. Rodya carefully plans to kill the landlady and goes to her flat, where he murders her with the axe.

What reasons would the following types of ethical philosopher give for the judgement that Raskolnikov's murder of the landlady was morally wrong?

1 A classic utilitarian
2 A preference utilitarian
3 A Kantian
4 A virtue ethicist

Abortion

> *Even if it is not true that abortion is murder, it still cannot be considered in the same light as mere contraception; an event has taken place that is a definite beginning, the progress of which is to be stopped ... Women will be haunted by the memory of this child which has not come into being.*[184]

Simone de Beauvoir, *The Second Sex*

Since de Beauvoir wrote *The Second Sex* in 1949, abortion has become socially and legally acceptable in most European countries. In England and Wales approximately 180,000 unwanted pregnancies are deliberately terminated by medical intervention each year. This procedure is legal for up to 24 weeks after conception if continuing with the pregnancy involves a greater risk to the physical or mental health of the woman, or the physical or mental health of her existing children, than having a termination. Abortion is also allowed after 24 weeks if there is a risk of grave physical and mental injury or to the life of the woman, or if there is evidence of severe foetal abnormality.[185] While the reasons for having an abortion are various, a woman's decision to terminate her pregnancy is unlikely to be an easy one. Terminating a pregnancy, after all, involves the deliberate killing of the developing foetus, and, as we have been seeing in our discussion of killing, the deliberate killing of human beings is generally regarded as morally wrong. And so, on the face of it at least, the killing of a human foetus would not appear to be morally justified. Thus in outline the basic argument against the moral justifiability of abortion would run as follows:

P1 The deliberate killing of human beings is wrong.
P2 A foetus is a human being.
C   Therefore, killing foetuses (abortion) is wrong.

Simple as this syllogism is, there is an important difficulty with it. As we were beginning to see in our discussion of killing above, it is not simply being members of a particular species which seems to give humans their right to life and not to be harmed. It is not our humanity as such which affords us the moral status we have, rather it is that being human tends to mean we have various other capacities which *do* constitute our moral worth. This can be seen if we consider a simple thought experiment. Imagine we discover intelligent life forms on one of Saturn's moons. Although these life forms are genetically very different from us, we are nonetheless able to learn each other's languages and so come to discover that they are remarkably similar to us in all sorts of ways: for example, they are social beings, they love their young, experience pleasure and pain, and have a recognisable sense of morally good and bad behaviour. We can even imagine discussing moral issues such as the ethics of killing with such beings. Now, suppose these creatures have built their cities on top of seams of rich mineral deposits which we could usefully exploit. Would we be justified in flattening their cities and killing these beings to get them out of the way? To answer yes is to regard non-human life forms as morally inferior, simply in virtue of not being human. But this is surely an irrational prejudice. For what seems to matter when it comes to treating others with moral respect is not their genes, but the kinds of capacities they have. We saw that there is some dispute about what these capacities might be. Classic utilitarians regard the important criterion as the ability to experience pain and pleasure; preference utilitarians take it to be the capacity to form preferences; Kant argued it is our ability to make rational autonomous decisions, and so on. But the key point here is that our judgement about whether a foetus deserves the same moral consideration as a human being after birth, does not hang on its being human, but rather on whether it possesses capacities we take to be necessary for a moral being, or in other words essential to being a *person*.

So here we are drawing an important distinction between *human beings* and *persons*. The term 'human being' refers to the whole class of beings conforming to a certain biological type, regardless of maturity, age, state of health, etc. That the term 'person' is not applicable to all human beings can be seen from the fact that a baby born without a brain would be human, but we might not call it a person. There may also be non-human persons. Dolphins or chimpanzees could be regarded as persons because of their relatively high level of intelligence, and, as we have seen, few would deny that any intelligent extra-terrestrials we might encounter would be persons, even though they might not be human. So rather than continue to talk of human beings we will from here on use the word 'person' to denote a being worthy of moral concern. So let's revise the argument against abortion to take account of this point.

P1 The deliberate killing of persons is wrong.
P2 A foetus is a person.
C   Therefore, killing foetuses (abortion) is wrong.

This revision now gives us a systematic way of evaluating whether abortion is indeed morally wrong, by assessing whether each of the premises is true in turn. So there are two basic responses to this argument for those who regard abortions as justifiable: we can deny that abortion is a case of wrongful killing, while accepting that a foetus is a person; or we can deny that a foetus is a person, and so reason that there can be no objection to killing one. We will begin by dealing with the latter approach.

ACTIVITY How do you think the following types of philosophers would approach the moral problem of abortion?

1 A utilitarian
2 A Kantian
3 A divine command theorist
4 A virtue ethicist

The traditional philosophical approach: is a foetus a person?

Finding an answer to the question of whether or not a foetus is a person has seemed to many philosophers the most obvious way in which to untangle the moral dilemmas which surround abortion. If a foetus can be shown to be a person, then we can straightforwardly draw on the principle that killing persons is wrong and condemn abortion as morally unjustifiable. On the other hand, if a foetus turns out not to be a person then to abort it would not be a breach of this principle and so would be justifiable. But for this approach to work it will be essential first to clarify our concept of a 'person'. If we can determine certain fixed criteria that a being must have in order to be a person and then assess whether or not a foetus fulfils those criteria, we should be able to determine whether it is morally permissible to kill one.

However, it is rare that philosophers can agree on a matter, and what the necessary conditions for personhood are is no exception. We have seen in the previous section that different normative moral theories regard killing differently, and reject it on different grounds. Those theories also view the concept of 'person' rather differently:

■ Classic utilitarians tend to regard a person as a sentient being capable of experiencing pleasures and pain.

■ Preference utilitarians and rights theorists regard a person as a being capable of self-consciousness and of concern for its future states.

■ Kantians regard a person as a rational, autonomous agent and as an end-in-itself.

■ Divine command theorists regard a person as a being with a God-given soul.

■ Virtue theorists may regard a person as a being possessing a character.

ACTIVITY   You are a United Nations scientist sent to investigate an unknown species that has been found in the outer reaches of our galaxy. It is unlike anything you have seen before. One of your tasks is to determine whether or not this alien is a person.

Which of the following features would suggest to you that the alien must be a person?

1 walks on two legs and looks rather like a human being
2 is as intelligent as a human being
3 is as intelligent as a dolphin
4 is artistic

5 has a functioning brain

6 eats in order to survive

7 saves money for its retirement

8 has a face with eyes, ears, nose and mouth

9 speaks English

10 has beliefs about the world around it

11 is able to communicate with you

12 is made of organic matter (rather than, say, wires or plastic)

13 has emotions

14 has a dress sense

15 has a sense of right and wrong

16 is good at maths

17 is good at football

18 is conscious

19 is self-conscious

20 can remember things it did several years ago

Now look again at the features you have selected. Which of these do you think are necessary to personhood? In other words, which do you suppose no person could do without or, if our alien lacked them, without which could it not possibly be counted as a person?

How then might we define 'person'? The English philosopher John Locke (1632–1704) famously defined a person as 'a thinking intelligent being that has reason and reflection and can consider itself as itself, the same thinking thing, in different times and places'.[186] In other words, a person must be able to consider freely how to behave and act, and must be self-aware, but must also be able to recognise itself over time, which is to say, have a sense of its past and future. As we saw above, philosophers often point to characteristics such as self-consciousness, concern with one's future states, rationality, the ability to make free choices, being an autonomous centre for sensations, emotions, volitions and so on. We also saw that it is often believed that most, if not all, other animals lack these capacities, and on this basis it is argued that they can be killed with impunity. However, few, if any, of such features apply to babies immediately after birth, and yet not many people would want to say that full term-babies are not persons, or at least few would want to countenance infanticide. So here we seem to have a problem. Why is it permissible to kill animals, but not neonates (i.e. new-born babies)? One solution, one adopted by Singer, is to deny personhood to babies and accept the conclusion that they may, in certain circumstances, be killed.[187] On this view, the only reasons why a new-born should not be killed are indirect, for example it may well be that its parents may not want it to be, and that to kill it would, therefore, go against their preferences to have a child. So it is not the preferences or rights of the infant itself which count, since it is not a person, but only the indirect rights or preferences of actual persons. It is perhaps worth noting that in the ancient world infanticide was common. During certain periods of Roman history, for example, it was customary for the new born to be brought to the head of the family who would decide whether the child would be kept or left to die by exposure. Moreover, Roman law dictated that a child that was visibly deformed should be put to death. Even after it became illegal in AD 374 with the rise of Christianity the practice continued and few prosecutions were brought. One method was to smear opium on the breasts so that the suckling infant would die without outward signs. This would presumably also ensure a painless death, although there is no evidence that this was a particular concern.

While nowadays such practices are viewed with moral abhorrence, they are consistent with the view that there is nothing intrinsically wrong with killing new-born babies. Nonetheless, it is hard for most to accept the idea that if the parents don't want their new born they should be permitted to kill it, so long as no one else is indirectly affected and no pain is caused. But why would it be wrong? The obvious answer is that a new-born baby is a person, and it is wrong to kill persons. In other words, the definitions of a person which exclude neonates are faulty: our moral horror at the prospect of infanticide demands that we revise our understanding of what capacities are required of a human being for them to warrant our moral concern. Perhaps it is the ability to experience pain and pleasure which is key, as Bentham's utilitarianism argued; or simply being a centre of awareness, albeit not *self*-awareness, is all that is important. Going along this route does, however, appear to commit us to affording any animal with at least as much conscious life as a new-born human infant equal moral concern, and so surely outlaws, among other things, eating animals for food.

Let us leave this consequence aside, however, for the time being (until we look at animal rights below) and focus on the new approach to the question of abortion that this leads us to. If it is wrong to kill new-born infants because they are persons, then it seems it must also be wrong to terminate a pregnancy before birth, since there seems to be no obvious place to draw a morally significant distinction between the fertilised egg and the newly born baby. So does the commitment to not killing babies mean we are obliged to regard the zygote[188] as morally equivalent to the newly born infant from the moment sperm and ovum unite? To be consistent, it seems that being against infanticide means we must also be against abortion.

Those who support a woman's right to choose to terminate her pregnancy will often try to tackle this difficulty by finding a morally significant dividing line between the newly born infant which it would be wrong to kill, and the newly fertilised egg, which it would not. So where and how might such a line be drawn? Let us look at various possibilities.

When does the zygote become a person?

Perhaps the most obvious initial place to look for a dividing line is the moment of *birth*. Since we tend not to encounter unborn foetuses in the everyday course of life and so have no direct dealings with them, it is perhaps inevitable that we be disinclined to accord them moral rights. So, perhaps, for as long as the foetus remains in the womb it is morally permissible to end its life (so long as no one else objects and no pain is caused). However, this approach faces an immediate difficulty. An unborn foetus is *prima facie* the same thing whether inside or outside the womb, and it doesn't seem that its environment can make any morally relevant difference to its status. New-born babies can recognise their mother's voice, which shows that they developed that memory before they were born, showing that they are already learning before birth. Consequently it would seem that the moment of birth cannot be morally significant.

Moreover, the argument that abortion is morally permissible up to the time of natural birth is vulnerable to the objection that foetuses are naturally viable several weeks before full term and so can survive if aborted or born premature. This consideration may incline us to entertain the possibility that a foetus' life should not be terminated beyond the point when it can survive and develop outside the womb, that is, beyond the point that it is *viable*. However, determining this point is not as straightforward as it might seem. After all, a baby brought to full term still requires constant care if it is to survive. Human infants are totally reliant on their caregivers and so cannot be considered fully viable anyway. So we have the problem of how to define 'viable'. Perhaps it could be defined as *capable* of survival outside the womb, given whatever care is needed, including incubators and so forth. However, viability so defined will not be precise either, since it will depend on what medical expertise is available to the infant and so will vary with time and place. Judgements about foetuses developing in wealthy countries with ready access to state-of-the-art hospitals would then be different from those concerning foetuses in the developing countries, or war zones. Surely it is absurd to suppose that it would be wrong to abort a foetus in London at 25 weeks, but permissible if you caught a plane to Kenya.

A cut-off point that can vary according to circumstances in this way can hardly be morally significant.

If we look more closely at the developing zygote it may be possible to discover some key developmental stage at which we may argue it begins to share a sufficient number of features with full fledged human persons to warrant our moral concern. Some have argued that the crucial stage is when the mother first feels the foetus move; however, it is now known that foetuses are able to move well before the mother is able to feel them. It is during the first eight weeks that all the organs are put into place so that the skeleton has formed and the appearance of the foetus is recognisably human. The remaining 20–30 weeks of gestation are devoted to growth and development. By this point the brain has begun to coordinate the movement of the muscles and organs, and brain waves can be measured. At eight weeks' gestation, the foetus will kick its legs and move its arms around. Recent developments with imaging techniques of foetuses in the womb have shown infants as young as 12 weeks sucking their thumbs and yawning. They will even appear to smile in the womb.

Such discoveries have led to calls for a reduction from 24 weeks, the time at which an abortion can normally take place legally in Britain. However, how are we to interpret such evidence? It is certainly plausible to argue that simply having the appearance or basic behaviours of a human being is not in itself morally significant. Having hands and legs or being able to stretch, yawn or smile cannot in themselves allow us to accord personhood to the foetus, since we can surely imagine persons who lacked these features. It would surely be grossly unfair to deny to an adult who didn't smile or who couldn't move his or her limbs the same moral status as other persons. This suggests that such behaviours in the foetus cannot be essential to what it is to be a person. Perhaps here it is our emotions rather than reason which incline us to consider the foetus more favourably in the light of such images. Of course, whether such emotion is irrelevant, as Kant and the utilitarians would argue, is a moot point. It may well be that we cannot divorce emotion from our moral judgements. But quite apart from this, couldn't it be that such abilities reflect some underlying capacities which *are* essential to our idea of a person? After all, the evidence suggests the foetus is sentient from eight weeks; the essential structures of its brain and nervous system are in place. Its movements show an awareness of its body and, while we surely cannot accord it self-consciousness, it is reasonable to suppose that it is sentient, that is, it can experience sensations such as those of touch or hearing and experience pleasure and pain. This line of reasoning might provide the basis for arguing that abortion is morally justified before the brain and nervous system have developed sufficiently to support sentience. And if this is what we take to be key in determining personhood, we might attempt to draw the line around this point. Of course, sentience is presumably itself a matter of degree, and so new difficulties are bound to arise here concerning precisely how to determine when this occurs. However, we will not explore such issues further. The basic difficulty should now be clear, namely that any dividing line drawn across a gradual process will be arbitrary to some degree. After all, if the evolution of embryo to person is a gradual one, then to fix any particular point as morally significant will always carry with it the difficulties of distinguishing it from the point immediately before or after.

experimenting with ideas

At what point on this line do you think a foetus becomes a person?

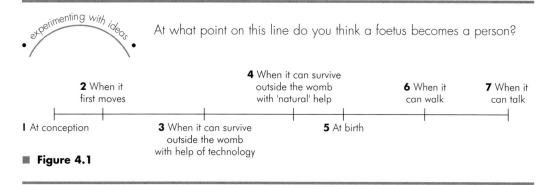

2 When it
first moves

4 When it can survive
outside the womb
with 'natural' help

6 When it
can walk

7 When it
can talk

1 At conception

3 When it can survive
outside the womb
with help of technology

5 At birth

■ **Figure 4.1**

Leaving questions of foetal development aside then, let's turn to some traditional religious approaches to the dilemma. Most of the major religions regard the human person as consisting of both a soul and a body. The soul is normally seen as an essential component of what it is to be a person since it carries with it the essence of what we are and of what it is to be conscious and alive. On this way of thinking, the crucial issue concerns when ensoulment takes place, i.e. when the soul is first united with the developing embryonic body. St Augustine (354–430) maintained that it is implanted 46 days after conception and on this basis we could argue that to abort before this time would not be to kill a person, and so would not be wrong. We mentioned earlier that it has been argued that when the mother first experiences the foetus' movements is significant, and the Catholic Church traditionally saw this stage, known as quickening, as the point at which the soul joined the foetus. However, in the seventeenth century the Catholic Church affirmed that ensoulment takes place at the moment of conception. The implication is that the fertilised egg is already a human person, and this led to the Church's opposition to abortion at any stage. Some Islamic scholars have argued that verses in the Qur'an imply that ensoulment takes place some time after conception and therefore that abortion is acceptable prior to this. However, the Qur'an doesn't specify precisely when this is, and working out when ensoulment takes place is no easy matter since it is not a physical phenomenon. In any case, if the soul is immortal, as Islam maintains, then abortion would never actually constitute killing the person, but simply preventing them from being born. This may incline someone to argue that abortion at any stage should be condemned as interfering with God's will to bring a person into the world. Natural law theory supports the idea that we should not interfere with God's will as revealed by our observation of processes such as pregnancy, with clearly recognisable goals. Foetal development has a definite end and purpose and so should not be deliberately interrupted.

This way of seeing the issue leads to the idea that what is really at stake is not whether or not a foetus ever actually attains personhood within the womb, but rather the fact that it has the *potential* to become a person. The fact that the foetus is capable of developing into a person may give us reason to condemn any action which prevents this. However, this approach leads us into the new difficulty of defining when this potential kicks in. Presumably, the potential to become a person exists before conception and so it can come to seem as though contraception is also morally wrong. This consequence of the natural law approach is indeed embraced by the Catholic Church, but the idea that an unfertilised ovum or individual sperm, both of which could be said to have the *potential* to become persons, should be given equal moral status with adult humans is certainly an extreme view.[189] Also, having the potential to become a person or a sentient being is not the same as actually being a person or a sentient being. Before sentience, the foetus may have the potential to acquire certain rights, but this is not the same as saying it already has them.

The examination of when a foetus becomes a person is only part of the debate, however. For, even if an embryo or foetus *is* regarded as a person, we may still not regard abortion as a case of wrongful killing. After all, many are already agreed that abortion is justified in cases where the mother's life is at risk from bringing the foetus to term. In cases such as this it is even legal in this country to allow abortion after 24 weeks, as we have seen, and the reasoning here may involve utilitarian considerations, which take the mother's preferences or happiness into consideration, or deontological approaches, which emphasise the rights of the mother to life. Could it be that such approaches may justify abortion in less extreme circumstances? Many feminist philosophers have argued that the traditional approach is wrong-headed, in that it focuses on only one side of the dilemma, namely the foetus. What is needed, they argued, was a new approach which fully considered the woman bearing the child.

A feminist perspective: the woman's moral right to choose

The feminist standpoint on the morality of abortion treats the woman's 'right to choose' as paramount over any rights of the foetus. Such a position is supported by considerations about the history of women as one of male domination and oppression. Women, it is pointed out, have traditionally been given little choice about taking on the role of being mothers, while men have been free to pursue a life outside the home. It is the woman who must carry the child in pregnancy, go through the pain of labour, bear the brunt of caring for the child, and so forth. Women were forced to bear many children in a life-time with the inevitable strain this put on their physical health, and many died young as a consequence. Thus a right to abortion is seen by many feminists as essential to the emancipation of women from slavery to their bodies.[190] A woman's body should be her own to dispose of as she sees fit, and arguments which suggest that control of her fertility should not be in her own hands represent an affront against her most basic rights as an autonomous agent. From this point of view, opposition to abortion, while often couched in the language of morality, appears actually to be a covert means by which society hopes to keep women in their place. In Kantian terms we might say it is a way of using women as a means to certain social ends. This pro-choice position can also be supported by a traditional utilitarian argument to the effect that abortion cannot be wrong so long as it does not cause suffering or reduce happiness. If abortion is the key to empowering women and freeing them to live fulfilling lives then it is a good thing. Unwanted childbirth leads to increase in child mortality, aggravates poverty, puts strain on the state's welfare services and damages women's health. Thus abortion is one tool society can use to increase the overall happiness of society. A preference utilitarian will make an equivalent argument. If the woman prefers to terminate her pregnancy she is the primary agent concerned in the matter, since the foetus is not in a position to have a preference one way or another.

One significant defence of abortion based on consideration of a woman's rights comes from Judith Jarvis Thomson, in a paper entitled 'A defence of abortion.'[191] In the paper Thomson proposed the following analogy. Suppose you were to wake up one morning, having been kidnapped by the Society of Music Lovers, only to find that a famous violinist had been plugged into your blood supply because his kidneys had failed. You are asked to support him for nine months to keep him alive after which he will be able to survive independently. According to Thomson, although it would be very decent of you to agree to the request, you would be under no *moral* obligation to do so. But surely, she argues, the situation is the same in pregnancy. The woman's right to life and her right of ownership of her own body are of far greater significance than the right to life which may be accorded to the unborn foetus. Carrying a baby to term is a dangerous undertaking. So we cannot in good conscience make a moral demand on the woman to bear it to term. There is no other situation, after all, in which we would require that someone give up their liberty, their autonomy, risk their health and even their lives for the sake of someone else. Thus while the mother may well choose to bear the child, and this would be a very generous act, she is not morally compelled to do so.

The feminist position, as articulated by Thomson, claims that there should be few if any restrictions on someone's rights to do with their own body as they wish. Not to allow someone the choice to abort is an infringement of their basic right to self-determination and not to be physically harmed. However, it may be objected that alongside any rights I may have, I surely also have certain responsibilities. After all I am not entitled to involve my body in negligent behaviour, such as sky diving from office buildings, in a way which may endanger the lives of others. And if I were to injure anyone through such antics, it would seem reasonable for me to be held responsible for the consequences. Moreover, individuals have to pay the price for actions which they later regret. If I get married and promise to be faithful to a particular person and later change my mind because I meet someone else, I cannot ignore the fact that I am married. And perhaps for similar sorts of reasons we might want to say that a woman has certain responsibilities as well as rights, and has obligations to live with the consequences of particular actions, in particular the consequences of sexual intercourse. In this respect the case of the violinist and the foetus are not really analogous, since the woman in Thomson's example has no way of knowing what she is getting into. But if I freely choose to engage in sexual intercourse without taking precautions against falling pregnant, then surely I am responsible for the foreseeable consequences. Also Thomson's analogy seems to treat the foetus as though it were just any human being, an unrelated stranger, and yet it can plausibly be argued that there are certain peculiar obligations that a mother has to her unborn child.

However, what Thomson's example does seem appropriate to are cases of rape, and perhaps also of accidental pregnancies when reasonable precautions have been taken. In the former case, the argument would go, we cannot be responsible for the consequences of what we are forced to do. And an unforeseen pregnancy need not be one a woman has any obligations to sustain, since she has not knowingly taken on any such obligations. While many would be sympathetic to this line with respect to rape, we should note that it may still be objected that our obligations do not necessarily depend on what we have decided to do. I may arrive by chance at the scene of an accident, but the facts that I did not decide to arrive and am not responsible for the accident do not mean that I have no obligations to help the injured and dying. Obligations do not necessarily depend on our voluntarily taking them on and so it may be argued that the mother still has a duty of care to her unplanned foetus. Whether or not such a line is persuasive in the case of rape, where the mitigating circumstances are so extreme, it certainly seems to have some force in the case of unplanned pregnancy.

Returning to the feminists' use of traditional utilitarian arguments to support the moral right to choose, we can object that there is no explanation as to why we should not take the future happiness of the foetus into account. To approach the issue of abortion in this way is again to deny significant rights to the foetus out of hand and begs the question. Any serious defence of the mother's right to abortion, it can be argued, should at least give some account of why the apparent victim (namely the foetus) need not be included in any calculations of utility. Of course, the feminist may argue that killing the foetus is simply to remove it from the equation – if it is killed painlessly it can no longer experience pleasure or pain – and so only the woman's happiness should be considered of relevance. But, as we saw above, even though the foetus may not be self-conscious and so not *concerned* about its future happiness it is not clear that this is a reason to ignore such happiness when doing our calculations. Similarly with preference utilitarianism: the foetus may not be able consciously to consider what it would prefer, but this doesn't seem by itself to be enough reason to ignore what would be in its best interests, since otherwise we seem to be committed to the moral acceptability of infanticide.

Moreover it is not just the interests of the foetus that may conflict with those of the mother. Conflicts may also arise with the happiness, preferences or rights of the father, the extended family and of society as a whole; and thus the interests of the mother, while they should be recognised and doubtless accorded the greatest weight, cannot be considered in isolation. Abortion, in other words, is not an isolated issue, but has social ramifications extending beyond the mother. So it seems that the utilitarian arguments are bound to lead into questions about the social consequences of abortion. Might a woman have a social obligation not to abort if her country's population is being depleted? Or by contrast, might she have an obligation to abort if the population were expanding out of control? We might also want to weigh up the social costs in terms of the utility principle of bringing so many unwanted pregnancies to term. Consider also that by making abortion illegal the consequences may be far worse since women will end up in back-street clinics where their lives are at risk.[192] This is, of course, not an argument to show that abortion in itself is morally justified, but only that it would be wrong to have laws preventing it.

Such utilitarian styles of reasoning, however, will strike the deontologically minded as morally callous, ignoring as they do any considerations of the right to life of the foetus or the rights and wrongs of the act of abortion itself. For many deontologists would also want to defend the rights of the unborn child even though it may not yet be regarded as a fully fledged moral agent. So opponents of abortion, while not denying that respect must be paid to the woman, insist that her rights cannot override the right of another person to life. Note that to concentrate on a woman's 'right to choose' at the expense of the rights of the foetus is to assume that the issue of abortion is no more than an issue of individual liberty. To treat the issue in this way is to put it on a par with so called *victimless* 'crimes', such as sado-masochistic relations between consenting adults. Many would argue that what adults freely choose to do cannot be regarded as morally wrong. In a similar vein it is often argued that the decision to abort, like the decision to commit adultery or to gamble, are beyond the ambit of the law and should be left to the individual's own conscience. Again, however, this is an argument about the rights and wrongs of legislation and not of abortion itself.

Here we have only been able to begin to explore the many avenues of thought which bear on this complex topic, but hopefully we have been able to give a sense of the terrain that moral philosophers have explored in debating it.

Euthanasia

On 13 March 1943 the Nazis finally liquidated the Jewish ghetto in the Polish city of Cracow. What 'liquidated' meant was sending all those Jewish men and women who were fit to work to slave labour camps, and sending all those who were unfit to work to be murdered in the gas chambers; people who tried to hide in the ghetto, or who refused to go or who were too sick to go were executed on the spot. In the ghetto's hospital a Jewish doctor, D, had stayed behind, despite being offered a possible escape route. Four of his patients were too ill to move – he knew the horrific fate (machine gunning or worse) that awaited them once the Nazis arrived. He had in his hand some cyanide, which he could give to the patients, killing them peacefully, with some left over for himself.

> *There was suicide, yes. But there was euthanasia as well. The concept terrified D. He suffered painfully from a set of ethics as intimate to him as the organs of his own body … To inject the cyanide or to abandon the patients to the [Nazis]? But D knew these things were never a matter of totting up columns, that ethics was higher and more tortuous than algebra.*[193]
>
> Thomas Keneally, *Schindler's Ark*

Deliberately killing or harming patients is forbidden by the Hippocratic Oath that doctors abide by.[194] But surely there are some instances, as in the terrible situation faced by D in the Cracow ghetto, where it is *better* for the patient to die than to live any longer. These are instances of euthanasia. The word 'euthanasia' derives from two Greek words (*eu* and *thanatos*) and means literally 'good death'. Today it refers to the act or practice of bringing about someone's death for their own good by someone else, normally in the face of some incurable or terminal illness which will otherwise cause them great suffering.

While euthanasia is rejected by the Hippocratic Oath, it was widely accepted in Greek and Roman times. The rise of Christianity contributed greatly, as we saw by its attitude to infanticide, to the feeling that human life is sacred and should not be taken. Consistent with this approach, the Christian tradition condemns euthanasia on the grounds that it amounts to the taking of a life which, as a gift from God, is not ours to take. Euthanasia is also opposed by natural law theory as a violation of the natural processes of living and dying; while Kant opposed it on the grounds that it amounted to ending one's own life without concern for the moral community as a whole. However, utilitarian arguments focusing on reducing suffering have been deployed in support of euthanasia. Before proceeding to a discussion of them we will need to outline certain distinctions which are traditionally made in discussions of euthanasia.

An initial distinction is between three types of euthanasia: voluntary, non-voluntary and involuntary.

Voluntary euthanasia

If a person freely chooses the termination of his or her life then this is termed *voluntary* euthanasia. Note that euthanasia can be regarded as voluntary even though the person may no longer be competent to make the decision (for example, if they have fallen unconscious) so long as they made it when they were competent. From a moral point of view, voluntary euthanasia is effectively a form of suicide, the only difference being that someone else's assistance is needed because the person is unable to perform the deed for themselves. So the issues of the moral permissibility of suicide and of voluntary euthanasia are closely intertwined. It is noteworthy that very different attitudes to suicide have emerged in different societies, some regarding it as the very worst of sins, others regarding it as the most honourable of deaths. In the West the moral arguments about the rights and wrongs of suicide have typically revolved around the deontological issue of whether or not suicide violates one or more of three obligations: namely to oneself, to others, and to God.

Taking the first of these, the idea is that voluntarily to end my own life prematurely is to abnegate a certain responsibility I have to live. My life is not something to be discarded lightly. Importantly, as we have mentioned, to commit suicide is to violate the proper order of living and dying, and so violates the 'natural law'. Secondly suicide has been regarded as a kind of betrayal of others. Since we are all members of some community, to kill oneself is to damage that community. We all have responsibilities to others – to our family and friends, to work colleagues and society at large – and the suicide should consider not only his or her own interests, but the interests of all those affected. This need not mean that suicide or voluntary euthanasia is always wrong, but rather that the social consequences need to be taken into account by the person contemplating suicide. And thirdly, because life is a gift from God, it has been argued that to commit suicide is an offence against the divine will. Because they are given by God, our lives are not our own to dispose of, so to destroy one's own life is analogous to stealing. A secular version of this argument might make appeal to the principle of the sanctity of life, arguing that life has an intrinsic value and should not be destroyed.

Note that the blameworthiness of suicide or voluntary euthanasia is normally thought to depend on the decision being autonomously made and in sound mind, since otherwise the person could not be held responsible for it. Since many suicides are committed while in the throes of severe depression or other mental illness, it may be that they cannot be condemned. Some have even argued that no suicide is rational, indeed that the very notion of a rational suicide is self-contradictory. The seventeenth century philosopher Spinoza, for example, held that suicide goes counter to the drive to survive, which is essential to human nature, and therefore can never be freely and rationally chosen. Similarly Freud regarded intended suicide as a symptom of some form of psychological dysfunction. It follows from such views that there can be no ethical problem of suicide, since for an agent to kill themselves entails that he or she has behaved irrationally and so not responsibly. Of course it also follows from this that it can never be right to assist someone in killing themselves, and so voluntary euthanasia can never be justified. For if no one can rationally choose to die, anyone who claims to want to die must be sick or confused. When confronted with such an unfortunate individual, therefore, our duty must always be to help them overcome their irrational urge, perhaps by reasoning with them, or treating their mental illness with counselling or drug therapies.

Involuntary euthanasia

Euthanasia is *involuntary* if a person who is capable of consenting to being killed, does not give that consent, either because they are not asked, do not respond to being asked, or choose to continue living. Since the motive for euthanasia is to alleviate suffering, it would be odd if the wishes of the person who is to be killed were not taken into account, and so cases of genuine involuntary euthanasia must be extremely rare. One example we have already looked at is Dr D's patients in the Cracow ghetto, and how D killed his patients with cyanide so that they might avoid being slaughtered by the Nazis. Although it may be argued that to increase doses of pain-killing drugs to the level where they become fatal, or to withhold life-sustaining treatments, amounts to involuntary euthanasia, generally involuntary euthanasia is not regarded as morally acceptable because it is difficult to distinguish such an act from murder, and consequently involuntary euthanasia plays only a minor part in current moral controversies.

Non-voluntary euthanasia

Finally a case of non-voluntary euthanasia occurs when a person is not capable, for one reason or another, of making the choice between life and death. Normally this would be because they are not mentally competent to make the decision, for example if they are a new-born infant, a coma victim, or suffering from brain damage. (However, as pointed out above, a patient who expressed a preference for life or death before succumbing to their present condition remains a case of voluntary euthanasia.)

ACTIVITY   How do you think the following types of philosophers would approach the moral problem of non-voluntary euthanasia?

1 A utilitarian
2 A Kantian
3 A divine command theorist
4 A virtue ethicist

Active and passive euthanasia

Another distinction that is often drawn is that between _active_ and _passive_ euthanasia. For there are two ways in which someone's death can be brought about: either _actively_ by administering, for example, a lethal injection; or _passively_ by withholding life-sustaining treatment. Cases of voluntary, involuntary and non-voluntary euthanasia can all be either active or passive. The difference is sometimes explained in terms of 'killing' and 'letting die'. The idea behind drawing this distinction in this way is that to kill someone appears, at least on the face of it, to be morally worse than simply to let someone die. So those who oppose active euthanasia may regard passive euthanasia as morally permissible on the grounds that in the one case the agent causes death, whereas in the other he merely allows nature to take its course. If killing and letting die were morally equivalent, the argument goes, then we would be as responsible for the deaths of those whom we fail to save as we are for the deaths of those whom we kill. Note that this line could be attractive to a natural law theorist, since it puts much store by the idea of allowing the natural course to run.

However, in practice, it is often not clear how we are to draw this distinction. For example, is unplugging a life support machine to be regarded as actively interfering to kill, or passively allowing things to take their course? You could argue, after all, that ending such life-sustaining treatment is actively to precipitate someone's death and so amounts to killing them; but it could also plausibly be maintained that unplugging the machine is really to stop interfering with the natural course of things and so merely allowing someone to die. Also to try to make the distinction simply in terms of what one actively does – 'acts' – and what one does not do – 'omissions' – is clearly implausible as an account of what should be permissible and what should not.[195] This is because we can be just as responsible for what we *omit* to do as for what we *actually* do. If, for example, a doctor fails to give emergency treatment to an otherwise healthy patient, who then dies, she can hardly be absolved of responsibility on the grounds that the person died as a consequence of what she *omitted* to do. She could hardly turn around and say: 'How can I be to blame? I didn't do anything!'

Ordinary and extraordinary means

If the active/passive distinction fails to identify accurately when euthanasia might be morally justified does this entail we are obliged to deploy whatever means we have in order to sustain life? Must we really do everything we can to prolong the life of a terminally ill patient even if for only a few extra days? Even strong opponents of euthanasia tend to agree that there must eventually come a point where life-sustaining treatment should be terminated. What is needed, therefore, are criteria by which to distinguish permissible and impermissible omissions of life-sustaining treatments. Traditionally the distinction has been made in terms of 'ordinary' and 'extraordinary means' of treatment. Thus while it would be wrong to withhold first aid from a patient, since this is obviously a very 'ordinary' way of keeping someone alive, it might not be wrong to withhold risky or painful surgery if there were few benefits to be gained in terms of prolonging life. Today this distinction is more often made in terms of 'proportionate' and 'disproportionate' means; that is to say, in terms of weighing up the likely benefits of different treatments to the patient's quality of life, against the complexity, expense and so forth of the treatments themselves. If the treatment is *disproportionate* to the expected benefits then it is permissible to withhold it.

The principle of double effect

Those who find euthanasia unacceptable may, however, want to distinguish intending death from foreseeing that death will occur. On this way of thinking, what determines the moral status of an action is in large measure the intention behind it. So if a doctor administers a lethal injection to end someone's suffering, this would be a case of *intentional* killing and therefore to be condemned. If, however, she intends to alleviate a patient's pain by administering increasingly large doses of morphine, for example, which, as a side-effect, will bring about the patient's death, then this is *not* intentional killing. For, it is argued, in the former case the patient's death is directly *intended*, but in the latter case, the death is merely *foreseen*. What the doctor intends in the case of administering morphine is to kill the pain, not the patient.

Aquinas uses this principle in his discussion of the moral justification of killing in self-defence. His argument is that if I kill in order to defend myself against attack, so long as my direct intention is to defend myself, and the death of my attacker is merely a foreseen (but not directly intended) consequence, then the action is permissible.[196] The notion that an action can have harmful and foreseen consequences, but still be justified so long as the primary objective of the action is good, is often termed the *principle of DOUBLE EFFECT*. It states that it is sometimes morally acceptable to perform a good act which will bring about bad consequences, but that it is always wrong to perform a bad act for the sake of good consequences. So it can be morally permissible to relieve pain (a good act) knowing that it may cause the patient's death (a bad consequence); but it is always wrong to kill (a bad act) for the sake of relieving suffering (a good consequence).

▶ criticism ◀ However, it is not clear whether such a distinction can be unambiguously drawn. Even in Aquinas' example we might ask whether doing something in the certain knowledge that a particular consequence will ensue is truly not to intend that consequence. There is also the difficulty of knowing for sure what our true intentions are. I may deceive myself into thinking my intentions are honourable, when in fact they are not. For example, I might try to justify agreeing to help my friend to die on the grounds that my direct intention is to alleviate their suffering, when in fact I am simply tired of caring for them.

With these distinctions in view let's now look at the basic arguments for and against euthanasia.

Arguments for euthanasia

(i) The basic utilitarian argument for euthanasia is straightforward enough: it increases the overall happiness because it brings to an end a life of suffering.

► criticism ◄ As always with utilitarian arguments, though, one difficulty concerns whether we can make safe predictions about the likely consequences of any particular act. Here there is the danger of making errors of judgement as to future happiness since medical prognoses may be inaccurate and people can make unexpected recoveries. It is also sometimes argued that modern techniques of hospice care undermine the utilitarian argument since people can now be helped to die painlessly. However, while this may turn out to be true in the future, in the meantime many do still die in great pain, and so for now we still have to wrestle with the moral issues of those who are not living pleasant lives as they await their deaths. And, while medicine is not an exact science, there will inevitably be cases where we can be very confident in the prognosis about someone's painful demise.

► criticism ◄ Nonetheless, we have already seen that there are other problems with the attempt to justify killing in terms of the net increase in happiness that may result. Deontological considerations can seem more in tune with our moral intuitions when it comes to examples such as killing a healthy patient to save five others. A deontologist is likely to regard one's right to life as paramount and so will urge that we all have a duty to defend this right. However, while killing someone is normally a violation of their right to life, if it is expressly asked for can we still speak of a right being violated? In general a person's rights only extend to the point at which they want them to be upheld. If, for example, you steal something that belongs to me, you violate my property rights; but if I ask you to take it you do not. Consent may therefore be sufficient for the right to life to be waived. So shouldn't the patient's express wishes be the determining factor here? Against this, it may be argued that consent is not sufficient in this case. After all if a worker gives consent to an employer to exploit her this would not be sufficient for her right to fair treatment to be waived. Similarly, we tend not to regard obtaining someone's consent as sufficient justification for buying their internal organs.

(ii) If we regard the autonomy of the individual as paramount, then we may follow J. S. Mill in arguing that the right to live or die is our own so long as no harm is done to others.[197] We might ask, after all, whose life it is anyway. Since this life is mine, and so long as I am of sound mind and fully cognisant of all the facts, then my free and rational decision to die should be respected.

▶ criticism ◀

One objection to this line of thinking which we have already mentioned is the view that no decision to die is ever rational since our most fundamental interests are always to stay alive. However, as an absolute claim covering all possible cases, this is not particularly convincing. It seems there will inevitably be some situations where it must be rational to choose a quick death over a slow painful one. Another objection points out that the fact that I call this 'my life' doesn't in itself mean that I own it or that I have the right to dispose of it as I will. After all, just because someone is 'my' uncle doesn't mean that I own *him*, or that I can do with *him* as I will. Furthermore, even if we accept that I own my life, it still doesn't follow that I have the right to destroy it. A parallel here might be with your ownership of a valuable commodity such as a famous painting. The fact that you own it does not mean you are permitted to destroy it. If a rich person owns a huge pile of food, they would not be permitted to destroy it when it could be used to feed hungry mouths. However, such analogies suggest that we have a duty to stay alive only so long as our life could be of value to others.

Arguments against euthanasia

A rule utilitarian may argue that euthanasia should not be permitted on the grounds that adoption of a rule outlawing it represents a stalwart against evil social consequences. For if euthanasia were permitted this would put pressure on the old and sick to die sooner rather than later because of the burden they represent to their family or to society. This would then open the door to the disposing of old people against their will. So, although particular acts of active killing can sometimes be justified on act utilitarian grounds, the social consequences of sanctioning practices of killing would run serious risks of abuse and misuse. Opponents of this argument can dispute whether such consequences need actually follow; they may invoke the case of the Netherlands where this doesn't seem to have happened following the legalisation of euthanasia in 1973.

Other arguments that might be deployed against euthanasia have already been considered as arguments against suicide, such as that life represents a gift from God, or that euthanasia distorts the 'natural' course of life.

Animal rights

Zaphod Beeblebrox and Arthur Dent are in the Restaurant at the End of the Universe wondering what to eat:

> *A large dairy animal approached [the] table.*
> *'Good evening,' it lowed ... 'I am the main Dish of the Day. May I interest you in parts of my body? ... the rump is very good ... I've been exercising it so there's plenty of good meat there.'*
> *... 'That's absolutely horrible,' exclaimed Arthur, 'the most revolting thing I've ever heard.'*
> *'What's the problem, Earthman?' said Zaphod ...*
> *'I just don't want to eat an animal that's standing there inviting me to,' said Arthur, 'it's heartless.'*
> *'Better than eating an animal that doesn't want to be eaten,' said Zaphod.*[198]

Douglas Adams, *The Restaurant at the End of the Universe*

Fortunately, we don't have to face this dilemma – the animals we kill for meat (or skin for leather, or experiment on for extra moisturising skin lotion) can't tell us whether they would like to be eaten, or skinned, or experimented on: fortunately for us, that is, but unfortunately for the animals. After all, you would surmise that if they could speak they probably wouldn't be offering up their rump to be sliced off and eaten. The question that most people in the Western world avoid asking every day is 'why, if it's morally wrong to kill, skin or experiment on humans, is it morally permissible to do these things to animals?' In other words, what are the moral differences between humans and animals, and at what point do we draw the line and say, 'No. Doing this thing to that creature is morally wrong'?

ACTIVITY   Where do you draw the line?

In the activity overleaf you need to apply each of the actions in the left-hand column of the table to each of the beings named at the top of the table.

Put a cross in the box if it is always or mostly WRONG to do this (below) to this (right)	An adult	A child	A foetus	A chimpanzee	A rabbit	An ant	A plant
Make life-changing decisions on its behalf							
Kill/destroy it because it interferes with your quality of life							
Own it (or deprive it of its freedom without any reason)							
Kill it in order to eat or use parts of it							
Perform harmful experiments on it							
Harm it for your own pleasure							
Kill/destroy it without any reason							

Where did you draw the line? The exercise gets you to think about which kinds of being you regard as worthy of moral concern, and which you do not. You may have found some cases about which you were unsure, and this highlights the difficulty with how we are to make this distinction. In our discussion of killing we began to consider the question of whether we should have moral concern for non-human animals. We saw there some of the ways philosophers have tried to justify humans' tendency to treat other animals differently. One possible way of drawing the distinction is simply to point out that animals come from different species from us. However, it does not seem morally acceptable to justify our lack of moral concern for animals simply on the grounds that they are biologically different. On the one hand, this is because the biological distinction between humans and other animals is not as clear-cut as it was once supposed to be. The theory of evolution tells us that humans are more or less closely related to all other living things; we are in genetic terms just a cousin of chimpanzees.[199] Whatever it is that differentiates us, it is a matter of degree, not of kind. In this light, humans appear as just one species among many thrown up by the processes of natural selection, and with no special status. On the other hand, and more importantly, biology doesn't have the relevant conceptual bearing on moral judgements. This can be illustrated by the thought experiment that any intelligent primate or alien we might happen upon would be thought to be worthy of moral consideration, even though it is not human. And similarly we do not confer moral consideration upon things just because they are human, otherwise we would be just as horrified at the abortion of a human zygote, or the switching off of a coma victim's life-support machine, as we are at the killing of an autonomous, self-conscious adult. Some argue that the appeal to biological distinctions is as morally arbitrary as the appeal to distinctions of race or sex between humans as justification for treating them differently. And just as such thinking is condemned as racist and sexist, philosophers such as Peter Singer have urged us to condemn such arguments about animals as *speciesist,*[200] speciesism being the prejudicial bias in favour of one's own species when weighing moral considerations.

In search of a morally relevant distinction, philosophers have not tended to look simply to biology, but rather to whether we should regard animals as *persons.* For, it has been thought, the moral consideration due to an animal (just as that due to a foetus) depends in large part on whether or not it counts as a person. So, here we will begin by trying to find an answer to the fundamental question of whether moral obligations extend to creatures which would seem to lack some of the basic characteristics associated with personhood. In other words, can we reasonably distinguish humans from other animals in any relevant way so as to make the latter not subject to the normal moral injunction on causing suffering and taking life? If animals lack rationality, self-consciousness, autonomy, the capacity for free choice, an interest in their future states and so forth, are we then permitted to use them as means to our own ends?

Aristotle regarded animals as devoid of any faculty of reason, defining man as the '*rational* animal'. Their lack of rationality he took to be evidence that the ultimate function of animals is simply to service the needs of man. Similarly the Christian tradition distinguished man in terms of possession of reason and of an immortal soul. And this led Aquinas, for example, to draw similar conclusions to Aristotle:

Aquinas

There is no sin in using a thing for the purpose for which it was meant ... Now the most necessary use would seem to consist in the fact that men use animals for food, and this cannot be done unless these be deprived of life: wherefore it is lawful to take life from animals for the use of men.[201]

Descartes regarded animals as having no soul or mind and therefore believed they were incapable of sentience. This, of course, meant that there could be no moral issue about how we treat them. Similarly, Kant wrote that we have no duties to animals, arguing that they 'are not self-conscious, and are there merely as a means to an end. That end is man.'[202]

More recently attempts have been made to make a morally significant distinction between man and other animals by pointing to our capacity for tool use, or the relative size of our brains. But such distinctions appear somewhat arbitrary as a basis for concluding that animals are not worthy of moral consideration. For there doesn't appear to be any conceptual connection between such features and ethical judgements, and consequently such distinctions haven't proved useful.

Another place to look for a significant difference which has perhaps more chance of success is language use. For without language, it is argued, a being cannot conceptualise and autonomously direct its own life. And if a creature is not able to represent its future states to itself it is unable freely to choose different courses of action or decide autonomously how best to live its life, and without such a capacity it seems inappropriate to treat it as an end in itself. Similarly, as we have already seen in our discussion of killing, utilitarians have argued that a being which cannot concern itself with its future is less valuable than one that can since it cannot suffer in the knowledge of what it will miss when it dies. Note, however, one significant consequence of this approach, namely that we should treat non-autonomous human beings who are not able to deliberate about their future states in the same manner as animals. We would therefore be morally permitted to conduct drug trials on people in comas – a consequence that many will find unpalatable.

Since the hoped-for distinctions are difficult to draw so as to include all borderline human persons, it may be an attractive option to argue that certain animals *do* count as persons, precisely on the grounds that they do have some capacity to use language, or to make autonomous decisions. Some chimpanzees have, with limited success, been taught to use sign language, which some believe indicates that they are self-conscious and can express future intentions. Despite this, most would be loath to hold animals responsible for their actions. It would surely be absurd to condemn a lion for killing an antelope, because lions do not engage in moral deliberation, just as coma victims, infants and mentally impaired people cannot. Thus, even though animals must have some ability to make choices, these are not ethical ones.

Rights arguments

Although animals may not be moral agents, this need not imply that they are not worthy of moral consideration. Tom Regan argues that beings only have *rights* if they have value independently of their usefulness to others, that is, value in themselves or inherently.[203] To have such value, he claims, an animal must be what he calls a 'subject-of-a-life', that is, it must be self-conscious, capable of having beliefs and desires, and of conceiving future goals. Regan figures mammals of more than a year old to be such subjects and therefore concludes they have the right to be treated as individuals with inherent value. The rights argument implies that we should not use animals as a means to an end – for example, for food or experimentation – since this is inconsistent with treating them as beings with inherent worth.

According to this view all beings with inherent value possess it equally in virtue of being subjects-of-a-life and not in virtue of anything they might do or be capable of doing. What this means is that questions of utility are not thought to be morally relevant in situations where we might have to choose between the life of a human being and an animal. Regan avoids the unhappy consequences of this (for example, that if forced to choose, one should save the life of two dogs rather than that of a human being) on the grounds that the death of a human is a greater harm, because their goals are more worthwhile. However, we may question whether this gets Regan off the hook, as it is not at all clear how we could dispassionately compare the different goals of different species. While we might regard reading a book as more worthy than chasing rabbits, it is not clear a dog would agree with us.

Utilitarian arguments

The utilitarian does not regard all beings as inherently equal in *value*, but does claim that the interest of all beings affected by an action should be considered equally. Thus what is relevant is the capacity of a creature to experience pleasure and pain regardless of species. As Jeremy Bentham has it, the question as to whether animals deserve moral consideration is *not* whether they can reason or talk, but whether they can *suffer*.[204] Thus the utilitarian agrees with the rights-based view that animals and humans have equal claims to moral consideration.

▶ criticism ◀

While this may be fairly straightforward with regard to suffering (slapping a person is surely a lesser evil than pulling a cat's eyes out) the utilitarian runs into difficulties when it comes to *death*. For surely a dog's life may well be happier than a depressive human being's. If we are forced to choose between saving a happy dog and saving a depressed human, are we really to choose the dog? Such a conclusion is difficult for most utilitarians to accept. Singer has modified the theory to escape this conclusion by arguing that self-conscious rational human beings are capable of entertaining a specific desire to continue living, while dogs, for example, are not.[205] And to thwart this desire would be to reduce the overall happiness more drastically than not to.

Utilitarian arguments can be marshalled on either side of the debate over whether it is morally permissible to eat meat. A utilitarian may object to eating animals on the grounds that killing them brings to an end any pleasure they gain from their lives. Moreover, it may be argued that farming methods designed to maximise meat production do not have the animals' interests at heart and so tend to cause distress and suffering. On the other hand, if the animals are raised humanely and live fulfilling and stress-free lives before being painlessly killed, it seems there can be no utilitarian objection to using them as food.[206] Moreover, there is an argument in favour of farmed meat production which points out that a greater amount of pleasure is produced by the very demand for meat. For, the argument goes, it is only because we eat them that farm animals exist at all. Thus although meat eaters are responsible for the death of animals and for putting an end to their pleasure, they are also responsible for the creation of many more animals than there would otherwise be, and so for a net gain of pleasure.

Those arguments which try to show that we owe to other animals the same sort of moral consideration that we do to each other ignore the role that kinship plays in much of our ordinary moral thinking. While Kant and others have argued that the logic of moral thinking demands that we universalise our principles and treat all people impartially, it also seems intuitively clear that we owe greater obligation to close friends and family than we do to strangers. While it may be argued that such obligation is not strictly *moral*, it is nonetheless a central factor bearing on our moral decision-making. So maybe the reason we feel that we ought to save a human being before another animal from a fire, is the same sort of reason that we would save a family member before a stranger. While reason is often regarded as integral to moral decision-making, emotional attachments and moral sentiments also play a crucial role. It is difficult to divorce emotions from morality. Indeed, without feelings of outrage and compassion it is hard to see how we would be motivated to act morally at all. If this is right and our capacity for sympathy is central to deciding who benefits from our moral concern, then it is to be expected that we will tend to show a species bias in making moral decisions. It may be natural for us, qua human, to place our own interests over those of other species.

Practical wisdom and the skills of ethical decision-making

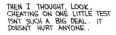

■ **Figure 4.2 How not to make a moral decision**

As Calvin acknowledges, making moral decisions is never easy, and an internal debate like this can go on endlessly. There are times when it's appropriate to dwell on both sides of the debate, perhaps do a bit of research, read what the experts have to say, talk to friends – for example, when confronted with the issues we looked at above (abortion, euthanasia, the treatment of animals). But there are other times when the urgency of the situation requires that a decision be made quickly – and if it isn't, then, as Calvin found, time runs out. So how do we go about making ethical decisions, and how can we make better, more effective ones?

Most of the time we don't have much difficulty identifying what the right thing to do is, or which course of action will bring about a morally better state of affairs. What we might call our 'moral intuitions', that is our pre-theoretical sense of what is right and wrong, are normally sufficient to make a judgement. (Of course it is an altogether different matter, once we have identified what it would be morally best to do, whether we actually go about *doing* this – all sorts of self-interested goals and desires, plus our own weakness of the will, conspire to get in the way of us doing the right thing. But that is another story.) However, there are many other occasions where we are confronted with a situation that our moral intuitions cannot deal with. These may be situations in which we feel pulled in different directions by two courses of action, or where the available options are morally unpalatable but where we must choose one. Situations such as these present us with a moral dilemma.

Dilemma 1. Read through the following moral dilemma[207], and then answer the questions below.

A woman was near death from a special kind of cancer. There was one drug that the experts thought might save her. It was a form of radium that a druggist in the same town had recently discovered. The drug was expensive to make, but the druggist was charging ten times what the drug cost him to make. He paid £200 for the radium and charged £2,000 for a small dose of the drug.

The sick woman's husband, Heinz, went to everyone he knew to borrow the money, but he could only get together about £1,000, which is half of what it cost. He told the druggist that his wife was dying and asked him to sell it cheaper or let him pay later. But the druggist said: 'No, I discovered the drug and I'm going to make money from it.' Heinz knew he could break into the lab and steal the drug without being detected. What should Heinz do?

1 Explain what the dilemma is here: what are the two basic options available to Heinz? What is problematic about each of these options?

2 Imagine you were Heinz. What would you do in this situation?

3 Write down, or draw as a 'concept map', all the issues you need to consider in order to help you make your decision in this situation.

■ **Figure 4.3 How would you approach this moral dilemma?**

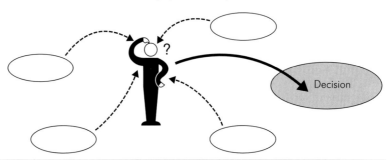

It is possible to identify different types of moral dilemma.[208] There are ones where we don't know what to do because there are 'reasons on both sides' and the evidence for a particular course of action is inconclusive. A second type is where we believe, on moral grounds, that a course of action both ought to be done and yet ought not to be done at the same time. A third kind of dilemma, faced by deontologists, is where there is an unavoidable conflict of obligations – for example, on the one hand Heinz ought not to steal, while on the other hand Heinz ought to try to save his wife, but he can't (apparently) meet both obligations.[209] In the case of such dilemmas our moral intuitions don't seem to contain the solution; they are simply not sophisticated enough.

Practical wisdom: looking beyond moral philosophy

We turned to moral philosophy with the hope that it might assist us in resolving moral dilemmas, clarifying how we should act and helping us to navigate through life. Now, having read most of this book, you might think that moral philosophy has confused things rather than clarified them. In this final section of the book we look at how we can improve our moral decision-making through developing certain skills; and for some contemporary philosophers this means looking beyond ethics.

> Bryan Magee: *Obviously moral philosophy done in this way … can't be done in a vacuum: you're going to get involved in psychological questions, anthropological questions, historical questions, institutional questions …*

> Bernard Williams: *Certainly. And the idea that there is a department of philosophy which is entirely autonomous called Moral Philosophy would seem to me to be obviously wrong, and indeed falsified by all the interesting history of the subject.*[210]

The suggestion here is that moral philosophy cannot be carried out in isolation from other academic disciplines. And this seems correct: those philosophers who have offered some of the most rounded normative theories were not just engaged in moral philosophy – they also drew on an understanding of human motivation, of the place of feelings in morality, and the role of reason. We too need to look beyond the musings of ethical theories if we are to equip ourselves with the skills necessary to make better moral decisions. Anthony Weston takes this kind of pragmatic approach, and Figure 4.4 overleaf indicates some of the skills that are the hallmarks of successful moral decision-making.[211]

■ **Figure 4.4**
Successful moral decision-making: the skills of practical wisdom (phronesis)

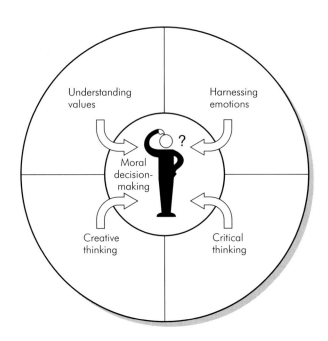

By recommending this practical approach we are returning to something close to virtue ethics. However, unlike Alasdair MacIntyre and others (pages 111–114 above), we are not advocating a return to a fully Aristotelian approach to ethics. But we are suggesting that we need to pay attention, as Aristotle did, to ethics as a practice which cannot simply be reduced to moral theories. And this means that, as Plato and Aristotle recommended, we need to develop our *phronesis*, i.e. the virtue of practical wisdom. For Aristotle, practical wisdom entailed skills in deliberation (determining what is good), understanding (seeing the whole context), judgement (coming to a decision) and cleverness (putting the decision into practice).[212] We examine below four different, though overlapping, sets of skills that should help us to develop practical wisdom, and so become better moral decision-makers.

1. Understanding values: the role of ethical theory

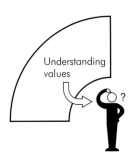

Ethics is not being recommended as a decision procedure, but as an essential resource for making decisions.[213]

The ideas that we have looked at in this book can play a crucial role in ethical decision-making. Most importantly an understanding of normative moral theories helps us to attend to the values at stake. Unless you have made a prior commitment to a particular ethical theory then the competing normative theories may be difficult to choose between, possibly because they seem so full of problems or possibly because they all seem to be right in some way. But we can find common ground between these theories, for example between rule utilitarian and deontological theories. Moreover the principles that these theories recommend also coincide with the dispositions that virtue ethicists recommend we develop. So, as a working rule of practice, we need to bear in mind a number of different and irreducible values that compete for our attention.

Nagel

Values come from a number of viewpoints … which cannot be reduced to a common denominator.[214]

Tom Beauchamp and James Childress, medical ethicists who are philosophers but also advise health practitioners on moral decision-making, identify at least four fundamental principles, which reflect four fundamental values, that are shared by the main normative theories.[215]

1 *Respect for autonomy* (we should value people as ends in themselves, respect them as rational decision-makers like us, minimise interference in their lives, and should promote their ability to be autonomous)
2 *Non-maleficence* (we should not inflict evil or harm)
3 *Beneficence* (we should help others and promote their welfare)
4 *Justice* (we should treat people equally, promote fairness and meet entitlements).

Principles 1 and 4 are broadly deontological (based on what is right), while principles 2 and 3 are broadly consequentialist (based on what is good). But it is crucial that all of them are embedded in us as action-guides that we are disposed to follow – in other words they are also virtues.[216] Beauchamp and Childress argue that from these basic principles others may follow or may be generated by combining them. For example, that we should be honest and tell the truth follows from respecting autonomy (if we lie, then we are denying others the opportunity to act with all the facts available to them). We may also think of other principles (promise-keeping, confidentiality, fidelity) that follow from these.

Beauchamp and Childress treat these principles along the same lines as W. D. Ross, i.e. as *prima facie* duties. In other words they are binding unless they conflict with other fundamental principles. Where there is a tension between two or more principles, then one *prima facie* rule may be overridden in favour of another rule that demands priority in this particular case. But it's not as if the overridden rule evaporates; instead the principle leaves behind what Robert Nozick refers to as 'moral traces'[217] – so there is a lasting impact on the agent, and remorse or regret from having overridden this rule. This ties in with the virtue ethicist's concern that we see all actions within the context of a whole life. So we are not robotically following these principles, nor are we treating the principles as rules of thumb to be broken whenever we feel like it. Instead we have a disposition to follow these principles, and we care to follow them, because we care about others.

Dilemma 2. Read through the following dilemma[218], then answer the questions below.

You are on a research trip to a foreign country, and during an expedition you find yourself in the central square of a small town. You are shocked to find that against one of the walls are twenty political protesters about to be executed by the army. The captain in charge explains that these people were protesting against his government and are going to be shot as an example to other potential protesters. But the captain would be happy for you to shoot one of the prisoners yourself (as a gesture of goodwill to you as a guest in his country) and he'll let the other nineteen go free. However, if you refuse, then the execution of all twenty will go ahead as intended. It looks like there are no other options available to you – you certainly couldn't kill the captain or the guards. You face a terrible dilemma: either you kill one prisoner, or you let twenty prisoners be killed.

1 Explain what you think is the dilemma here.
2 Identify all the values or moral principles you think are at stake in this dilemma. You may draw on any of the normative theories that you've studied, and any other moral values that you think come into play here.
3 Are you able to make a decision about which value or principle should override the others? What is this decision based on?
4 What would be the 'moral traces' (as Nozick says) of making the decision?

2. Critical thinking: the role of practical reason

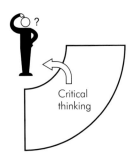

Critical thinking

Moral debate about a particular course of action may stem not only from disagreements about the relevant action-guides and the facts of the case but also about the correct scientific, metaphysical, or religious description of the situation.[219]

Critical thinking in ethics means treating our moral decisions as based on reasons. In other words we are thinking critically about processes that lead us to the decisions and actions we make. Our claim here is that moral decisions are a type of argument. The moral decisions that we make should be built on reasons – things that justify and support our decisions. In this sense, our moral judgements (about other people, or about our own course of action) are 'conclusions' supported by reasons, and they are subject to all the problems that face other, less important, types of argument. So if you wish to strengthen the reasoning that led to your moral judgement, or if you want to criticise someone else's decision, then you should look out for these problems.

An argument can be seen as a conclusion supported by premises, or as premises leading to a particular conclusion. Premises are *reasons* given to support a conclusion. We are in trouble if, when making a moral judgement, our argument is unsound because we have based it on faulty premises (see Figure 4.5). As there are many different types of premise, we need to watch out for the following mistakes:

- a fact could be wrong
- evidence could be lacking
- a false assumption could be made
- one reason could be inconsistent with (contradict) another reason
- we may be confused about the words being used – for example, ambiguities or unclear definitions.

■ **Figure 4.5 An argument based on a false premise**

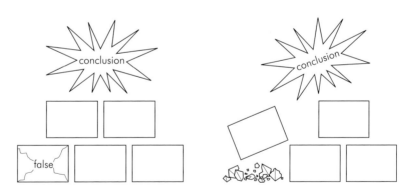

We are also in trouble if the case that supports our moral judgement doesn't 'add up', in other words where the conclusion does not follow from the premises (Figure 4.6 overleaf). We saw above, on page 138, that philosophers who believed in the autonomy of ethics thought that any argument which consisted of factual premises, but then leapt to a moral conclusion, was a fallacious argument.

From the point of view of a virtue ethicist we should become well practised at critical thinking so that, when the time arises, we do not have to spend ages thinking about

■ **Figure 4.6 A fallacious argument**

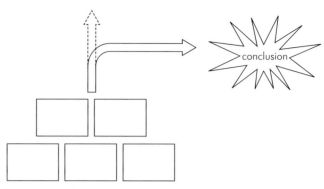

whether our judgement is based on fallacious reasoning. However, even once we have reached that ideal state, we may still need to practise the following:

- identifying and ironing out inconsistencies in our own beliefs
- clarifying and justifying the (metaphysical, religious, scientific, etc.) assumptions that we are making
- weeding out any unreliable evidence
- getting our facts straight (and not arriving at a hasty conclusion)
- considering the acceptability of our reasons
- being clear about our definitions of contested terms
- working out the grounds for our conclusions
- reconsidering any faulty conclusions.

Dilemma 3. Read through the following dilemma[220], then answer the questions below.

You wake up in the morning and find yourself back to back in bed with an unconscious violinist – a famous unconscious violinist. He has been found to have a fatal kidney ailment, and the Society of Music Lovers has canvassed all the available records and found that you alone have the right blood type to help. They have therefore kidnapped you, and last night the violinist's circulatory system was plugged into yours, so that your kidneys can be used to extract poisons from his blood as well as your own.

The director of the hospital now tells you, 'Look, we're sorry the Society of Music Lovers did this to you – we would never have permitted it if we had known. But still, they did it, and the violinist now is plugged into you. To unplug you would be to kill him. But never mind, it's only for nine months. By then he will have recovered from his ailment, and can safely be unplugged from you.'

1 How might you construct an argument to support the judgement that you ought to let the violinist remain plugged into you for the next nine months?

2 How might you construct the opposite argument, to support the judgement that you are not obliged to support the violinist and can unplug yourself?

3 What assumptions are being made in each argument? Make these explicit and then include them as premises in the arguments.

4 Do either of the arguments violate Hume's law (no 'ought' from an 'is' – see page 138)?

5 What facts do you think need to be gathered in order to make your decision a better informed one?

3. Harnessing emotions: the role of feelings

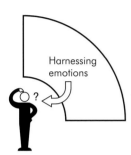

Harnessing emotions

It is easy to get angry – anyone can do that … but to feel or act towards the right person to the right extent at the right time for the right reason in the right way – that is not easy.[221]

Aristotle

The history of moral philosophy tells us that philosophers are uncomfortable with feelings. Ever since Socrates inspired Plato to search for the criteria that enabled us to make proper judgements, philosophers have been reason-oriented. There are exceptions to this – Aristotle saw feelings (appropriately contained and expressed) as an essential part of the good life, and David Hume went so far as to say our goals and values are determined by our feelings and not by reason. But by and large it is reason that has dominated moral philosophy.

One of the problems you may have had with both utilitarianism and Kantian ethics is their failure to include feelings in their systems: both types of theory are coldly calculative. But this emphasis on reason sits uneasily with our experience of moral decision-making. When faced with a terrible real-life dilemma, such as whether or not to have an abortion, our feelings flood us. We cannot ignore them and pretend that what's necessary is either to calculate utility or to follow the categorical imperative. So, if we are going to deal with the brute fact that moral dilemmas impact on us in an emotional way, we are going to have to deal with feelings. The emotions of ethics (sympathy, compassion, disgust, guilt, respect, love, empathy) are crucial in moral decisions, possibly even more so than our reasoning skills. So we need to know how to make use of emotions, how to identify useful and unhelpful emotions, how to reason about emotions, how to shape our selves (character, habits, dispositions).

At least one area where we could learn to be more 'emotionally intelligent' (as Daniel Goleman terms our harnessing of emotions[222]) is in the process of moral debate. Above we claimed that moral judgements were made on the basis of argument. But all too often, and for good reason, we confuse a moral argument with a quarrel, or shouting match –

issues like abortion and euthanasia, particularly if they've touched our own lives, hit sensitive emotional buttons which means all of us, even academic philosophers, find their voices being raised or their thoughts becoming muddled or their sarcasm more biting. What we need to be able to do is identify the buttons that we know cause us to flood with emotions and have calming strategies in place to prevent an argument becoming a quarrel.

Another practical way in which we can harness our emotions is through reflecting on the feelings that a particular situation has generated in us. Writing these down, or talking to friends about them, is particularly helpful in teasing them out. Through this reflection, once we have identified the feelings, we can go about examining which of them are helpful in moving us forward, which of them should be given weight in the decision we need to make, and which of them are unhelpful or are bound up with peripheral factors (for example, the feeling that by making a particular moral judgement we may be losing face or looking uncool in front of our peers). This process enables us to be responsive to values, and to use our sympathies in 'specific, directed and effective ways'.[223]

---

experimenting with ideas

Dilemma 4. Read through the following moral dilemma[224], then answer the questions below.

Sherman is a stockbroker living in New York. He is an obscenely wealthy man with a wife who appears in the 'Society' pages of glossy magazines at all the right parties. He has it all; he is, as he says, a Master of the Universe. He's phoned his wife to say he's working late. Except he's not – he's meeting his lover Maria from the airport – she is also married to someone rich, powerful and very important. They take a wrong turning coming back from the airport and end up in the Bronx, a place of poverty, deprivation and racial tension. There is a tyre in the road blocking their path and Sherman gets out to move it. Two men approach him asking if he needs help. Sherman panics, he hurls the tyre at one of them and gets back in the car. Maria reverses and 'thok', one of the men disappears under the back of her car, beneath the wheels. They drive away quickly, away from the man lying in the road, away from the scene of the crime. A simple case of hit and run.

1 Write down all the emotions that you think Sherman must be feeling as they drive away from the Bronx.

2 How do you think these emotions will affect what he does next (whether he goes to the police, whether he tells his wife, whether he keeps quiet)?

3 Which of these feelings do you think would be helpful in deciding what he ought to do; which are unhelpful? Why?

4. Creative thinking: multiplying your options

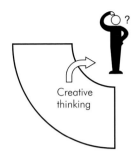

Creative
thinking

Can't you see
Life's easy
When you consider things
From another point of view.[225]

D. B. Boulevard, *Point of View*

Sometimes we face moral dilemmas where there seem to be only two or three options open to us, each of which compromises our moral integrity, or each is something that feels like the wrong thing to do. For example, in the case of a young teenager who is pregnant, she may feel (and may be advised by friends) that if she has the baby then she will not be able to flourish, nor will she be able to provide the baby with an environment in which it will flourish; yet on the other hand she may also feel that she cannot kill the foetus. The issue is, are these two options the only possibilities or is she, or are we, missing something? One of the best ways of generating more options is to apply some of the techniques of creative thinking to a dilemma.

Creative thinking is a way of thinking that enables us to generate new ideas, approaches and solutions. At the centre of creative thinking is the 'fundamental principle that to get a different result you need to do something different'.[226] However, creative thinking is not the same as creativity. Someone painting a picture is doing something creative (in the sense that a new object is being formed – the painting), although they may not be doing it in a creative way. It is only if they paint it differently from the norm (for example, using an unusual pigment, or a different form of application, or a new type of subject matter) that they are applying creative thinking to the task.

When we are confronted with a moral dilemma we may feel as though we are caught in a trap. The metaphor of a lobster that's been caught is a useful one here: to a lobster, once it has climbed into the trap there is no way out – it just doesn't have the capacity to think to itself 'well, I must have got in here, so why don't I just escape the same way?' Because of the limitations of its behaviour and representation of the world, the lobster *is* trapped (Figure 4.7). However, if the lobster could somehow free up its way of thinking then it might be able to escape.

When we face a moral dilemma sometimes we can't see the way out either, because of our limitations. So how might we use creative thinking to get out of the trap, and to reframe our moral dilemma? Like the lobster, we might not be able to see the full range of options available because we are 'set' in

■ **Figure 4.7 The lobster pot is only a trap because of a lobster's limitations**

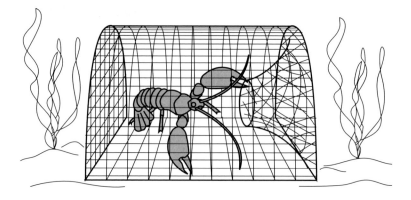

our beliefs. This 'set' refers to our habitual ways of looking and thinking about the world, which prevents us from seeing things a different way. The job of creative thinking is to break this set to help find our way out of the trap. So how do we break 'set', and so make possible other ways of looking at the problem? How, in other words, can we multiply our options? Here are some suggestions:[227]

- Asking around is a simple way to start – other people have different sets and their perspective (worn and familiar to them) may throw new light onto our dilemma.
- Brainstorming – use a group to write down as many ideas as possible, however bizarre or odd, without censorship or criticism.
- Edward DeBono suggests random association: go to a dictionary, flick open a page, choose a word at random, and see how that word might be connected to the dilemma you are in.
- Thinking 'What if … ': Here you select an absurd idea with a view to pushing your mind in new directions; this might mean coming up with absurd solutions that you then make practical or applicable to this case.
- Problem-shifting: this means attending to the problem as it stands, rather than the options open to you. Sometimes this may mean identifying what caused the problem and working preventatively on that, so that it doesn't occur again.
- Turning the problem into an opportunity: again this is difficult for us, as we may be inclined to view the dilemma as a problem. But perhaps it isn't such a problem, perhaps the narrow options available are advantageous in some way, perhaps one option will result in important long-term benefits.

There are many more ways of multiplying options, but these should be enough to break our set ways of thinking. That is the fundamental goal here: to consider things from another point of view. The important thing is to experiment with these methods without worrying about absurd solutions, because once you have a dozen or so absurd solutions you may find that one of them opens the door to another more practical solution, one that hadn't occurred to you before. So, as a final activity, try your hand at multiplying options by revisiting the four moral dilemmas described above.[228]

Re-read dilemmas 1, 2, 3 and 4 from the activities above. The situations as presented appear to give you only a narrow range of options:

Dilemma 1. Steal the drugs or let your wife die.

Dilemma 2. Shoot one prisoner yourself, or allow all twenty to be executed.

Dilemma 3. Cut yourself loose from the violinist (who will then die) or support him for nine months.

Dilemma 4. Inform the police about the accident and see your life destroyed, or keep quiet about it (thus avoiding scandal and imprisonment).

A) Take the following methods of creative thinking and apply to each of the dilemmas in turn. Try to generate as many ideas as possible.

   1 Asking around – read out the dilemmas to friends and family and see what they come up with, what they would try to do.

   2 Random association – flick open a dictionary, choose the first word that leaps out at you. Try to make a connection between that word and the dilemma. Now see if that connection twists the dilemma in any way so that new solutions are suggested.

   3 Ask yourself 'What if …?' and see how this changes the situation. For example, in dilemma 1, you could consider what if … a) Heinz wanted his wife to die, or b) the druggist accepted things other than money, or c) the newspapers found out about Heinz's terrible situation, or d) the drug hadn't had any clinical trials?

   4 Can the problem be turned into an opportunity – what might be the long-term benefits of each course of action?

B) Now that you have a list of ideas, is there any that provides options which satisfy more of our moral values than the two options stated?

Key points: Chapter 4

What you need to know about **practical ethics**:

1 Practical ethics deals with real-life moral problems and decisions. It examines how ethical theories can be applied to genuine issues of moral concern. The three such issues we discuss here (abortion, euthanasia, animal rights) all deal with the ethics of killing. So why is killing regarded as morally wrong? And why is the killing of human beings normally seen as morally worse than killing other animals?

2 The utilitarian answer to the first question is relatively straightforward: killing any sentient creature is wrong because it prevents it from enjoying further pleasure. However, to explain why it is worse to kill a human is more difficult since it is not clear that other animals enjoy life less than we do. Two indirect reasons may be that the loved ones of humans suffer more than the companions of other animals when one of them dies, and humans suffer more from knowing they are going to die. Preference utilitarians answer the second question by pointing out that human beings have a greater number of preferences than other animals. Moreover, they can recognise that death will deprive them of realising their preferences and so their primary preference is to stay alive. Other animals are incapable of explicitly recognising such a preference. However, answering the first question from this perspective is more difficult since if animals don't have a preference for life it would seem their lives can have no value.

3 Rights-based theories may stress the importance of a creature's ability to consider its future states and claim that a right to life depends upon having a concept of one's future state and of death. Since animals other than humans, as well as foetuses, don't have such a concept it is permissible to kill them, so long as it is painless. For Kant, killing a person is the *worst* violation of their autonomy, because choosing life is the fundamental choice of an autonomous agent. It is fundamental because it underlies all other choices and by choosing life I choose to have choices. But killing a non-autonomous creature is not so bad because they have not chosen to remain living. Animals, he claims, exist merely as a means to man's ends.

4 The approach of virtue theorists to moral dilemmas is different from that of consequentialists or deontologists. Virtue ethics does not provide us with a formula. Instead it requires us to embark on a programme of 'moral education' – of training ourselves to do the right thing, through painful experience, and through observing those wiser than us and learning from them. To the virtue

ethicist each situation we face is different, and we must discern what the right thing to do is, basing our decision on the many virtues that may be required in the situation (helping others, preventing harm, telling the truth, etc.) When it comes to judging others we should judge what they did within the light of their character as a whole, and whether it fits in with their character, or whether there were special circumstances that led them to act out of character.

5 Issue 1: abortion. The core of the argument against abortion is that it is wrong to kill an innocent human being, and a human embryo is an innocent human being. However, while an embryo clearly is human, it can be questioned whether it has the same moral status as human persons. So a central point of contention has been over the point in its development when the embryo becomes a person. Definitions of personhood have traditionally involved characteristics such as self-consciousness, concern with one's future states, rationality, and being an autonomous centre for sensations, emotions and volitions. However, many such definitions will also exclude new-born infants and this means either that we should permit infanticide, or that any animal with as much conscious life as a neonate should have the same moral status as human persons. Because the evolution of embryo to person is a gradual one, all attempts to fix a particular point as morally significant can appear somewhat arbitrary. However, the examination of when a foetus becomes a person is only part of the debate. For even if an embryo or foetus *is* regarded as a person, we may still not regard abortion as a case of wrongful killing as it can be argued that the mother's moral right to choose whether or not to bear the child should be paramount.

6 Issue 2: euthanasia. There are several conceptual distinctions made in the debate over the moral permissibility of euthanasia. *Voluntary euthanasia* is where the patient gives consent to being killed; *involuntary euthanasia* is where the patient does not give consent; and *non-voluntary euthanasia* is where the patient is incapable of giving consent. *Active euthanasia* involves acting to bring about someone's death, while *passive euthanasia* means withholding life-sustaining treatment and allowing someone to die. It is often argued that, while *ordinary means* of treatment with a reasonable chance of prolonging life are morally obligatory, there will come a point where *extraordinary means* with very little chance of prolonging life should not be undertaken because such treatment is *disproportionate* to the expected benefits. The *principle of*

double effect states that it is sometimes morally acceptable to perform a good act which will bring about bad consequences, but that it is always wrong to perform a bad act for the sake of good consequences. So it may be permissible to cause someone's death, so long as one's direct intentions are honourable.

7 Issue 3: animal rights. Concerns over the moral acceptability of our treatment of animals centre on whether we should use them for food and clothing, or perform experiments on them. The main issue is whether it is morally acceptable to treat non-human animals differently from humans, or whether the prevailing attitude today is to be condemned as 'speciesist'. If we are to treat animals differently we will need a principled way of distinguishing humans from other animals. If animals lack rationality, self-consciousness, autonomy, the capacity for free choice, an interest in their future states and so forth, then it may be argued that we may use them as means to our own ends. On the other hand, it can be argued that any differences between us and the rest of the animal kingdom are inevitably a matter of degree and not kind, and so animals should be accorded some degree of moral concern.

8 Moral philosophy is supposed to throw light on three important questions: what should I do? What should we do? And what sort of person should I be? But it is also supposed to help us answer these questions in terms that are relevant to our own lives. The ancient Greeks stressed the importance of the virtue of *phronesis*, practical wisdom, in helping us answer these questions. Developing the skills of practical wisdom can help us to become better moral decision-makers. These skills include: 1) understanding the values at stake in a situation, and being able to judge which have priority; 2) critical thinking, being clear about the reasons for a judgement, and about the facts of the matter, avoiding inconsistency and fallacious argument; 3) harnessing your emotions, so that they are not completely ignored, but nor do they flood your judgement; 4) creative thinking in dilemmas and other situations where the options seem limited, the goal being to multiply those options and offer an alternative way out.

Glossary

AGENT/AGENCY   A being who is capable of action. Agency and action are typically restricted to human beings, because human beings have the capacity to reason, make a choice between two courses of action, then do what they've chosen.

ANTI-REALISM   See **realism and anti-realism**.

APPLIED ETHICS   See **practical ethics**.

A PRIORI   A Latin term that usually describes a belief (or knowledge) that is known prior to or independently from experience. *A priori* beliefs are contrasted with *a posteriori* beliefs, which are ones derived from experience.

ARGUMENT   An argument is a series of propositions intended to support a conclusion. The propositions offered in support of the conclusion are termed **premises**.

AUTONOMY   (From the Greek *auto* – self, and *nomos* – law) An agent has autonomy insofar as it is rational and free. For Kant, moral autonomy was only achieved through following the categorical **imperative**.

AUTONOMY OF ETHICS   See **is/ought gap**.

CATEGORICAL IMPERATIVE   See **imperative**.

COGNITIVISM AND NON-COGNITIVISM
Cognitivism in ethics is the view that moral **judgements** are **propositions** which can be known – they refer to the world and they have a **truth-value** (they are capable of being true or false). Non-cognitivism is the view that moral judgements cannot be known, because they do not say anything true or false about the world (they do not have a truth-value). There are many different forms of non-cognitivism such as **emotivism**, **prescriptivism** and **nihilism**. See also **realism and anti-realism**.

CONCLUSION   A belief or statement that an **argument** tries to prove. If an argument is sound or valid and all of the **premises** are true, then the conclusion will also be true.

CONSEQUENTIALIST ETHICS   A type of normative moral theory which views the moral value of an action to lie in its consequences. So an action is judged to be good if it brings about beneficial consequences, and bad if it brings about harmful ones. This is in contrast to **deontology**. **Egoism** and **utilitarianism** are two examples of consequentialism.

DEONTOLOGICAL ETHICS   A type of normative moral theory which views the moral value of an action to lie in the action itself. So an action is right or wrong in itself, whatever the consequences. Generally deontologists (such as Kant) propose certain rules or principles that guide us as to which actions are right and which are wrong. This is in contrast to consequentialism. **Divine command ethics** and **Kantian ethics** are two examples of deontological theories.

DESCRIPTIVE   See **prescriptive and descriptive**.

DILEMMA   See **moral dilemma**.

DISPOSITION   Our tendency to behave in certain ways, our character traits. This term is used by virtue ethicists, who believe we ought to develop virtuous dispositions.

DIVINE COMMAND ETHICS   A type of deontological ethical theory, which views that the moral value of an action is determined by the commands of God. So an action is right if it follows one of God's commands.

DOUBLE EFFECT   The principle of double effect is one which accepts that there are side-effects of action, and that we should judge the original intention of the action, rather than these side-effects. People who are against abortion might not judge as wrong an abortion which results as a side-effect of the efforts to save the mother's life.

DUTY   An action which we are required or impelled to carry out. Kant's deontological theory places duty at its centre. For Kant, duties are experienced as **imperatives**. See also *prima facie* **duties**.

EGOISM   The view that our actions are

essentially self-interested. Psychological egoism claims that it is a matter of fact that humans are motivated solely by self-interest. Ethical egoism goes a stage further and claims that we ought to do whatever is in our self-interest.

EMOTIVISM/EMOTIVIST   A non-cognitivist theory of the meaning of moral terms and judgements. In its basic form emotivism claims that moral judgements do not refer to anything in the world, but are expressions of feelings of approval or disapproval.

EMPIRICISM/EMPIRICIST   The claim that our beliefs and knowledge must be based on experience.

ETHICAL EGOISM/EGOISTS   See **egoism**.

EUDAIMONIA   According to many Ancient Greek philosophers *eudaimonia* is the goal or 'good' we are all striving for. Sometimes translated as 'happiness', it is probably closer in meaning to 'flourishing'. Aristotle's virtue ethics is centred around *eudaimonia*.

FALLACY   This refers to an **argument** which has gone wrong, either because a mistake has been made, rendering the argument invalid; or because the argument has a form, or structure, which is always invalid (see also the **naturalistic fallacy**).

GOOD   Actions are good according to whether they bring about certain positive outcomes – these may be pleasure or happiness, or something more intangible (Moore believed that love of friendship and beauty were goods). Consequentialists believe that moral value lies in the good (or bad) consequences of an action. But 'good' also has a functional meaning, in the sense that 'good' means 'fulfilling your function well'. Aristotle believed that we had a function and hence could be good in both senses: by being good (fulfilling our function) we could reach the good (*eudaimonia*).

GOLDEN RULE   Versions of this rule have been proposed at various points within religion and moral philosophy (e.g. by Confucius, Jesus, Hobbes and Kant). The basic idea is that we should be impartial, and not afford ourselves special treatment: we should treat others as we should like to be treated. See also **universalisability**.

HEDONISM/HEDONISTIC   The claim that pleasure is the **good**. Many utilitarians are hedonists, in that they believe we ought to try to maximise pleasure (for the majority).

HUME'S LAW   See **is/ought gap**.

HYPOTHETICAL IMPERATIVE   See **imperative**.

IMPERATIVE   In **Kantian ethics** we experience our duties as commands (imperatives) which are categorical, or absolute. These categorical imperatives are commands that we are obliged to follow no matter what, and according to Kant only these are moral imperatives. As rational agents we can work out the categorical imperative by asking whether the maxim that lies behind our action is universalisable. Other imperatives, things we should do in order to achieve some goal, are conditional or hypothetical imperatives, and they are not moral according to Kant.

INTUITIONISM/INTUITIONIST   A realist theory which claims that we can determine what is right or good according to our moral intuitions. For intuitionists, the terms 'right' and 'good' do refer to something objective, but they cannot be reduced to naturalistic terms.

IS/OUGHT GAP   Hume argued that we cannot draw a conclusion which is evaluative (containing 'ought') from **premises** which are purely factual or descriptive. To some philosophers this indicated the autonomy of ethics, i.e. that the ethical realm was entirely distinct from other, factual or naturalistic, realms.

JUDGEMENT   A moral judgement is a decision made (in advance or retrospectively) about the rightness or goodness of a course of action (our own or someone else's) or, for virtue theorists, of someone's character.

KANTIAN ETHICS   A **deontological** ethical theory developed by Kant or influenced by Kant. At the heart of Kantian ethics is the claim that we can determine what is right, and what our duties are, through the categorical **imperative**.

META-ETHICS   Sometimes called 'second-order ethics', this is the study by moral philosophers of the meaning of moral **judgements**. This covers issues such as **realism/anti-realism**, **cognitivism/non-cognitivism**, the **is/ought gap**, the **naturalistic fallacy**, and the objectivity/subjectivity of moral judgements.

MORAL DILEMMA   Any situation that an agent faces where there is a difficulty choosing between two or more courses of action. This difficulty arises when there are moral reasons for both choosing and not choosing a course of action. It also arises when there are moral reasons against all courses of action, but where a choice has to be made.

MORAL SENSE THEORY An early form of **intuitionism**, this type of **normative** theory was prevalent in the eighteenth and nineteenth centuries, and claimed that a special moral sense that we possessed enabled us to identify **good** or **right** actions.

NATURALISM The view that we can explain moral concepts, such as **good**, in naturalistic terms, such as happiness or pleasure.

NATURALISTIC FALLACY G. E. Moore attacked naturalism because he claimed that it committed a **fallacy**, namely of trying to define the indefinable. Moore believed that moral terms such as **good** could not be defined (he held they were non-natural), and that naturalists tried to define them in naturalistic terms. He particularly singled out the utilitarians in his attack.

NIHILISM/NIHILIST This term has come to refer to the rejection of morality (at least in its conventional form). Some philosophers who have been termed nihilist (for example, Nietzsche and the existentialists) have urged that we replace conventional morality with another type of morality.

NON-COGNITIVISM See **cognitivism and non-cognitivism**.

NORMATIVE ETHICS Sometimes called 'first-order ethics', this term covers moral theories that offer action-guides. These are rules, principles or standards by which we make moral **judgements**, and according to which our conduct is directed. There are three general forms of normative theory: **deontological**, **consequentialist** and **virtue ethics**.

ONTOLOGICAL Ontology is the study of 'being' or 'existence'. If you have an ontological commitment to something then you believe that it exists independently of you (for example, some moral realists have an ontological commitment to moral values).

PERSON In ordinary language this refers to human beings, but recently some philosophers have asked what is special about persons and whether a) all human beings are persons and b) some non-human beings might count as persons. The sorts of qualities that characterise persons might include **agency**, **autonomy**, rationality, self-consciousness, etc.

PRACTICAL ETHICS Like **normative ethics** this is also a type of 'first-order' theory. It looks at the application of ethical theories to concrete situations and **moral dilemmas** that people face, such as abortion, euthanasia and the treatment of animals.

PREMISE Any reason given (usually in the form of a statement or claim) to build or support an **argument**.

PRESCRIPTIVE AND DESCRIPTIVE A prescriptive statement is one that guides action, it tells us what to do. A descriptive statement, on the other hand, simply tells us the way things are.

PRESCRIPTIVISM A non-cognitivist view of the meaning of moral terms and **judgements**. Like **emotivists**, prescriptivists believe that moral language has a special use, but they believe that the purpose of moral judgements is to prescribe actions, in other words to urge others to act in a certain way.

PRIMA FACIE A Latin term meaning 'at first sight' or 'as things first appear'.

PRIMA FACIE DUTIES A term used by W. D. Ross to describe the 'rough and ready' obligations that we know that we have in advance of any particular situation (such as the obligation to be honest, keep promises, not harm others). Sometimes we face dilemmas where our *prima facie* duties clash, and we have to decide what our actual duties are in these circumstances, i.e. which **duty** has the stronger claim over us.

PROPOSITION A proposition is a sentence that makes a claim about the way the world actually is. Non-cognitivists such as the **emotivists** claim that moral **judgements** are not propositions, in other words they are not making claims about the world and are neither true nor false.

RATIONALISM/RATIONALIST The claim that our beliefs and knowledge are properly based on reason (and not, for example, on sensory experience as the **empiricists** claim).

REALISM AND ANTI-REALISM Moral realists believe that in some sense moral terms refer to something real, for example pleasure, or happiness, or utility, or the moral law or God's command. So, from a realist position, morality is discovered. Moral anti-realists believe that moral terms do not refer to anything real, but are something else entirely – for example, expressions of feelings (**emotivism**), prescriptions to other people (**prescriptivism**) or they refer to nothing at all (**nihilism**). See also **cognitivism and non-cognitivism**.

RELATIVISM   Moral relativism is the view that moral **judgements** vary according to (are relative to) the social context in which they are made. So moral values or standards of conduct are different in different society: what is right for you may not be right for me etc.

RIGHT   Actions are right according to whether they ought to be done, irrespective of the particular situation, or the consequences that result from a course of action. Deontological theorists believe that moral value lies solely in what is right (rather than in what is **good**) and that we have obligations or duties to do what is right. However, consequentialist theorists are quite happy to redefine 'right' to mean 'actions that bring about the good'.

RIGHTS   A right is an entitlement that I have to the protection of certain powers, interests or privileges. It is debatable whether we can have rights only because we make a contract within society, or whether we have 'natural rights' which exist independently of any contract. Rights may be seen as the converse of duties; thus if I have a right to X then you have a duty to promote X or at least not interfere in my access to X.

SYMPATHY   Hume believed that we could give a psychological account of morality, through understanding moral **judgements** in terms of the feelings that certain actions or characteristics arouse in us. It is through sympathy (in modern terms, empathy) that we feel the pains and pleasures of others and that we then judge others as virtuous or vicious.

TELEOLOGICAL   Purpose, goal or end, deriving from the Greek word *telos*. A teleological ethical theory is one that says we should be striving to achieve certain moral goals – for Aristotelians this would be virtue, for utilitarians the goal would be happiness. See also **consequentialism**.

TRUTH-VALUE   The truth or falsity of a **proposition**. Only propositions can have truth-value. Some philosophers (cognitivists) claim that moral judgements are propositions, but other philosophers (non-cognitivists) claim that moral judgements are not propositions and hence do not have a truth-value.

UNIVERSALISABILITY   A fundamental feature of most ethical theories, and a version of the **golden rule**. A principle is universalisable if it is applied to all people equally and in the same way. Some philosophers (including prescriptivists) have seen this as part of the very meaning of a moral **judgement** – it applies to everyone in the same situation. Consequentialists (Bentham and Mill), deontologists (Kant) and even existentialists (Sartre) have all appealed to universalisability at some point in their theories. For Kantians, the principle of universalisability has to be a more rigorous version of the golden rule: it says that we should only act on those rules which we can will to be universal laws (i.e. without contradiction or inconsistency).

UTILITARIANISM   A consequentialist moral theory, perhaps inspired by Hume (although he is closer to **virtue ethics**) and developed first by Bentham and then by Mill and Sidgwick. In most of its forms it is a **hedonistic** theory claiming that what is **good** (i.e. what we ought to strive to bring about) is as much pleasure or happiness as possible for the majority of people. In its negative forms it says we ought to strive to reduce pain or harm to the majority of people.

UTILITY   Welfare or use for the majority of people. For Bentham and Mill, utility came to mean 'pleasure' or 'happiness'.

VIRTUE   A character trait or **disposition** which is to be valued (for the Ancient Greeks, it is a disposition which is excellent). Common virtues include wisdom, courage, self-control, honesty, generosity, compassion, kindness.

VIRTUE ETHICS   A normative ethical theory which locates value not in an action or its consequences, but in the agent performing the act. Virtue ethicists stress the need to develop virtuous **dispositions**, and to judge actions within the broader context of what someone is inclined to do. So a person may be judged to be virtuous or vicious through noting how they are disposed to act. Frustratingly, for many people, virtue ethicists fail to give us a formula (unlike consequentialists and deontologists) that guides us in what we ought to do in any particular situation.

Notes

1 George Orwell, *1984*, Penguin 1984, pp. 230–231.
2 Plato, *The Republic*, 352d, Penguin 1987, p. 98.
3 William Golding, *The Lord of the Flies*, Faber and Faber 1954, pp. 31–32.
4 Aristotle, *Politics*, 1253a, Penguin 1992, p. 59.
5 John Donne, *Devotions upon Emergent Occasions* XVII, in *John Donne: Selections from Divine Poems, Sermons, Devotions, and Prayers*, Paulist Press 1990, p. 272.
6 Aristotle, *Ethics*, 1094b5, Penguin 1988, p. 64.
7 Jim Thompson, *Pop 1280*, Vintage 1990, pp. 64–65.
8 The Greek word *ethica* (from which our word 'ethics' derives) means 'character', meaning the kind of person I am.
9 A recent exception to this convention is Bernard Williams, who uses the term 'morality' in a technical sense, to refer to a particularly modern system of moral obligations – a system that, for example, the Ancient Greeks did not have. See Williams, *Ethics and the Limits of Philosophy*, Fontana 1985, Ch. 10. For a critique of Williams' claim see Julia Annas, 'Ancient ethics and modern morality' in James Sterba (ed.), *Ethics: The Big Questions*, Blackwell 2004, pp. 305–315.
10 Homer, *The Iliad*, opening paragraphs of Book 24, Penguin 1987, pp. 393–394. For further discussion of the issues this passage raises in terms of our understanding of Ancient Greek ethics, see J. O. Urmson, *Aristotle's Ethics*, Blackwell 1991, pp. 1–2.
11 Alasdair MacIntyre, *A Short History of Ethics*, Routledge 1967, pp. 10–11.
12 For more on the Sophists see Chapter 6 of Edward Hussey, *The Pre-Socratics*, Duckworth 1972.
13 Anthony Burgess, *A Clockwork Orange*, Penguin 1972, pp. 99–100.
14 William Rowe, 'The Problem of Evil and some varieties of atheism' in Charles Taliaferro and Paul Griffiths (eds), *Philosophy of Religion*, pp. 368–373.
15 G. Jones, D. Cardinal and J. Hayward, *Philosophy of Religion*, Hodder Murray 2005, pp. 114–132.
16 Thomas Nagel argued that part of our conception of ourselves as agents is to see ourselves as existing over time – as having 'future selves'. Thomas Nagel, *The Possibility of Altruism*, Oxford University Press 1970.
17 Adam Morton, *Philosophy in Practice*, Blackwell 1998, p. 120.
18 For a book about someone obsessed by making judgements about the minutiae of everyday life, such as choosing a checkout queue or a pair of shoelaces, read the brilliant little novel *The Mezzanine* by Nicholson Baker (Granta 1998).
19 Woody Allen, 'The condemned' in *The Complete Prose*, Picador 1997, pp. 309–310.
20 For more on the distinction between act-centred and agent-centred ethics see Julia Annas, *An Introduction to Plato's Republic*, Oxford University Press 1981, pp. 157–158.
21 C. D. Broad proposed this distinction between deontological and teleological ethical theories in *Five Types of Ethical Theory* in 1930, and many philosophers have found it a useful distinction, for example John Rawls, *A Theory of Justice*, Oxford University Press 1971, pp. 24–30.
22 Some forms of virtue ethics, most notably Aristotle's and Aquinas', can also be described as teleological because they claim that the virtues we should be striving to develop are determined by our function or our purpose – i.e. by our *telos*.
23 From the film *Do The Right Thing*, directed by Spike Lee, 1989.
24 The Bible, Exodus 20: 3–17. For a modern response to these commandments see the ten brilliant short films by Krzysztof Kiesloswki entitled *Decalogue* (1989).
25 http://www.un.org/Overview/rights.html
26 Bentham wrote that 'Natural Rights is simple nonsense; natural and imprescriptible [Absolute] rights – nonsense on stilts.'

Jeremy Bentham, 'Anarchical fallacies' in *Collected Works* II, W. Tait 1843, p. 501.

27 The Bible, Genesis 22: 1–3.

28 Plato, *Euthyphro* 10a ff, in *Last Days of Socrates*, Penguin 1981, p. 31.

29 John Stuart Mill, *Examination of Sir William Hamilton's Philosophy, Collected Works*, volume 9, ed. J. M. Robinson, Toronto University Press 1979, p. 103.

30 Plato, *Euthyphro* 7E, p. 28.

31 For a more detailed discussion of the Problem of Evil see Jones, Cardinal and Hayward, *Philosophy of Religion*, pp. 114–132.

32 For two attempts to apply the commandments of the Bible to biomedical issues see Norman Geisler, *Christian Ethics: Options and Issues*, Apollos 1989, and John Stott, *Issues Facing Christians Today*, Harper Collins 1990.

33 Immanuel Kant, *Critique of Practical Reason*, trans. T. K. Abbott, Longman 1873, p. 260.

34 Immanuel Kant, *Groundwork of the Metaphysic of Morals*, in H. J. Paton (trans.), *The Moral Law*, Hutchinson 1972, p. 78.

35 Heinrich Hoffman, *Struwwelpeter or Pretty Stories and Funny Pictures*, Belitha Press 1997.

36 Kant, in Paton, *The Moral Law*, p. 65.

37 Ibid. p. 66.

38 From the film *This is Spinal Tap*, directed by Rob Reiner, 1983.

39 Kant, *Foundations of the Metaphysics of Morals*, trans. L. W. Beck, in Johnson, *Ethics*, Harcourt Brace College 1994, p. 198.

40 For example see the Bible, Matthew 7:12 and Luke 6:31. Another version of the golden rule can be found in the writings of K'ung-fu-tzu (Confucius) 'What you do not like when done to yourself do not do to others' in *Analacts* Book 15:3.

41 Kant, *Foundations of the Metaphysics of Morals*, in Johnson, *Ethics*, p. 190.

42 Kant, in Paton, *The Moral Law*, pp. 85–86.

43 Ibid. p. 95.

44 See Plato, *The Republic*, 331c, Penguin 1987, p. 66, and Kant's essay 'On a supposed right to lie from altruistic motives', extract in Christine Korsgaard, 'Kant on dealing with evil', in James Sterba (ed.), *Ethics: The Big Questions*, Blackwell 2004, p. 199.

45 Bernard Williams, *Ethics and the Limits of Philosophy*, Fontana 1985, pp. 66–69.

46 From the film *Dr Strangelove: or How I Learned to Stop Worrying and Love the Bomb*, directed by Stanley Kubrick, 1964.

47 Plato, *Gorgias* 492c, Clarendon Press 1995, p. 66.

48 Thomas Hobbes, *Leviathan, English Works* 3, p. 113.

49 Ian McEwan, *Enduring Love*, Vintage 1998, pp. 14–15.

50 For more on the rationality of each course of action see R. M. Sainsbury, *Paradoxes*, Cambridge University Press 1995, pp. 66–69.

51 See, for example, Richard Dawkins, *The Selfish Gene*, Oxford University Press 1999, pp. 228–233.

52 Joseph Heller, *Catch-22*, Vintage 1994, p. 561.

53 Jean-Paul Sartre, *Existentialism and Humanism*, Methuen 1987, pp. 35–38.

54 See Jones, Hayward and Cardinal, *Existentialism and Humanism: Jean-Paul Sartre*, Hodder Murray 2003, pp. 63–67.

55 Aldous Huxley, *Brave New World*, Penguin 1959, p. 66.

56 Jeremy Bentham, *Introduction to the Principles of Morals and Legislation*, in John Stuart Mill, *Utilitarianism*, ed. Mary Warnock, Fontana 1985, p. 33.

57 Ibid. p. 34.

58 Jeremy Bentham, *Introduction to the Principles of Morals and Legislation*, in *Collected Works*, Hafner 1946, pp. 310–311.

59 Quoted by Mill in *Utilitarianism*, p. 79.

60 Jonathan Swift, *A Modest Proposal*, Dover 1996, p. 53.

61 Fyodor Dostoyevsky, *Crime and Punishment*, Oxford University Press 1995, p. 354.

62 Mill, *Utilitarianism*, p. 257.

63 Ibid. p. 257.

64 Ibid. p. 260.

65 Ibid. pp. 254–255.

66 Ibid. p. 288.

67 Ibid. pp. 288–289.

68 G. E. Moore, *Principia Ethica*, Cambridge University Press 1986, p. 67.

69 Mill, *Utilitarianism*, p. 255.

70 David Hume, *Treatise of Human Nature*, Book III, Part I, Section 1 (III.1.1), ed. L. A. Selby Bigge, Oxford University Press 1955, p. 469.

71 John Stuart Mill, *System of Logic*, quoted in W. D Hudson, *Modern Moral Philosophy*, second edition, Macmillan 1983, pp. 75–76.

72 Ibid. pp. 76–79.

73 Moore, *Principia Ethica*, p. 10.

74 Mill, *Utilitarianism*, p. 26.

75 *The Letters of John Stuart Mill*. See F. H. Bradley, *Ethical Studies*, second edition, Oxford University Press 1977, p. 113.

76 Henry Sidgwick, *Methods of Ethics*, in *Consequentialism*, ed. Stephen Darwell, Blackwell 2003, p. 72.

77 Bertrand Russell and Father F. C. Copleston, 'The existence of God – a debate' in *Why I am Not a Christian*, Routledge 1996, p. 140.

78 Mill, *Utilitarianism*, p. 276.

79 John Stuart Mill, *On Liberty*, ed. Mary Warnock, Fontana 1985, p. 209.

80 The case for treating Mill as a rule utilitarian is strongly put by J. O. Urmson, 'The moral philosophy of J. S. Mill' in Philippa Foot (ed.), *Theories of Ethics*, Oxford University Press 1970, pp. 128–136.

81 Joe Simpson, *Touching the Void*, Vintage 1997, pp. 94–106. In one of the most incredible escape stories ever, Joe, despite his broken leg, eventually found a way to climb out of the crevasse and crawled down the mountain to base camp to be reunited with Simon.

82 See, for example, Aristotle, *Ethics* 1175b22, p. 324.

83 Jean-Paul Sartre, *The Wall and other Stories*, New Directions 1969.

84 Mill, *Utilitarianism*, p. 275.

85 Aristotle, *Ethics*, 1095b16, p. 68.

86 Samuel Coleridge, 'Kubla Khan' in J. Hayward (ed.), *The Penguin Book of English Verse*, Penguin 1982, p. 255.

87 See Robert Nozick, *Anarchy, State and Utopia*, Chapter 3, Basic Books 1977. For a brief, lively discussion of this machine, see Julian Baggini, *The Pig that Wants to be Eaten*, Granta 2005, pp. 292–294.

88 Plato, *Gorgias*, 493e–494a, p. 68.

89 Ibid. 493c, p. 67.

90 Ibid. 494d, p. 68.

91 The term 'ideal utilitarian' was coined by Hastings Rashdall to describe his own non-hedonistic, multi-valued version of utilitarianism – *The Theory of Good and Evil*, Clarendon Press 1907.

92 Moore, *Principia Ethica*, p. 183.

93 Peter Singer, *Practical Ethics*, Cambridge Universiy Press 1979.

94 In *On Liberty*, John Stuart Mill proposed the principle that individuals should be free to pursue whatever goals they wanted to so long as the pursuit didn't harm anyone. See *Utilitarianism*, p. 135.

95 The opening lines from the labyrinthine gangster film *Miller's Crossing*, directed by Joel Coen, 1990.

96 Julia Annas, 'Ancient ethics and modern morality' in James Sterba (ed.), *Ethics: The Big Questions*, Blackwell 2004, pp. 311–312.

97 Aristotle, *Ethics*, 1102a17, p. 88.

98 Plato, *The Republic*, 434e–441c, pp. 208–217.

99 Plato, *Phaedrus*, 253d, Oxford University Press 2002, p. 38.

100 Aristotle, *Ethics*, 1102a30–1103a10, pp. 88–90.

101 Plato, *The Republic*, 441d, p. 218.

102 Ibid. 442b, p. 219.

103 See, for example, Aristotle, *Ethics*, 1106a22–1106b33, pp. 100–101.

104 Aristotle, *Ethics*, 1098a15, p. 76.

105 Ibid. 1096a10 ff, pp. 69–72.

106 David Hume, *An Enquiry Concerning the Principles of Morals*, ed. Tom Beauchamp, Oxford University Press 1998, p. 83.

107 Hume, *Treatise of Human Nature*, II.3.3, p. 415.

108 Ibid. II.3.3, p. 416.

109 Although perhaps we shouldn't expect so much of moral philosophers, as Nicholson Baker writes 'you can be eloquently virtuous in one sphere while tolerant of nastiness, or even nasty yourself, in another', *The Mezzanine*, Granta 1998, p. 121.

110 Hume, *Treatise of Human Nature*, III.1.1, p. 468.

111 Hume, *Enquiry Concerning the Principles of Morals*, p. 114.

112 Choderlos de Laclos, *Dangerous Liaisons*, Penguin 1989, p. 58.

113 Hume, *Enquiry Concerning the Principles of Morals*, p. 156.

114 Ibid. p. 145.

115 Ibid. p. 146.

116 Wallace Matson draws a similar distinction between morality which is common to all humans because we are social animals and morality which is constructed by individual cultures. The former he calls 'low morality' and the latter 'high morality'. See Wallace Matson, 'The expiration of morality' in E. F. Paul, F. D. Miller and J. Paul (eds), *Cultural Pluralism and Moral Knowledge*, Cambridge University Press 1994, pp. 159–178.

117 Hume, *Enquiry Concerning the Principles of Morals*, p. 77.

118 But the twentieth century is not unique. Such has been the frequency of genocide

throughout human history that Jared Diamond identifies genocide as one of the 'hallmarks' of human beings – i.e. what distinguishes us as animals from other animals. Jared Diamond, *The Rise and Fall of the Third Chimpanzee*, Vintage 1992, pp. 250–276.

119 Elizabeth Anscombe, 'Modern moral philosophy', *Philosophy* 33 (1958), pp. 1–19.

120 Bernard Williams agrees that something has gone wrong with moral philosophy, and it is not well adjusted to modern life. But, unlike MacIntyre, he believes a return to the more meaningful ethical approach of the Ancient Greeks simply isn't possible. Bernard Williams, *Ethics and the Limits of Philosophy*, Fontana 1985, p. 197.

121 For more on the discussion of virtue ethics in relation to act-centred ethics see Walter Schaller, 'Are virtues no more than dispositions to obey moral rules?' in James Sterba (ed.), *Ethics: The Big Questions*, Blackwell 2004, pp. 297–303.

122 Aristotle, *Ethics*, 1109a26, p. 109.

123 Ibid. 1094b31, p. 65.

124 Primo Levi, *If This Is A Man*, Abacus 1987, p. 92.

125 Ibid. p. 177.

126 In philosophy the prefix 'meta' has come to mean something like 'beyond' or 'at a more abstract level'. This is quite odd because 'meta' in ancient Greek in fact means 'after'. The story goes that in the first century BC Andronicus of Rhodes was wondering what to name a work by Aristotle in his catalogue. This unnamed work dealt with certain theoretical issues about the fundamental nature of the universe, and it was placed in the catalogue after Aristotle's work on physics. Hence it was called *Metaphysics* (i.e. 'after physics').

127 W. D. Hudson, *Modern Moral Philosophy*, second edition, Macmillan 1983, p. 1.

128 Ibid. Hudson's point reflects remarks that A. J. Ayer made forty years previously in *Language, Truth and Logic*, Penguin 1980, p. 137.

129 It seems as if 'moralist' has long had a derogatory history. Mill praises his predecessor Bentham as a progressive *philosopher*, while criticising Kant by referring to him as a moralist. See Mill, *Utilitarianism*, p. 79 and p. 254.

130 Jonathan Swift, *Gulliver's Travels*, Penguin 1985, pp. 230–231.

131 Another particularly brilliant invention is a huge machine, manually operated, which could write philosophy books by printing out every combination of word that there is. Ibid. pp. 227–229.

132 Another lung-saving device for philosophers was suggested by the novelist Rabelais when he described two philosophers arguing in silence by using only rude gestures and signs. François Rabelais, *The Histories of Gargantua and Pantagruel*, Penguin 1955, p. 231.

133 Hume, *Enquiry Concerning the Principles of Morals*, pp. 73–74.

134 We deal with this topic in great detail in another book in this series: Cardinal, Hayward and Jones, *Epistemology: the Theory of Knowledge*, Hodder Murray 2004, pp. 37–83.

135 Immanuel Kant, *Groundwork of the Metaphysic of Morals*, in Paton, *The Moral Law*, pp. 82–83.

136 Samuel Clarke (1675–1729) is the most famous of these rationalists, while many other names have been lost to history, for example John Balguy (1686–1748) and William Wollaston (1659–1724).

137 Mill, *Utilitarianism*, p. 257.

138 Moore, *Principia Ethica*, pp. 39–40.

139 Hume, *Treatise of Human Nature*, III.1.1, p. 469.

140 J. R. Searle, 'How to derive an ought from an is', in W. D. Hudson (ed.), *The Is/Ought Question*, Macmillan 1969, pp. 120–134.

141 Alasdair MacIntyre, *After Virtue*, Duckworth 1981, p. 54.

142 Mary Warnock, *Ethics Since 1900*, Oxford University Press 1979, p. 132.

143 Moore, *Principia Ethica*, Preface, p. x.

144 Ibid. p. 15.

145 Well, maybe not that absurd. Some philosophers, clearly ones with too much time on their hands, have doubted whether all unmarried men are in fact bachelors. See Terry Winograd's article 'Moving the semantic fulcrum', *Linguistics and Philosophy* 8:1 (1985), pp. 91–104.

146 Moore, *Principia Ethica*, p. 67.

147 Ibid. p. 224.

148 These are the words of the economist J. M. Keynes, as quoted in S. P. Rosenbaum, *The Bloomsbury Group*, Toronto University Press 1975, p. 52.

149 H. A. Prichard, 'Does moral philosophy rest on a mistake?' in *Moral Obligation*, Oxford University Press 1949, p. 8.

150 Prichard, like many of his fellow moral philosophers of that time, puts forward

slightly more gentile examples, such as wondering whether we have a duty to slow down as we approach a main road! For Mary Warnock it was examples such as these that revealed the impoverished and trivialising nature of much meta-ethical philosophy, and its failure to address the real moral issues that confronted humanity in the twentieth century: genocide, starvation, the exploitation of developing nations, the threat of nuclear holocaust. See Warnock, *Ethics since 1900*, pp. 132–133.

151 Hudson, *Modern Moral Philosophy*, p. 91.
152 J. L. Mackie, *Ethics: Inventing Right and Wrong*, Penguin 1977, p. 38.
153 G. J. Warnock, *Contemporary Moral Philosophy*, Macmillan 1970, p16.
154 William Golding, *Lord of the Flies*, Faber and Faber 1958, pp. 98–99.
155 For example, see Charles R. Pidgen, 'Naturalism', in Peter Singer (ed.), *A Companion to Ethics*, Blackwell 1997, p. 423.
156 Hume, *Treatise*, II.3.3, p. 416.
157 Ibid. III.1.1.
158 Ayer, *Language, Truth and Logic*, p. 143.
159 Alasdair MacIntyre, *After Virtue*, p. 16.
160 Ayer, *Language, Truth and Logic*, p. 142.
161 C. K. Ogden and I. A. Richards, *The Meaning of Meaning*, Kegan Paul 1923, p. 125.
162 MacIntyre, *After Virtue*, p. 17.
163 R. M. Hare, *The Language of Morals*, Oxford University Press 1952, p. 168.
164 Although we haven't mentioned him, the ghost of Wittgenstein is present throughout this chapter, as throughout twentieth century philosophy of language. It was Wittgenstein who urged philosophers to turn their attention to the meaning of terms in ordinary language usage. It is only by looking at how terms are used that we will understand their meaning, and Wittgenstein says terms are used in very many different ways. So any theory such as emotivism which claims to have found the 'single' meaning is bound to be oversimplifying the case.
165 See Jones, Hayward and Cardinal, *Existentialism and Humanism: Jean-Paul Sartre*, pp. 104–105.
166 Jared Diamond, *The Rise and Fall of the Third Chimpanzee*, p. 267.
167 Diamond gives a brilliantly lucid account of which cultures these were, and how they happened to become world cultures, in his book *Guns, Germs and Steel*, Vintage 1997.

168 Keith Windschuttle, who has a horror of all things culturally relativist, goes into some detail about the practice of human sacrifice among the indigenous civilisations of Central and South America in *The Killing of History*, Encounter 1996, pp. 62–70.
169 Wallace Matson argues for the existence of fundamental moral values (what he terms 'low morality') in his paper 'The expiration of morality' in Paul, Miller and Paul (eds), *Cultural Pluralism and Moral Knowledge*, pp. 164–166.
170 From the film *The Long Goodbye*, directed by Robert Altman, 1973.
171 Bret Easton Ellis, *Less Than Zero*, Picador 1985, pp. 186–187.
172 Albert Camus, *The Outsider*, Penguin 1983, p. 97.
173 Ibid. p. 118.
174 Sartre, *Existentialism and Humanism*, p. 33. This 'quote' is actually a conflation of two quotes from Fyodor Dostoyevsky's novel *The Brothers Karamazov*, Bantam 1970, p. 80 and p. 381.
175 Sartre, *Existentialism and Humanism*, p. 49.
176 For a detailed analysis of the lecture in which Sartre first outlined his existentialist ethic see Jones, Cardinal and Hayward, *Existentialism and Humanism: Jean-Paul Sartre*.
177 Joseph Campbell, who studied hundreds of myths and stories from around the world, referred to these moments of decision as the 'Call to adventure'. See Joseph Campbell, *The Hero With A Thousand Faces*, Paladin 1988, pp. 49–58.
178 Nicholson Baker, *The Mezzanine*, p. 101.
179 The Bible, Genesis 1:26.
180 Quoted in Singer, *Practical Ethics*, p. 96.
181 Aristotle, *Ethics*, 1105a22, p. 99.
182 Tom Beauchamp and James Childress, *Principles of Biomedical Ethics*, Oxford University Press 1989, p. 376.
183 Fyodor Dostoyevsky, *Crime and Punishment*, p. 73.
184 Simone de Beauvoir, *The Second Sex*, Penguin 1987, p. 508.
185 The current law on abortion is based on: the Abortion Act (1967) and Section 37 of the Human Fertilisation and Embryology Act (1990).
186 John Locke, *Essay Concerning Human Understanding*, Ch. 27, Section 9, Dent 1976, p. 162.
187 Singer, *Practical Ethics*, pp. 169 ff.
188 A zygote is the term used to describe the

cell that results from the fertilisation of the ovum, and the organism that then develops from it.

189 Mary Anne Warren, 'Abortion', in Peter Singer (ed.), *A Companion to Ethics*, Blackwell 1991, p. 311. (For a more detailed discussion of the argument from potential see Singer, *Practical Ethics*, pp. 152 ff.)

190 See Simone de Beauvoir, *The Second Sex*, p. 510.

191 In J. Rachels (ed.), *Moral Problems*, Harper & Row 1979.

192 See Simone de Beauvoir, *The Second Sex*, p. 506.

193 Thomas Keneally, *Schindler's Ark*, Hodder 1983, p. 194.

194 An oath taken by doctors to observe a code of conduct which derives from the Greek physician Hippocrates (c. 460–c. 377BC).

195 See Jonathan Glover, *Causing Deaths and Saving Lives*, Penguin 1988, pp. 92–112.

196 Thomas Aquinas, *Summa Theologica*, II.ii.64.7.

197 Mill, *On Liberty*, in Warnock (ed.), *Utilitarianism*, p. 135.

198 Douglas Adams, *Restaurant at the End of the Universe*, Pan 1980, pp. 92–93.

199 For a discussion of the blurred line between humans and other animals see Diamond, *The Rise and Fall of the Third Chimpanzee*.

200 Singer, *Practical Ethics*, pp. 55–62.

201 Aquinas, *Summa Theologica*, II.ii.64.

202 Immanuel Kant, *Lectures on Ethics*, The Century Co. 1930, p. 239.

203 Tom Regan, 'The case for animal rights', in Rosalind Hursthouse (ed.), *Humans and Other Animals*, Open University Press 1999, pp. 222 ff.

204 Jeremy Bentham, *Introduction to the Principles of Morals and Legislation*, Ch.17n.

205 Singer, *Practical Ethics*, p. 107.

206 Similarly the utilitarian could justify animal experimentation so long as the expected benefits outweighed the suffering caused. But note, as Singer puts it: 'an experiment cannot be justifiable unless the experiment is so important that the use of a retarded human being would also be justifiable.' P. Singer, *Animal Liberation*, Random House 1990.

207 From Lawrence Kohlberg, 'Stage and sequence: The cognitive–developmental approach to socialization' in D. A. Goslin (ed.), *Handbook of Socialization Theory and Research*, Rand McNally 1984, p. 379.

208 See, for example, Beauchamp and Childress, *Principles of Biomedical Ethics*, pp. 4–5.

209 Another type of dilemma arises for ethical

egoists, i.e. those who believe we ought to do whatever benefits ourselves. This is Catch–22, i.e. a lose–lose situation in which whatever we do we suffer. Joseph Heller coined the phrase in his novel *Catch-22*, p. 62.

210 Bernard Williams in conversation with Bryan Magee, *Modern British Philosophers*, Paladin 1973, p. 197.

211 Anthony Weston, *A 21st Century Ethical Toolbox*, Oxford University Press 2001.

212 Aristotle, *Ethics*, 1142a30 ff, pp. 216–223.

213 Thomas Nagel, 'The fragmentation of value', in *Mortal Questions*, Canto 1992, p. 141.

214 Ibid. p. 132.

215 Beauchamp and Childress, *Principles of Biomedical Ethics*, pp. 44–45.

216 Ibid. pp. 380–381.

217 Robert Nozick, 'Moral complications and moral structures', *Natural Law Forum* 13 (1968), pp. 1–50.

218 Adopted from Bernard Williams, 'A critique of utilitarianism' in J. J. C. Smart and Bernard Williams (eds), *Utilitarianism For and Against*, Cambridge University Press 1973.

219 Beauchamp and Childress, *Principles of Biomedical Ethics*, p. 7.

220 From Judith Jarvis Thomson, 'A defence of abortion' in Joel Feinberg (ed.), *The Problem of Abortion*, Wadsworth 1984, p. 153.

221 Aristotle, *Ethics*, 1109a26, p. 109.

222 Daniel Goleman, *Emotional Intelligence*, Bloomsbury 1996, p. 34.

223 Anthony Weston, 'Toward a really practical ethics', paper given at The Society for the Advancement of American Philosophy Conference, March 2002: http://www. american-philosophy.org/archives/ 2002_papers/dp-6.htm

224 From Tom Wolfe's novel *The Bonfire of the Vanities*, Bantam 1988.

225 D. B. Boulevard, *Point of View*, 2002. (See p. iv.)

226 Gerard Darby, 'Encouraging creative thinking', in Gerald Jones (ed.), *Gatekeepers, Midwives and Fellow Travellers*, Mary Ward Centre 2005.

227 Weston, *A 21st Century Ethical Toolbox*, pp. 186–199.

228 Beauchamp and Childress provide 38 dilemmas, most drawn from biomedical ethics, which can be used to hone your moral decision-making skills. See Beauchamp and Childress, *Principles of Biomedical Ethics*, pp. 400–454.

Selected bibliography

Recommended reading

Aristotle, *Ethics*, Penguin 1988

Beauchamp, Tom and Childress, James, *Principles of Biomedical Ethics*, Oxford University Press 1989

Blackburn, Simon, *Being Good*, Oxford University Press 2001

Frankena, William, *Ethics*, Prentice Hall 1973

Glover, Jonathan, *Causing Death and Saving Lives*, Penguin 1988

Hudson, W. D. (ed.), *The Is/Ought Question*, Macmillan 1969

Hudson, W. D., *Modern Moral Philosophy*, second edition, Macmillan 1983

Hume, David, *An Enquiry Concerning the Principles of Morals*, ed. Tom Beauchamp, Oxford University Press 1998

Kant, Immanuel, *Groundwork of the Metaphysic of Morals*, in H. J. Paton (trans.), *The Moral Law*, Hutchinson 1972

MacIntyre, Alasdair, *A Short History of Ethics*, Routledge 1967

Mackie, J. L., *Ethics: Inventing Right and Wrong*, Penguin 1977

Plato, *Gorgias*, Clarendon Press 1995

Plato, *The Republic*, Penguin 1987

Singer, Peter, *Practical Ethics*, Cambridge University Press 1979

Singer, Peter (ed.), *A Companion to Ethics*, Blackwell 1997

Smart, J. J. C. and Williams, Bernard, *Utilitarianism: For and Against*, Cambridge University Press 1973

Sterba, James (ed.), *Ethics: The Big Questions*, Blackwell 2004

Warnock, Mary (ed.), Jeremy Bentham, *Introduction to the Principles of Morals and Legislation*, and John Stuart Mill, *Utilitarianism* and *On Liberty*, Fontana 1985

Warnock, Mary, *Ethics Since 1900*, Oxford University Press 1979

Weston, Anthony, *A 21st Century Ethical Toolbox*, Oxford University Press 2001

Williams, Bernard, *Morality*, Cambridge University Press 1980

Further reading

Books on ethics have a tendency to be a bit earnest; so here are some other, more gripping, books that you should read, which touch on many of the issues raised by moral philosophy.

Nicholson Baker, *The Mezzanine*
Anthony Burgess, *A Clockwork Orange*
Albert Camus, *The Outsider*
Truman Capote, *In Cold Blood*
Fyodor Dostoyevsky, *Crime and Punishment*
Bret Easton Ellis, *Less Than Zero*
William Golding, *The Lord of the Flies*
Graham Greene, *The End of the Affair*
Joseph Heller, *Catch-22*
Aldous Huxley, *Brave New World*
Thomas Keneally, *Schindler's Ark*
Choderlos de Laclos, *Dangerous Liaisons*
Primo Levi, *If This is a Man*
Ian McEwan, *Enduring Love*
George Orwell, *1984*
Joe Simpson, *Touching the Void*
Jonathan Swift, *Gulliver's Travels*
Jim Thompson, *Pop 1280*
Tom Wolfe, *Bonfire of the Vanities*

Index